THE PRIVATE SECTOR

Also by George O'Toole:

THE
PRIVATE
SECTOR

Private Spies, Rent-a-Cops,
and the Police–Industrial Complex

by GEORGE O'TOOLE

W · W · NORTON & COMPANY, INC., *New York*

Library of Congress Cataloging in Publication Data

O'Toole, George.
  The private sector.

  Bibliography: p.
  Includes index.
  1. Police, Private—United States. 2. Wire-tapping—United States. 3. Detectives—United States. 4. Civil rights—United States. I. Title.
HV8091.08   363.2   77-16495
ISBN 0-393-05647-3

designed by Paula Weiner
1 2 3 4 5 6 7 8 9 0

For Mary Ann, who made it possible.

Contents

Acknowledgments

It would not have been possible to write this book without the cooperation of many people who work in the private security industry. I especially want to thank the following for generously permitting me to draw on their experience and tap their expertise: Richard Bast, Allan Bell, Jr., Lake Headley, Martin Kaiser, Harold Lipset, C. R. McQuiston, Anthony J. Pellicano, Arnold E. Preston, and William Turner. I am also indebted to "Major James Valentine" and several other individuals who prefer to remain unidentified. I hasten to add that none of those named or unnamed should necessarily be assumed to agree with my views and conclusions regarding the private security industry or related matters.

Credit for uncovering the political dirty tricks in Indianapolis detailed in Chapter Eleven should go to James M. Davis and J. Michael Sara of the Marion County, Indiana, Prosecutor's Office, and to the Indianapolis *Star*'s investigative team: William E. Anderson, Harley R. Bierce, Richard E. Cady, and Myrta J. Pulliam. I am indebted to all of them for their help in putting together an accurate account of the case.

I want to thank Robert Ellis Smith of the *Privacy Journal* and David Klaus of the Privacy Protection Study Commission for helping me trace some of the pathways through which personal dossiers are exchanged in the Private Sector. The generous cooperation of John Marks of the Center for National Security Studies, and the Rev. John Adams of the United Methodist Church led to the discovery of some links between Private Sector organizations and federal government intelligence agencies. My thanks also to Jim Hougan and to Kevin Walsh for important information.

A large part of the research that went into this book was done by Mary Ann Werntz, without whom it would have been impossible to undertake, much less complete, this project.

Finally, I want to thank my editor, Starling Lawrence, for his patience, encouragement, and suggestions.

Introduction

A few years ago I had occasion to hire a private detective to locate several people who had played apparently minor roles in a newsworthy event some years earlier and had since dropped out of sight. I was researching a book about the subject, and I hoped they could provide me with some valuable firsthand information. Before I completed my project, I had reason to deal with several other private detective agencies in different parts of the country. In the process, I got my first glimpse of a fascinating world I hadn't known existed.

Most of the private detectives I met had some kind of background in public law enforcement. They were retired police officers, military policemen, or intelligence agents. All seemed to have good current connections in official law enforcement agencies. And all seemed to have access to official files and records not usually available to private citizens. As in any industry, many of the detectives knew each other and had mutual friends among the senior ranks of related businesses, such as guard services, electronic surveillance, lie detection, and the manufacture of police equipment. Taken together, they seemed to form a kind of subculture: white, middle-class, middle-aged males with half a lifetime in police work, now employed in some security-related job in the private sector.

Out of curiosity about this "police–industrial complex," I did some research into the private police industry; my perspective quickly changed. I had thought of private security as the civilian fringe of public law enforcement, but I found that the two are more like mirror images of each other. If anything, the private police establishment may be a bit mightier than the public police. For example:

There are about a million police officers in America; roughly half of them are private cops.

The General Motors Corporation has a force of 4200 plant guards. That's larger than the municipal police forces of all but five American cities.

While federal agencies maintain 3.9 billion dossiers on American citizens—an average of eighteen files on every man, woman, and child—substantially more records are kept on Americans by private detective agencies, credit bureaus, political blacklisting services, and other private institutions.

Police and federal agents are required to get court orders before tapping telephones; during a typical year a few hundred wiretap warrants are issued. But the telephone company can legally tap a phone without any warrant, and during one five-year period Ma Bell's private cops listened in on 1.8 million telephone conversations.

Large multinational corporations like Citibank and IBM operate their own corporate intelligence services along the same lines as the CIA, but the information they turn up is often better than that collected by the government.

The most secure installation in the United States may be a new X-shaped building in East Hanover, New Jersey. It's protected by some of the most sophisticated electronic security systems in the world, but it's not occupied by the CIA or the National Security Agency. It's the corporate headquarters of a leading cookie manufacturer.

All this was just for openers. On delving further into the statistics, I learned that private security is a $5 billion per year industry that's growing at an annual rate of 10 to 15 percent. I found that a police consultant has estimated that, by 1990, some 1,431,000 Americans will be working in private sector security, outnumbering by two to one the projected number of public law enforcement officers.

At about this point I realized the subject of private police deserved to be the subject of a book. In my notes I frequently used the term "private sector" to refer to the private police industry, so I chose that as a working title. In the following pages I have capitalized the term to distinguish it from what is generally used to designate the private sector of the economy. But by the Private Sector I mean something more than the industry that provides goods and services for law enforcement and security; the private police subculture transcends those boundaries. It includes, for example, the 6600-member Society of Former Special Agents of the FBI, an influential Old Boy Network that links many of the most powerful figures in both public law enforcement and private security. The Private Sector subculture also includes the Law Enforcement Intelligence Unit network; LEIU members are all public police officers, but the organization itself is a private network through which members of the intelligence squads of some 225 North American police departments exchange dossiers and coordinate investigations. And the Private Sector cannot exclude *Posse Comitatus,* the loose organization of 10,000 armed vigilantes across the country who preach and practice do-it-yourself law enforcement. In general, I mean the term "Private Sector" to include any individual or group involved with law enforcement or security, but lacking official police authority.

Apart from its sheer size, the thing that most impressed me on first examining the Private Sector was its age and the many ways it has left its mark on our history, our literature, and even our folklore. For instance, I was surprised to learn that a private detective thwarted a pre-Inaugural assassination attempt against Abraham Lincoln, or that years later the same man was stalked through the streets of Chicago by Jesse James. I was delighted to discover that the real-life adventures of Private Sector heros were the basis of many of the exploits of Sam Spade and Sherlock Holmes, or that a private detective's 1907 investigation in San Francisco led to the birth of the "Mutt and Jeff" comic strip, and added the word "beanie" to the dictionary.

Despite such diverting nuggets, much of what I learned of the Private Sector was disturbing. The prospect of a shadow army of a half-million private cops ready to do the bidding of whoever will pay their wages is enough to make even the most ardent law-and-order advocate a little nervous. In Latin America, where the police have embraced private allegiances, the result has been the Death Squad: public law enforcement officers who moonlight as political murderers. Perhaps it can't happen here, but it is disquieting to note that the line separating public police from the Private Sector has been blurred in many places.

The prospect of retirement in early middle-age is used to recruit young men into the public police. An ex-cop with fifteen or twenty years of police experience behind him, and many more of useful working time ahead of him, will often gravitate to a second career in private security. An identical route leads retired military police and intelligence agents into the Private Sector. And a considerable number of FBI agents serve in the Bureau for only a few years before moving on to private practice. One survey reports that over 40 percent of corporate security officers are former policemen, FBI agents, military intelligence officers, or other veterans of public law enforcement.

Police aren't the only public employees who migrate into private positions somehow related to their old jobs. Retired admirals and generals populate the marketing departments of aerospace companies doing business with the Pentagon. Former members of federal regulatory agencies often find lucrative employment in the industries they used to oversee. And Justice Department attorneys often go into private practice and work the other side of the legal street. None of it is very reassuring, but the movement of public police officers into the Private Sector seems especially disturbing. Consider this:

In Indianapolis, a retired air force lockpicking expert broke into the offices of a United States senator; his accomplices in the burglary planted bugging devices and collected political intelligence. The operation was part of a political espionage and dirty-tricks campaign carried out by a private detective firm.

In Maryland, a state senate investigating committee heard testimony that a former police officer employed in the security department of the Chesapeake and Potomac Telephone Company helped the Baltimore police install illegal wiretaps.

In California, a former police officer committed seventeen political burglaries during a two-year period. He says he did it under the direction of the FBI.

In Houston, several police officers say their illegal wiretaps were installed with the help of Southwestern Bell's security force, a staff about one-third of whom are former FBI agents. The FBI itself was allegedly a major customer for the information gleaned from the illegal taps.

And there is much more, detailed at length in the following pages. Most such incidents highlight the same hazard: the Private Sector can serve as an informal and invisible nexus, linking both public and private police outside officially regulated channels. It can become de facto a national police force; what it lacks in organization and formal structure, it makes up for in ubiquity.

To be balanced, however, I must report that of the many inhabitants of the Private Sector I've come to know well, none impresses me as a likely *putsch* participant. Most are mildly conservative people who look askance at much of the current scene, but wouldn't consider taking the law into their own hands. Of course, they are only a few out of a half-million, but I believe the reason the Private Sector has thus far realized a remarkably small fraction of its potential for mischief is due largely to a preponderance of this kind of person among the ranks of its leaders. But one should keep in mind that things can always change.

The real danger of the Private Sector lies in its obscurity; we cannot do much to safeguard ourselves against something if we don't know it exists. There is no reason to remain ignorant of it; the Private Sector has been the inspiration of generations of storytellers and screenwriters, but the reality is no less absorbing than the myth. Because of this, I have tried to make this book as much an exposition as an exposé. Here, then, is an unhurried tour of the Private Sector.

THE PRIVATE SECTOR

1

Law and Order, Inc.

"I'm going to shoot you and I'm not going to miss," said the three-year-old.

From his front porch vantage point, George Barcroft glanced at the little boy standing on the lawn. The child was pointing a gun at Barcroft's daughter.

"I thought it was a toy gun," Barcroft later recalled.

It was not. It was a .357 magnum Sturm-Ruger revolver. As the little boy stood holding the two-and-a-half-pound weapon, seven-year-old Jeffrey Krauch approached. The toddler turned, pointed the pistol at Jeffrey, and pulled the trigger. The quiet of the blue-collar suburb was shattered by the report. Jeffrey stood for a moment looking down with astonishment at the gaping wound in his chest, then fell to the ground dead.

The little boy had taken the loaded weapon from the dining room closet of a nearby home where his mother was visiting her boyfriend, a 36-year-old convicted felon who worked as a security guard for a private detective agency. The man used the weapon in his work. It happened in Baltimore in August 1976.

A recent Rand Corporation study indicates that about half of the several hundred thousand private security guards in the United States carry

3

guns, but less than 20 percent of them ever receive any instruction in how and when to use them, or how to keep them out of the hands of children.

At a private lake outside Washington, D.C., a security guard shot and killed a child who ignored the man's command to get out of the water. In Orlando, Florida, a private guard shot up an exhibit of life-sized paper dolls in a darkened classroom when they failed to obey his order to step out of the shadows; the guard believed he was outnumbered ten to one. In Sacramento, California, a security guard tried to cure a young woman's hiccups by whipping out his pistol and pointing it at her. He succeeded—the gun went off and shot her between the eyes.

Unfortunately, such incidents are all too common among the thousands of untrained and unqualified men and women who have been recruited to meet the growing demand of business and industry for protection that the official, or "sworn" police officer doesn't give. The private cops' wages run as low as $2 per hour, sometimes lower, and at those prices you don't get Wyatt Earp.

The security guard is the Private Sector's counterpart of the cop on the beat. He is on hand in banks, factories, shopping centers, race tracks, and virtually everywhere else private assets are concentrated. The sworn officer will try to catch a thief, but he's too busy doing that and other duties simply to stand around and frighten off crooks. Private guards are hired for that purpose, but often the uniform contains nothing more than a warm body.

No one knows exactly how many private guards there are in America, but most estimates range between a quarter and a half million. One thing is certain: there are as many or more private cops as there are sworn officers. There are 50,000 private guards in California, but only 45,000 official police officers. New York City has 30,000 officers on its police force and between 75,000 and 100,000 private guards. In New York's financial district, where cash, gold, and negotiable paper are concentrated, the private guards outnumber the cops by twenty to one.

Faced with the growth of such crimes as shoplifting, employee theft, and vandalism, businessmen have increasingly turned to contract guard services and detective agencies that deal in "rent-a-cops," or have hired their own "in-house" guards. Between 1963 and 1969, American business doubled the money it spent on rent-a-cops. Pinkerton's, Inc., one of the more reputable contract guard services, increased its gross receipts from $37 million to $193 million between 1965 and 1975. Overall, the rent-a-cop business has been steadily growing at an annual rate of 11 or 12 percent. The International Association of Chiefs of Police estimates that by 1990 some 1,431,000 people will be employed in some kind of security work in the private sector.

The *Washington Post* described the typical security guard working in the nation's capital as "a transient from North Carolina en route to Detroit, who stopped here for a few days because he had run out of money." The Rand Corporation, which has studied the private guard, describes him as "an aging white male, poorly educated, usually untrained, and very poorly paid . . . he averages between 40 and 55 years of age, has had little education beyond the ninth grade, and has had a few years of experience in private security." Forty percent of the private cops interviewed by the Rand researchers said they were unemployed immediately prior to accepting their guard jobs.

The annual turnover rate among contract guard services ranges from 20 to 200 percent, so it is not surprising that the rent-a-cops' employers are reluctant to spend much time and money training new recruits. Of the 275 private guards interviewed by the Rand researchers, two-thirds had received no training prior to starting work, and only 7 percent received more than eight hours of training. Almost one in five guards was turned loose to perform his duties alone the first day on the job. As noted before, few of the armed guards had received any training in the care and safe use of their weapons, but a guard ignorant of the limits of his authority can be a dangerous individual even when unarmed.

Most private guards have no more authority than any other private citizen to arrest, detain, search, or use force on a suspect; half of the guards interviewed by Rand did not know this, and 6 percent of them were firmly convinced they had the same legal powers as a sworn police officer. Larger portions of the group were ignorant of such things as the circumstances in which a citizen's arrest can be made, the difference between a felony and a misdemeanor, and the justification for the use of deadly force. Forty-one percent thought drinking on the job is a crime if the employer has a rule against it, and almost a third believed that calling a security guard a pig is a misdemeanor. Ignorant of the limits of their authority, the rent-a-cops often exceed it, and even those who are aware of the bounds of their legal power often go beyond it, secure in the knowledge that most of the public is unsure of how much authority a private guard wields. Many people mistakenly assume anyone wearing a police-type uniform and badge and carrying a sidearm has all the authority of a sworn police officer. More than 20 percent of the private guards interviewed by the Rand researchers admitted to having witnessed or taken part in incidents of false arrest, improper detention, illegal searches, excessive force, or impersonation of a sworn police officer.

In 1972, a twenty-four-year-old bank teller was seized leaving a New York City department store by members of the store's security force. She was accused of shoplifting and was taken to the store's security office where a shopping bag she was carrying was searched. No stolen merchandise was found in it. The security guards contended the bank teller was working with two other women whom they had arrested, searched, and found to be carrying merchandise from the store; the guards claimed the teller had passed the stolen goods to her accomplices. The two women admitted to shoplifting, but denied even knowing the bank teller. They repeated their denials to police later, when they and the bank teller were taken to the local police station. Nevertheless, the store's security man pressed charges and the bank teller was booked, arraigned, and brought to trial on shoplifting charges. Besides the testimony of the two women that they were not working with the bank teller, the defense pointed out that the shopping bag the young woman allegedly used to conceal the store's goods before passing them on to her accomplices happened to be constructed of transparent plastic, and made an unlikely shoplifting tool. After deliberating for ten minutes, the jury acquitted the teller, who then slapped the department store with a suit for false imprisonment, pointing out that her newly acquired arrest record prevented her from working in banks anymore. The young woman was awarded $1.1 million in damages.

The same store was involved in a worse incident in 1976, when a young woman refugee from Mainland China was arrested and allegedly assaulted by the store's security guard force. The woman had bought a pants suit in another department store earlier in her shopping trip, and she took it from the bag she was carrying in order to compare it with a similar one she found on sale. A security guard who was watching her believed she was shoplifting, grabbed her, and hauled her off to the security office. The young Chinese woman didn't fully understand what was happening, and she struggled with the guards as they attempted to search her. At one point, she says, her blouse and bra were pulled up around her neck.

Finding no stolen merchandise on her person, the security guards tried to make the young woman sign a statement admitting her guilt and releasing the store from any liability in the incident. She refused and, she says, the store's twenty-three-year-old assistant security director beat her, causing cuts and bruises and loosening several teeth. Another shopper who was passing the store's security office at the time says he witnessed the beating and tried to stop it, but was informed that the security man was a New York City police officer—which apparently was considered an adequate explanation.

The security guards filed shoplifting charges against the young woman, who was arrested and spent the night in jail. However, after the district attorney investigated the case, he dropped all charges against the woman, arrested three of the security men, and charged them with perjury and assault. The assistant security director was also charged with criminal impersonation of a police officer. The woman sued the store for $7 million.

A few months prior to this incident, a security guard tried to arrest an alleged shoplifter in the Queens branch of another New York department store. The suspect, a seventeen-year-old boy, resisted and was beaten by the guard. He died of a fractured skull, contusions and lacerations of the brain, and cerebral edema. No criminal charges were placed against the guard, but the parents of the dead boy are suing the store for $10 million.

Also in 1976, a young man was shot and killed by a private guard in the back seat of a car in a Bronx, New York, housing project. The victim had been arrested by the guard for assault and disorderly conduct after a shoving incident. The guard's gun accidentally discharged, killing the handcuffed prisoner while he was being driven to the police station. The guard was charged with second-degree manslaughter. Three other security guards present in the car at the time of the shooting were charged with obstruction of justice for lying to the police about the details of the incident.

All private citizens, including private security guards, have some legal powers to arrest, detain, interrogate, or search others. However, anyone choosing to exercise those powers had better understand thoroughly the legal intricacies limiting them if he doesn't want to end up in a much worse predicament than the object of his attentions. The private citizen who attempts to exert police power is skating on some very thin legal ice, often unsupported by much in the way of precedent. Indeed, he may find his name immortalized in the lawbooks as part of a landmark civil or criminal case that better defines this legal *terra incognita*.

It varies from state to state, but—generally—a citizen has the power to arrest a person who is committing or has committed a crime, and to turn that person over to the proper authorities, *if the crime was committed in his presence*. In some states, if the crime is a misdemeanor rather than a felony, it must involve a breach of the peace. A sworn police officer can arrest someone on the strength of reasonable grounds for believing he has committed a crime; a private citizen has got to catch his man in the act and be able to prove it. Otherwise it's false arrest and the arresting citizen can be prosecuted and sued.*

Most states recognize the shopkeeper's right to detain suspected shoplifters. Detention differs from arrest in that the latter includes turning the suspect over to the police; detention means keeping the suspect on the premises for a reasonable period of time when there is probable cause to believe he has stolen something. Reasonable force may be used to detain the suspect while attempting to discover whether he is a shoplifter. But the law contains no precise definitions of the terms "reasonable period of time" or "reasonable force," and the security guard may

---

*A recent recommendation by the General Accounting Office would expand to a terrifying degree the police powers of private guards at commercial nuclear plants, however. The GAO, in a study of ways to improve security at nuclear plants, suggested that guards be given the authority to shoot to kill "if such action is necessary to prevent special nuclear material from being stolen."

find his definition of "probable cause" differs from that of a judge if the detention results in a charge of wrongful imprisonment.

The power of a private citizen to search another is the worst defined of all such citizens' police powers. Generally speaking, a security guard is only safe in searching the person or belongings of a suspected shoplifter if he has obtained the person's consent. A guard who searches a customer against his or her will may be starting a sequence of events that will make legal history and, at his employer's expense, enrich the suspect beyond any foreseeable future need to engage in petit larceny.

Interrogation of a suspect is just about the only area in which the private cop's powers are, in one sense, greater than his sworn counterpart. He is free to question a suspected thief as much as he wishes, and he isn't required to first advise him of his right to an attorney or to keep silent, as an official police officer would be. Of course, the suspect is equally free to refuse to answer. And if the private security guard asks such questions as "What did you do with the merchandise?" or "Did you take that dress?" within earshot of other customers or store clerks, his employer may have to pay the customer damages for slander, as did one department store in those circumstances.

A Harvard law degree would be a very helpful asset to anyone contemplating conducting a citizen's arrest, and few $2-per-hour rent-a-cops can be expected to tiptoe through the legal minefield of private police action without opening themselves and their employers to serious litigation. Nevertheless, retail merchants are increasing their use of private guards and ordering them to take aggressive action against shoplifters. The United States Department of Commerce estimates that for every shoplifter caught, thirty-five others get away, and that between $2 and $5 billion worth of goods are stolen annually. Industry estimates put the individual store loss at about 2 or 3 percent of total sales, on the average, and much higher in ghetto neighborhoods. So despite the awarding of considerable damages in a few cases of private police abuses, the economic equation still favors the aggressive and widespread use of rent-a-cops. Soon, however, the increase in the number of such suits, as wronged customers become aware of their rights, will force the employers of private guards to take some steps to limit their legal liability.

One such step is deputization, a process by which some private citizens can be invested with full or partial police powers. The law in many states permits the deputization of private guards and other security personnel as "special officers" or "special deputies." Such officers are the employees of private companies, but have the same arrest powers as a sworn policeman. Armed with these broader police powers, the guard who is also a special officer can arrest, search, or detain someone in circumstances that would constitute false arrest or some other offense by a regular private guard.

The New York City Police Department has deputized some of the security staffs working in the fourteen largest department stores in the city as special patrolmen. Security guards in Las Vegas casinos are commissioned as "special deputy sheriffs." In Maryland, the governor can appoint "special policemen" to work for private businesses; their police powers are limited to their employer's premises. North Carolina has the same arrangement. In Oregon, the company policemen can only work in the railroad and steamboat industries. The District of Columbia has 2600 "special officers" who are commissioned by the mayor.

But the most elite corps of deputized private police is the Texas Special Rangers. Not to be confused with the Texas Rangers, the near-legendary force of official law enforcement officers, the Special Rangers were instituted in the 1930s as a means of deputizing private policemen in Texas. The Texas Department of Public Safety—the state police—is authorized to commission Special Rangers, who have the full arrest and firearms powers of an official policeman and are empowered to enforce all laws protecting life or property, except highway traffic laws. The Special Rangers work for private employers, although, in theory, they can be called to special duty by the governor.

The Special Rangers are not private guards or rent-a-cops; they are often the managers and directors of the security forces of some of the largest industries holding assets in Texas, including Gulf Oil, Continental Oil, Exxon, Texaco, Hughes Tool Company, the King Ranch, Braniff Airways, Dow Chemical, S. S. Kresge, Southwestern Bell Telephone Company, and several railroads. They are not uniformed, and are identified only by a small badge or tie tack. By law, the size of the Special Ranger force cannot exceed 300.

There were 225 Special Rangers in 1974 when liberal elements in the Texas state legislature tried to pass a law abolishing the force. The move was unsuccessful, but it did result in the reduction of the number of Special Rangers to thirty, all of whom work for the Texas and Southwestern Cattle Raisers Association. However, the Department of Public Safety is free to deputize additional Special Rangers at any time, and is expected to do so after the political pressure is off.

In testifying in favor of the law to abolish the Special Rangers, John Duncan, the executive director of the Texas Civil Liberties Union, said, ''There can be no justification in clothing employees of private economic interests with the police powers of the state. [The commissioning of Special Rangers] does just this and in so doing, places this police power in the hands of many of the largest corporations in Texas. . . . Law enforcement officers are presumably the servants of the public and not the servants of private economic interests.'' The same might well be said of all specially deputized private cops.

Deputization of private citizens was a law enforcement necessity in the Western frontier communities of the nineteenth century, where one sheriff or marshall was responsible for keeping the peace throughout a vast expanse of territory; in modern America it should be an ad hoc procedure, reserved for those rare situations in which there are not enough sworn officers to deal with some unexpected law enforcement crisis. To empower one group of private citizens with special police powers is to create a privileged elite whose property rights are somehow greater than those of others.

Deputization as a means of evading the legal consequence of heavy-handed methods by private police doesn't always work. It boomeranged on one New York City department store that stationed a deputized security guard—a woman—to watch women customers covertly through a grated air vent in one of the store's dressing rooms. The practice of spying on customers in store dressing rooms is widespread because many shoplifters take advantage of the privacy the rooms afford to conceal stolen items. In this case, two customers were arrested and brought to trial for shoplifting, but the case was thrown out on constitutional grounds. The testimony of the security guard that she saw the defendants stealing would have been perfectly admissable if she were a private citizen; as a deputized special officer, however, she was acting as a sworn public police officer when she spied on the shoppers. That made it an illegal search, the judge said, a violation of the Fourth Amendment. The guard's testimony could not be entered as evidence, and the case was dismissed. There was even the possibility that the store could be sued.

This incident points up another curious anomaly in the legal powers of private police as compared to sworn officers. An undeputized private cop who conducts an illegal search of a suspected thief may have to face the consequences of a civil suit, but the fruits of the illegal search can be entered as evidence if charges are brought against the suspect. The exclusionary rule by which courts reject evidence seized by the official police as "tainted" if it was acquired improperly or illegally doesn't apply to private cops. By the same token, a private cop may question a suspect without first informing him of his rights, obtain a confession, and use it in court as evidence against the suspect; a confession obtained in the same circumstances by a sworn officer would be thrown out of court. The legal theory behind all this is that the constitutional safeguards of the Fourth and Fifth Amendments are intended to protect the citizen from the government, not from another citizen; a sworn officer is the government, but a private cop—unless deputized—is just another citizen.

Another means used by the employers of private guards to avoid the legal pitfalls of citizens' arrests is to hire off-duty sworn police officers to serve as security guards. A sworn police officer's legal powers are not suspended when he goes off-duty; he retains them even while "moonlighting" for a private employer. But the real advantage of the moonlighting cop as private guard is the training and experience he brings to the job. Presumably he is well versed in firearms and police procedure, and would be much less likely to overstep his legal authority than a private citizen in a guard's uniform would be.

The use of moonlighting cops as guards by private employers is open to much of the same criticism as the deputization of private police; it places public police power under the control of private economic interests. Some critics of the practice see it as a conflict of interest for a police officer to perform virtually the same job on both public and private payrolls. A Maryland state policeman who owns a rent-a-cop service in neighboring Virginia recently tried to extend the guard service into Maryland, where the State Police are responsible for regulating private detective agencies and guard services. The Maryland Board of Ethics saw this as a potential conflict of interest and denied the officer permission to open a Maryland branch. The Rand Corporation study of private police sidestepped the question of whether ''public police who moonlight as private security officers are a problem or an asset,'' recommending the matter be given further study.

Some private sector employers find that undercover agents are less troublesome and more effective than uniformed guards in fighting many types of business crime. Typically, an undercover agent will be ''hired'' by the client and assigned to a plant or office where some employees are suspected of stealing from the company. Often the client is satisfied simply to identify the dishonest workers, fire them, and bring the pilferage to a halt, rather than prosecute. Undercover agents posing as shoppers are also used against shoplifters.

The undercover agents who work for an Ohio detective agency known as The Multi-State Unit, Inc., hunt a very different kind of quarry. Multi-State agents don't chase white-collar criminals or shoplifters; they hire out to small-town police departments to catch users and dealers of illegal drugs. The thirteen-man Multi-State force is headed by Dwight Joseph, former Columbus police chief and one-time head of the Ohio Bureau of Criminal Investigation. Multi-State was founded on the theory that many small police forces lacked any narcotics expertise, but would be willing to hire some ''rent-a-narcs'' to come in and make a few drug busts in their communities. The idea paid off.

Some federal narcotics agents disdain the rent-a-narcs as bounty hunters, and one Midwestern prosecutor charges that many of their busts are kids caught with marijuana, not the important hard-narcotics dealers. Yet the Multi-State agents are doing nothing illegal and, as they readily point out, they didn't write the laws making possession of a single marijuana cigarette a felony. But they are managing to make a living off them.

Licensing is not now an effective factor in reducing abuses by private police. As of 1975, nine states did not regulate any part of the private security industry. The Rand Corporation study found spotty and usually inadequate regulation in most of the others. Generally, private guard firms are licensed, not the guards themselves, although many states require as a minimum a police check to insure that the prospective rent-a-cop has no criminal record. The owner of a Seattle, Washington, private detective agency obtained a private investigator's license for his thirteen-year-old son to demonstrate that the local Department of Licensing and Consumer Affairs would issue such a license to anyone. Matters are even worse among in-house security personnel—private cops who work directly for the businesses they guard; the Rand study found that no state licenses or otherwise regulates such private cops.

The Law Enforcement Assistance Administration, which sponsored the Rand study, set up a Private Security Advisory Council to recommend uniform state legislation that would alleviate the abuses discovered by the Rand researchers. However, the Council consists mostly of representatives from the major contract guard agencies and other private sector security interests. It published a Model Private Security Guard Licensing and Regulatory Statute, which falls far short of the reforms suggested in the Rand study. Milton Lipson, a private security specialist who teaches the subject at New York University, said of the model statute, ''[it] is not an attempt to install basic regulations for the industry, but rather [is] intended to foreclose further criticism.''

Yet another LEAA-funded panel, the Task Force on Private Security, was created in April 1975 to study the private police problem. The task force was chaired by Arthur Bilek, former vice-president of Pinkerton's, Inc., the oldest rent-a-cop agency. In a 580-page report released in April 1977, the panel acknowledged that the Private Sector's personnel quality is ''often inferior.'' The task force report proposed a comprehensive set of standards and goals for the private security industry, which, if adopted, would do much to correct the problems identified in the Rand study. Among the task force's recommendations were detailed criteria for state licensing of guard firms and state registration of private guards.

Of those states which currently try to regulate the private security industry, all find that the most frequent cause for denying a license to an applicant is the discovery that he has a criminal record. Fifteen percent of the applicants for state licenses are denied, suggesting that a significant number of professional criminals are attracted by the fox-in-henhouse opportunities afforded by private security work. Where licensing and screening procedures are lax or nonexistent, i.e., in most states, professional criminals may be infiltrating contract guard services and related companies to a dangerous extent.

One of the largest heists in American history was the October 1974 break-in at the Chicago vault of Purolator Security, Inc., an armored-car service. The thieves displayed an astonishing knowledge of burglar alarm systems, and succeeded in neutralizing the sophisticated electronic equipment set to protect the more than $3.9 million Purolator had picked up from its clients after the close of banking hours on a Friday afternoon. When the police finally identified some suspects in the case, one turned out to be a former Purolator guard.

Purolator Security was also the target of another record theft at London's Heathrow Airport in June 1976. Two men wearing Purolator guard uniforms presented themselves at the airport vaults used by British Airways and Sabena Airlines to store valuables in transit. The two produced papers authorizing them to receive five packages being held for pickup by Purolator couriers. The packages contained $3.5 million in U.S. dollars, French francs, and other currencies; some of the money was due to be shipped out of England, and the rest was to be delivered to Purolator clients within the country. The uniformed men collected the five packages and drove off in an armored truck. Two days later the real Purolator guards turned up at the vaults to pick up the money; it was only then that the authorities realized the first pair had been phonies.

"We are sick, very sick," lamented the Purolator general manager.

One reason for the security executive's sickness was the realization that the theft was almost certainly an inside job. After a brief investigation, Scotland Yard came to the identical conclusion and issued a nationwide alert for a former Purolator manager.

With private cops guarding currency shipments, payrolls, negotiable certificates, and other big-ticket items, it should not be surprising if the private security industry has attracted organized crime. Exactly how far the Mob may have penetrated into the rent-a-cop business can only be guessed at, but an incident that took place in Brooklyn, New York, in March 1976 may be the tip of an iceberg.

At 8:30 one morning, a middle-aged man escorted two little girls from a house in the Bath Beach section of Brooklyn and into a waiting station wagon. The man was a private guard in plainclothes, assigned to protect the children. As he slid behind the wheel, a late-model Chrysler pulled up and two men got out, approached the station wagon, and identified themselves to the guard as FBI agents.

"I know you have a gun," said one of the men. "I have one too. Let's have yours."

As the guard surrendered his .38 caliber revolver, the older girl, a seven-year-old, began to cry. One of the men patted her reassuringly, saying, "Cathy, it's O.K."

The two children were transferred to the automobile. The men jumped back into the car and the Chrysler disappeared into the flow of morning rush-hour traffic, leaving the guard standing alone at the curb.

The little girls were the daughters of Seward Prosser Mellon, the thirty-three-year-old heir to the Mellon fortune, and his ex-wife Karen Leigh Boyd Mellon. The couple were divorced in 1974. At the time, Mrs. Mellon was a patient in a private psychiatric clinic in Connecticut, so the children remained with their father. In December 1975, the two girls visited their mother, who had been discharged from the clinic and was then in Durham, North Carolina. Mrs. Mellon took the girls, chartered a private airplane, and flew to New York. There she made contact through her lawyer with Superior Investigations and Claim Service, a private detective firm. The detective agency installed Mrs. Mellon and her daughters in a private house in Brooklyn under the pseudonym of "Roberts," and assigned plainclothes guards to protect the children from reabduction by their father, who had been given legal custody of the girls under a Pennsylvania court ruling. In February 1976, Mrs. Mellon was awarded custody of the children by a New York State Supreme Court justice, thus creating a clouded and confused legal situation.

The Mellon family's lawyers hired Joseph Presti, a private investigator and retired New York City detective, to locate the girls. Armed with photographs of the children and a list of private schools they might be enrolled in, Presti located them and followed Mrs. Mellon's plain-clothes guard when he took the children home from school. He reported his findings to his client. Exactly what happened after this is unclear, except that the children were abducted and returned to their father, and each parent accused the other of trafficking with the Mafia.

It is a fact that two weeks before the abduction, Assistant U.S. Attorney-General Richard L. Thornburgh, head of the Justice Depart-ment's Criminal Division, was contacted by a Mellon family represen-tative who reported receiving an offer from the Mafia to deliver the two girls to their father for a fee of $250,000. It is also a fact that Superior Investigations and Claims Service, the detective agency hired to protect Mrs. Mellon and her children, is owned by Bruce Romanoff, who pleaded guilty in 1973 to attempting to sell $8.4 million in stolen cashier's checks. And it is also true that the detective firm has worked for the Joseph Columbo family in Brooklyn: Peter Diapoulas, a former member of the Joey Gallo gang, recalls that Romanoff ''did things for us like getting us bullets and he was involved in deals with us.'' Finally, it's a fact that the house Mrs. Mellon and her children were living in at the time of the kidnapping was rented from the Cantalupo Realty Com-pany, a firm that once carried Joseph Columbo on its payroll, and that Cantalupo was recommended to Mrs. Mellon by Bruce Romanoff.

The Mellon family lawyers say all this means that Mrs. Mellon had involved herself and her children with the Mafia and it was for this reason the father ordered the abduction. But Mrs. Mellon denies any significance to Romanoff's record of association with the Mob. And the *New York Post* says Seward Prosser Mellon paid $275,000 to the Mafia to kidnap the little girls and deliver them to him.

Because of the confused legal situation, it's unlikely that Seward Mellon can be charged with kidnapping or custodial interference. The men who carried out the abduction might be charged with imperson-ating federal agents and theft of the guard's gun if they could be iden-tified, but there is only the guard's word, and the weapon was never re-covered, so even this prosecution is improbable. The extent of Mafia involvement, if any, in the incident will probably remain a mystery to all except the members of the grand jury that investigated the abduction.

But there is no question that a New York private detective agency, owned by a convicted felon, had close ties to powerful Mafia families.

The secret partnership of private police and the Mafia may be one of the most ominous developments in the history of American law enforcement, but it is only the fruit of seeds that have always existed in private sector security. The private cop is, quite literally, a hired gun, no matter how much he is dignified by the mercantile respectability of corporate America. He's the mercenary soldier of business and industry whose allegience is for rent by the hour to anyone willing and able to pay his price. Whether he works for Macy's or the Mafia is less significant than the fact that he does not work for the voters and taxpayers.

Like the criminals who create a need for them, private cops only become a major social problem when their numbers increase much more rapidly than the total population, as they have in the last decade or so. Private police are a side effect of the rising crime rate, a symptom of social illness. As a vice-president of the William J. Burns International Detective Agency explained, ''We exist because public police departments are not big enough and don't have a large enough budget to provide protection for private industry.''

It could be argued that private industry *should* pay for its own protection, but the cost of rent-a-cops ultimately comes out of the public's pocket anyway, in the form of increased prices. Michael Klare, a student of the private police establishment, points out that private security is, in effect, funded by a kind of regressive sales tax, because the cost is passed on to the consumer. Better, perhaps, to pay the social and economic price of a larger public police force that, at least in theory, is answerable to the public and elected officials.

It is likely, however, that the private cop will be a part of the security and law enforcement scene for a long time to come. One can only hope that the current rent-a-cop abuses will soon be answered by better standards for recruiting, training, licensing, and managing private security personnel. Meanwhile, the private police must be given their due; the image of the rent-a-cop as reckless, incompetent, arrogant, and dishonest is by no means universally applicable. In a section of upper Manhattan near Columbia University, for example, a team of twenty-five rent-a-cops hired by a neighborhood association has made a significant dent in the area's traditionally high crime rate. In Washington, D.C., seven ex-convicts attached to a rehabilitation program have been working as unarmed security guards in an apartment complex; the owner says they've proved very effective at reducing burglaries and vandalism.

And let's not forget Frank Wills, that lowly paid rent-a-cop who did his job in Washington's Watergate complex one June night in 1972 and knocked over the first in the line of dominoes that eventually tumbled from office a president of the United States.

2

The Giants

In 1921, $200,000 in gold was missing from an Australian ship when it docked in San Francisco. The insurance company that had underwritten the bullion shipment suspected it was stolen by some of the crew and hidden away on board the ship. But a thorough search of the vessel failed to turn up the missing gold and the scheduled sailing date for the return trip to Australia was drawing near. The company called in Pinkerton's National Detective Agency, and a Pinkerton's man soon found the gold secreted inside one of the ship's stacks. It was a routine job for Pinkerton's, but it happened to be the detective's last case; he quit and turned to writing whodunits. The Pinkerton's man was Dashiell Hammett.

It is especially fitting that the creator of Sam Spade, perhaps the most famous of fictional private eyes, was once a Pinkerton's detective, for the very term "private eye" is said to be derived from the Pinkerton agency's trademark, "The Eye That Never Sleeps." Pinkerton's is the oldest and largest private detective agency; its one-and-a-quarter-century history is a map of the growth and development of hired police in America.

Police, public or private, are not one of America's oldest traditions; the Republic was nearly seventy years old before the first public police force was organized. The infant nation had few laws to enforce, and the protection of life and property was largely a do-it-yourself matter in the tiny wilderness communities that made up the frontier. In the cities, night watchmen roamed the streets while the populace slept, ready to raise an alarm if there were a fire or other emergency. In 1838, Boston added a six-man day watch; six years later, New York City combined its day and night watches into the first American municipal police force.

The early constabularies were intended as a local deterrent against crime. They considered their job done if they simply succeeded in keeping miscreants beyond the city limits and maintained law and order in town. If, despite their presence, someone was robbed or murdered, the police had little capability to solve the crime, and no jurisdiction to pursue the criminal if he fled across the city line. The bustling young metropolis of Chicago, for example, had not a single detective on its police force until 1849 when it appointed one man to the job. His name was Allan Pinkerton.

Allan Pinkerton was a Scot who emigrated to the United States in 1842. He settled in a small town near Chicago and started his own business as a barrel-maker. Almost by accident, the young cooper was instrumental in catching two local rings of counterfeiters. His success as an amateur sleuth led the sheriff of Cook County, Illinois, to recruit him as a deputy. In 1849, the mayor of Chicago appointed Pinkerton as the city's detective, a job he held for a year before resigning to form the North-Western Police Agency. For a fee, the detective agency would "attend to the investigation [of] depredation, frauds and criminal offenses; the detection of offenders, procuring arrests and convictions, apprehension or return of fugitives from justice, or bail; recovering lost or stolen property, obtaining information, etc." It was the first private detective agency in America. The Private Sector had been born.

Pinkerton found a strong demand for his agency's services among the many railroad companies serving Chicago. The railroads were large interstate enterprises, and their security problems extended to every town and village where the railroad tracks went. In Canada, the railroads linking the frontier to the settled eastern provinces were protected by a centralized national police force, but the American companies had to rely on a haphazard array of sheriffs and other local law enforcement officials, each tethered by the boundaries of his own jurisdiction along the railroad's right of way. The criminal who remained on the move found the railroads a lucrative target involving little risk.

Pinkerton put together a small staff of nine detectives, including Mrs. Kate Warne, the first woman to work in the detective field. The agency soon grew to include a far-flung network of informants and a force of uniformed guards, the first of their kind in America. It was, in effect, a privately chartered national police force. Among the railroads that hired Pinkerton's agency for protection were the Michigan Central, the Michigan Southern and Northern Indiana, the Chicago and Galena Union, the Chicago and Rock Island, and the Chicago, Burlington, and Quincy. But the largest account—amounting to $10,000 per year—was with the Illinois Central. Pinkerton's business dealings with the Illinois Central led to his deep personal friendship with the railroad's vice-president, George Brinton McClellan, who was to be a Union commander during the Civil War. Pinkerton also made the acquaintance of an Illinois lawyer named Abraham Lincoln who handled much of the railroad's legal work.

In February 1861, Pinkerton's agency learned of a plot to assassinate Lincoln—then president-elect—as he traveled to Washington, D.C., for his first inauguration. Lincoln was due to travel from Harrisburg, Pennsylvania, to Baltimore by rail, then change to a New York–to–Washington train for the last leg of his journey. The conspirators, who were in league with the Baltimore police, planned to shoot Lincoln as he rode in an open carriage from the Calvert Street Station to the Washington Branch Depot.

Pinkerton met Lincoln in Philadelphia and warned him of the plot. The information confirmed warnings the president-elect had already received from two other sources, one of whom was a New York City police superintendent. (In a macabre historical coincidence, the superintendent's name was John Kennedy.)

There was at the time no Secret Service or other presidential protective force, so Lincoln agreed to put himself under Pinkerton's protection for the journey to Washington. The detective's plan was simple but effective. While attending a banquet in Harrisburg, Pennsylvania, Lincoln would excuse himself, pleading illness. Pinkerton would arrange to have all telegraph lines out of Harrisburg cut so that word of Lincoln's changed plans could not be sent ahead. Then, traveling incognito with Pinkerton and another guard, the president-elect would return to Philadelphia and board a sleeping car on a New York–to–Washington train. Pinkerton's plan went off without a hitch, and at 6:00 A.M. on the morning of February 23, 1861, Lincoln arrived safely in Washington while his would-be assassins waited vainly in Baltimore for their victim.

It was more than a month later before Lincoln again heard from Allan Pinkerton. Six days after the fall of Fort Sumter, Pinkerton wrote to the president:

"When I saw you last I said that if the time should ever come that I could be of service to you I was ready. If that time has come I am on hand.

"I have in my Force from Sixteen to Eighteen persons on whose courage, Skill and Devotion to their country I can rely. If they with myself at the head can be of service in the way of obtaining information of the movements of the Traitors, or Safely conveying your letters or dispatches, on that class of Secret Service which is the most dangerous, I am at your command."

Less than a month after making this proposal, Pinkerton and his detectives were operating behind Confederate lines, relaying reports of Southern troop strengths to Union commanders. Pinkerton's small staff of detectives had become America's first intelligence agency.

Adopting the *nom de guerre* of Major E. J. Allen, Pinkerton reported to his old friend and former client, General George McClellan. Pinkerton's Secret Service not only carried out espionage assignments behind Confederate lines, but also served a counterintelligence function back in Washington—the hunting and catching of confederate spies. The mixing of these two activities, however, led to the loss of one of Pinkerton's most trusted men, Timothy Webster.

Webster was a guard at New York City's famed Crystal Palace when Pinkerton recruited him into his detective agency in 1853. The young detective had taken part in many of Pinkerton's most important cases, including the discovery of the plot against Lincoln. Immediately after Pinkerton put his agency in Lincoln's service, Webster infiltrated the Confederate lines and began to build his cover as a Southern sympathizer. Within six months he had worked his way into the confidence of Confederate Secretary of War Judah P. Benjamin and other Southern officials and was given the job of secret courier, carrying messages between Confederate headquarters in Richmond and Southern sympathizers in Baltimore. It was an ideal arrangement, for it not only enabled Pinkerton to read the Confederate dispatches, it also permitted Webster to report his own observations of Southern troop movements and other tactical information.

When Webster was taken ill in Richmond, Pinkerton sent a woman agent to nurse him and two detectives to help carry on his work. Unfortunately, the two men had earlier assisted Pinkerton in the arrest of Mrs. Rose Greenhow, a Confederate spy, in Washington, D.C. Mrs. Greenhow had been sent to Richmond in a prisoner exchange, and chanced to recognize one of the two Pinkerton detectives. He and his associate were arrested and one of them apparently betrayed Webster in exchange for his life. Webster was tried on charges of espionage and hanged.

In November 1862, after the failure of the Peninsula Campaign and other military errors, General George McClellan was relieved of his command by President Lincoln. Pinkerton immediately resigned his commission and withdrew his detective force from the army. He spent the duration of the war working for the government in New Orleans, but his assignments were standard police work, rather than espionage or counterintelligence.

After the war, Pinkerton reopened his detective agency and was joined in the business by his two sons, William and Robert. The post-war Pinkerton's Agency prospered, largely because of the increased number of bank, stagecoach, and train robberies. In July 1873, a gang of outlaws derailed a train near Adair, Iowa, killing the engineer and badly injuring the fireman. The gang robbed the safe in the baggage car and relieved the passengers of their money and valuables before riding off into the darkness. The Adams Express Company hired Pinkerton's to track down the bandits, and Allan Pinkerton and his son William trailed the gang through several states before losing them in Missouri. However, the detectives succeeded in identifying the gang members: Jesse and Frank James, the Younger brothers, and several lesser known outlaws.

During the next two years, three undercover agents sent by Pinkerton to infiltrate the James gang were killed by the outlaws. In January 1875, a posse led by Pinkerton's detectives surrounded the Missouri home of Dr. and Mrs. Reuben Samuels, the James brothers' stepfather and mother. As the posse approached the farmhouse, the occupants extinguished the lights. The detectives tossed a flare into the building, accidentally causing an explosion. When the smoke cleared, the posse found eight-year-old Archie Samuels—Jesse and Frank's half-brother—dying from the wounds he received in the blast. Mrs. Samuels had lost her right arm. Jesse and Frank James were not in the farmhouse; they had learned of the trap and fled before the posse arrived.

Jesse James swore vengeance against the Pinkertons and stalked Allan Pinkerton in Chicago for four months. He had several chances to shoot the detective from ambush, but he did not. Jesse later told a friend, "I wanted him to know who did it. It wouldn't do me no good if I couldn't tell him about it before he died. I had a dozen chances to kill him when he didn't know it. I wanted to give him a fair chance, but the opportunity never came."

Jesse James was later often heard to say, "I know that God will someday deliver Allan Pinkerton into my hands." But the outlaw's faith was never rewarded. Nor was Allan Pinkerton destined to capture Jesse James, who was murdered by one of his own gang seven years later.

Pinkerton's pioneered the use of photographs for criminal identification and compiled the first "rogues' gallery." A Pinkerton's detective visiting a Fort Worth, Texas, photographic studio discovered a group portrait the famous Wild Bunch posed for while hiding out in the area. The photograph included Butch Cassidy and the Sundance Kid (whose real names were Robert Parker and Harry Longabaugh, respectively), and the thousands of wanted posters Pinkerton's had printed from the picture were a major factor in convincing Cassidy and Sundance to leave the country and ply their trade—robbing banks—in South America.

The exploits of the Pinkertons were glamorized in a series of eighteen books published in the name of Allan Pinkerton. In fact, the books were written by a stable of six writers hired by Pinkerton to promote the legend of his detective agency.

Bank and train robbers weren't Pinkerton's only quarry in the years after the Civil War. Business and industry faced a much greater threat to profits—the growing demands by employees for decent wages and working conditions. Rather than give in to these demands, businessmen found it cheaper to hire undercover agents to spy on and disrupt labor unions, and private police to beat strikers into submission. To its lasting disgrace, Pinkerton's National Detective Agency was a major supplier of such services.

But many of the working men were made desperate by their plight and resorted to violent acts; in fairness to Pinkerton, it must be admitted that some of the cases in which he was employed against labor were essentially investigations of murder or other serious crimes. The Molly Maguires investigation is a case in point.

The Molly Maguires was a secret society that had its origins in the poverty and hunger of nineteenth-century Ireland. Many of the Irishmen who fled famine and oppression in their native land ended up in the coal mines of Pennsylvania where conditions were little better, sometimes worse. As in the Old Country, the secret Molly Maguires society was a means of striking back at the exploiters. Like many insurgent groups, it sought to achieve its ends through terrorism, including murder. That was where Pinkerton's came in.

In 1873, Pinkerton sent an agent—James McParlan, a young Irish immigrant—to infiltrate the Molly Maguires. McParlan became Jim McKenna, a hard-drinking drifter fleeing a murder charge in Buffalo, New York. McParlan/McKenna succeeded in penetrating the Molly Maguires and spent three years in his role as undercover informer. After he surfaced in 1876, his testimony led to the conviction and execution of several of the society's leaders.

Shortly after the turn of the century, Pinkerton's son William recounted the story of McParlan and the Molly Maguires to a fellow passenger during a transatlantic voyage. The man was so intrigued by the tale he later obtained a copy of Allan Pinkerton's ghostwritten *The Molly Maguires and the Detectives*. A writer himself, he decided to incorporate the case into one of his own stories. The man was Arthur Conan Doyle and the story was that Sherlock Holmes classic, *The Valley of Fear*.

Not all of the Pinkerton's Agency's labor cases were as heroic, or even as successful, as the Molly Maguires investigation. The very name of the firm became synonymous with labor spying and strikebreaking. Perhaps the worst such incident occurred in 1892 when the Carnegie Steel Company was hit by a strike at its Homestead Works near Pittsburgh. The company hired Pinkerton's to protect the plant, and the agency brought in 300 armed guards from New York and Chicago. When the Pinkerton's guards attempted to enter the plant grounds from barges in the Monongahela River, they were met by thousands of angry strikers. A pitched battle ensued in which three Pinkertons and five strikers were killed and many more injured. The Pinkertons finally surrendered to the superior force and were escorted to the local railroad station by the strikers, many of whom administered vicious beatings to the guards along the way. For Pinkerton's the incident was a complete debacle.

The Homestead Massacre, as it was called, became an issue in the presidential campaign of 1892 and may have helped Grover Cleveland defeat President Benjamin Harrison. It was also the subject of a House Judiciary subcommittee investigation, which questioned the propriety of law enforcement by hired police. Perhaps as a consequence of the unfavorable public attention the private detective agency had received, Congress passed the Pinkerton Law, which prohibited the federal government from hiring Pinkerton's Detective Agency or similar firms.

Four decades later, in 1936, Pinkerton's was again called on the congressional carpet by the Senate over the agency's anti-labor activities. A Judiciary subcommittee headed by Senator Robert LaFollette, Jr., of Wisconsin was set up to investigate violations of free speech and labor's right to organize and bargain collectively, resulting from management's use of private police. The hearings inspired a congressional resolution that "the so-called industrial spy system breeds fear, suspicion and animosity, tends to cause strikes and industrial warfare and is contrary to sound public policy." Pinkerton's might have added that labor spying assignments were a headache and far more trouble than they were worth. On the heels of the congressional resolution, the detective agency announced it would no longer work for either side in labor disputes. Pinkerton's maintains that policy to this day.

Allan Pinkerton died in 1884. The business was carried on by his sons William and Robert, then by his grandson, Allan Pinkerton II, and then by his great-grandson Robert Pinkerton II. In 1967, a non-Pinkerton was appointed president of the company for the first time.

Throughout the first half century of its history, the Pinkerton law enforcement dynasty provided America with something we have always boasted we didn't need and never had: a national police force. Until the Federal Bureau of Investigation was formed in 1909, only Pinkerton's ranged from coast to coast in the investigation of crime and the pursuit of criminals. It was Pinkerton's that, in 1897, formed the first centralized criminal records system, the National Bureau of Criminal Identification under the auspices of the International Association of Chiefs of Police; the collection was turned over to the FBI's Identification Division in 1924.

The curious set of circumstances that made our first national police force a private one tells us something about the dynamics of private police power in America. We have always left law enforcement to state and local governments, an arrangement that has proved adequate to meet most requirements of public order and safety. But big business transcends local jurisdictions and state lines, and holds large concentrations of private property, an attractive target for professional criminals who also operate interstate. Given these basic factors, it is easy to understand the parallel growth of private capital and hired police.

Pinkerton's remained virtually unchallenged in its role of national police force until 1909, the year in which the Justice Department's Bureau of Investigation was created, the agency that later came to be known as the Federal Bureau of Investigation. But it was not the embryonic Bureau that threatened Pinkerton's primacy in the Private Sector, but the creation of a new private detective agency under the leadership of William J. Burns. Three months after it was formed, the Burns agency took away Pinkerton's most prized customer, the American Bankers Association and its contract for the protection of 11,000 member banks.

William Burns started out as a freelance private detective at age thirty in 1888. Three years later, he joined the U.S. Secret Service and soon chalked up an impressive record catching counterfeiters. As Burns's reputation grew and his fame spread, he was often in demand by other federal agencies in need of detective work. In 1903, President Theodore Roosevelt sent Burns to investigate federal land fraud in Oregon. Before he completed his assignment three years later, Burns had turned up corruption at every level of the Interior Department's General Land Office, and brought about the conviction of many prominent persons, including a U.S. senator from Oregon.

Burns's success in the land frauds case caught the attention of Fremont Older, editor of the *San Francisco Bulletin*. Older was concerned about the totally corrupt municipal government in his city and the stranglehold several large corporations had on San Francisco. He and California banker Rudolph Spreckels persuaded President Theodore Roosevelt to grant Burns and his men a leave of absence from federal service to come to San Francisco and clean up the city.

Burns and his team of detectives had been given a formidable task. Arrayed against them was a national trolley car trust called United Railroads, several other public utilities that had bought the city officials, the San Francisco Police and Sheriff's Departments which were also in the pockets of the grafters, and a city administration riddled by a labyrinthine pattern of corruption.

Also working against the Burns group was newspaper publisher William Randolph Hearst who hired cartoonist Ed Fisher to satirize them. Fisher drew a comic strip featuring a tall, gangling character named Colonel A. Mutt, and added a detective known as "Hot Tobasco Burns," much to the delight of the real-life Burns. Francis Heney, a Burns associate appointed as deputy district attorney for the corruption probe, became a grinning dwarf named Beany in the strip, who always wore a little cap. University of California students adopted the cap and added the word "beanie" to the language. Ed Fisher's strip survived the affair; later he added a short, bald character to complement the tall, thin Colonel Mutt, and the strip became the now-familiar "Mutt and Jeff."

After a three-year campaign in San Francisco, Burns could point to at least partial success: the corruption had been exposed and some of the grafters were behind bars. But rather than return to federal service, Burns decided to go into business with his detective team. Thus began the second Private Sector dynasty, a national detective agency today still controlled by members of the Burns family.

William Burns was in his sixties in 1921 when he came out of retirement to accept the post of director of the Justice Department's Bureau of Investigation. Unfortunately, Burns's three-year tour as director added nothing to his distinguished career, and he was unable to keep the Bureau from becoming involved in the political scandals of the Harding administration. In 1924, he resigned and was succeeded by his assistant, a young man named John Edgar Hoover, who was to enjoy a somewhat longer and more successful tenure in the position.

Today Pinkerton's and the William J. Burns International Security Services are the two largest contract security firms in the Private Sector. Pinkerton's has offices in ninety-three North American cities; Burns has ninety-nine branch offices throughout North and South America. Each does close to $200 million worth of business annually and employs almost 40,000 people, roughly half of whom work full-time. Both firms are now engaged primarily in rent-a-cop services; detective work comprises only a small fraction of their revenues. Together the two giants collect about a third of all the money spent on hired police each year.

Third place among the Private Sector giants is occupied by the Wackenhut Corporation, which is also the fastest growing private security firm in the country. Compared to Pinkerton's century and a quarter and Burns's nearly seven decades, Wackenhut is a relative newcomer. It was founded in 1954 during the height of the Cold War and the McCarthyite obsession with suspected domestic subversion. If the stories of Pinkerton's and Burns delineate the history of hired police in America, Wackenhut's brief record tells us much about the Private Sector in our own times.

Originally known as Special Investigations, Inc., the company was founded in Miami, Florida, by former FBI special agent George Wackenhut. Wackenhut had served with the Bureau for three years, from 1951 to 1954, and his job didn't really entail investigation; the robust six-footer worked as a physical education instructor, training agents in hand-to-hand combat. Still, the FBI image was a valuable Private Sector asset, regardless of the kind of experience it actually represented, and Wackenhut enhanced his company's expertise by bringing in three other former agents.

But neither image nor expertise was the key to Wackenhut's success; rather, it was devising a legal means to circumvent the 1893 Pinkerton Act. The law, passed in the wake of the Homestead Massacre, states, "An individual employed by the Pinkerton Detective Agency, or similar organization, may not be employed by the Government of the United States or the government of the District of Columbia." The comptroller-general of the United States in 1928 and 1946 further ruled that detective agency employees could not be hired by the government even to work as guards or in other nondetective jobs. But Wackenhut knew the government was going to become a prime customer for rent-a-cop services, and he sought some way around the restrictions of the Pinkerton Act.

Wackenhut hired the law firm of Senator George A. Smathers, a conservative Florida Democrat, to look into the problem. The attorneys came up with a simple solution: create a wholly owned subsidiary company to provide guard services, but no detectives. It worked; Wackenhut's subsidiary dodge withstood the legal challenges of his competitors, and he was soon providing guards to federal agencies. The Atomic Energy Commission signed a $3-million-a-year contract with Wackenhut to guard its Nevada nuclear test site. The National Aeronautics and Space Administration paid the firm $1 million annually for guards at Cape Kennedy, and another $400,000 for protective services at its Greenbelt, Maryland, facilities. By 1965, Wackenhut was doing $17 million annually, more than a third of which was from federal government clients. The former FBI jock had become a multimillionaire, with a palatial home in Coral Gables and a yacht called the *Security Risk*.

Despite this whimsical use of the term, Wackenhut takes the matter of security risks very seriously. His agency's files are said to contain dossiers on every name in the files of the old House Committee on Un-American Activities, and the firm distributes a monthly bulletin called *The Wackenhut Security Review: Communism and You!* The Wackenhut Corporation's board of directors has included such prominent personalities of the political right as the late Captain Eddie Rickenbacker, General Mark Clark, and Ralph E. Davis, a member of the John Birch Society's national council. In addition to Wackenhut himself, thirty former special agents of the FBI hold down senior positions in the detective firm.

Mixing business with right-wing politics has proved an effective formula for Wackenhut's private sector success. One of his principal allies in the political arena is Claude Roy Kirk, Jr., a businessman who made his personal fortune in insurance and stock brokerage before going into politics. Wackenhut supported Kirk in several of the politician's bids for public office in the 1960s. In 1966, Kirk won the Florida gubernatorial race with a campaign against crime and corruption. After he took office, Kirk announced his crusade against crime in Florida. He said he was going to employ "a task force of untouchables" to clean up the state. The untouchables were not to be state, county, or local cops, he revealed: Governor Kirk's war on the Mob was to be waged by the Wackenhut Corporation.

It was not the first time Wackenhut had accepted public sector assignments. In 1957, he talked the foreman of a Dade County grand jury into hiring him to investigate crime and corruption in Miami. Wackenhut dramatized his probe with such stunts as 2 A.M. telephone calls to the jury foreman to hint about the risk of personal danger, and the implication that prominent persons were involved in government scandals. In the end he produced, for a $2500 fee, a 340-page report filled with hearsay and information from the newspapers, but nothing the grand jury could use to obtain even a single indictment. The jury foreman recalls, "My impressions were that you couldn't have a sorrier investigator."

But Wackenhut's performance in the 1957 investigation did nothing to deter Kirk almost ten years later from using the former FBI gym instructor and his agency to investigate Florida's organized crime problem. Kirk didn't actually put Wackenhut on the public payroll; instead, he hired him as a dollar-a-year employee and asked some of his rich friends to chip in to a private trust fund to pay the detective agency's $1000-per-day fee.

Twenty-six "Wackencops"—as they came to be called—were assigned to Kirk's private war on organized crime. Each was issued official credentials, signed by the governor, authorizing the private eyes to conduct investigations on behalf of the State of Florida. All regular law enforcement agencies in the state were directed to cooperate with the private detectives, including throwing open all their files to them. The governor sought to drum up public support for the project through a statewide billboard advertising campaign, which produced a steady stream of leads phoned in by helpful citizens. George Wackenhut made a daily report to Governor Kirk from his Miami office over a special red scrambler telephone connected to an identical instrument in the Talahassee statehouse.

Many of Kirk's political oppenents charged that the Wackencops were really the governor's personal Gestapo, a claim that was supported by the private detectives' probing into political matters having no apparent connection to organized crime. One county elections supervisor revealed that the Wackencops had been snooping into voting records, which contained such information as party affiliation, property ownership, and frequency of voting. Other Wackenhut agents trailed a prominent Democratic politician to the Bahamas to document reports he had engaged the services of prostitutes there. And Florida Secretary of State Thomas B. Adams, a Democrat, said he had been warned by hotel owners that Wackenhut investigators had asked them to keep track of his visitors and telephone calls. Other officials reported the same thing.

Nineteen of the Wackencops were former FBI agents, but the only investigator with any real knowledge of the Mob seems to have been Hank Messick, a highly respected investigative reporter Wackenhut hired from the *Miami Herald*. Messick had earned his reputation uncovering organized crime in Kentucky, and had compiled extensive files on the Mob in Florida. He knew the state was in the grip of organized crime and he believed the Kirk–Wackenhut claims that they were going to do something about it. After six weeks he quit, declaring, "A hoax is being perpetrated on the people of Florida and I will not be a party to that hoax."

The Wackencops' record over the first month and a half of their war on organized crime was, in fact, rather unimpressive. The only tangible result the untouchables had achieved was the nailing of a Titusville school superintendent who had stolen a $400 washer-dryer and some other items from the school system. If the black hand of La Cosa Nostra had manipulated the washing machine thief, it was well hidden.

The Kirk–Wackenhut war on crime had achieved little more when, after four months, it collapsed from lack of funds. The private donations Kirk had counted on to support the Wackencops never materialized, and the Florida legislature refused to appropriate funds for the project. The Wackenhut Corporation's $1000-per-day bills were, for the most part, never paid, but the detective agency had reason to view the episode as something other than a total loss. Publicity from the company's role in the project had increased Wackenhut's private investigative work by 63 percent over the same three-month period of the previous year. The war on crime had been good advertising.

The Wackenhut Corporation continued to prosper and grow at the phenomenal annual rate of 28.4 percent during the late sixties. Subsidiaries were opened in the Caribbean and in several Latin American countries. By 1969, the company was servicing 6000 clients from seventy offices in thirty-six states. In 1974, its twentieth year of operation, the Wackenhut Corporation plucked one of the juiciest plums in the history of the Private Sector, a $15 million contract to guard the trans-Alaska pipeline during construction.

If Pinkerton's and Burns represent the Private Sector's past and Wackenhut its present, then some dim image of its future may be read in the operations of a relative newcomer to the scene, International Intelligence, Inc. Intertel, as it is more commonly known, is not a giant rent-a-cop company; it is, in effect, an intelligence agency for hire, and it is staffed by a small group of the Private Sector's elite. Its founder and president is Robert Dolan Peloquin, a private police entrepreneur very much in the tradition of Allan Pinkerton and William Burns.

Peloquin is a veteran of Naval Intelligence and the National Security Agency, and a graduate of Georgetown University Law School. In 1955, he joined the Justice Department and soon became one of the government's bright young investigating attorneys. He was part of the Justice Department team that nailed Jimmy Hoffa on a jury-tampering charge and sent the Teamster boss to prison. In 1966, Peloquin became chief of the first government strike force against organized crime, a group of agents from several federal law enforcement agencies working together as a team. Four years later, when he formed Intertel, he described the firm as ''the first organized crime strike force in the private sector.''

Peloquin wasn't exaggerating; the Intertel staff included John D. O'Connell, a twenty-four-year FBI veteran who specialized in organized crime investigations; William A. Kolar, former director of the IRS's intelligence division and an eight-year FBI man; Fenelon Richards, formerly director of enforcement for the U.S. Bureau of Customs; David Belisle, formerly deputy director of security for the State Department and also formerly director of investigation for the National Security Agency; James Golden, an ex-Secret Service agent; and Warren Adams, formerly of the Las Vegas sheriff's gaming squad. Intertel's board of directors included Sir Ranulph Bacon, formerly head of Scotland Yard. It was the greatest collection of recycled brass ever to be assembled in the Private Sector.

Intertel's pitch was that it was a management consulting firm which specialized in advising client businesses on how to keep the Mafia out. Peloquin and his staff are well qualified to provide such services, and many of their clients have probably benefited from their collective background in official Mob-busting law enforcement agencies. But Intertel's expertise goes well beyond the field of industrial security and includes such specialties as economic intelligence, data processing, systems engineering, and the behavioral sciences. It is more an intelligence agency than either a management consulting firm or a private detective outfit.

The seed that was to grow to be Intertel was planted in the mid-1960s by a man named James M. Crosby. Crosby was a partner with A&P heir Huntington Hartford in the Mary Carter Paint Company, which owned a desolate strip of sand in the Bahamas known as Hog Island. Crosby and Hartford had big plans for Hog, including a resort and gambling casino. There was one problem that had to be surmounted first: how to keep the local Bahamian gamblers from dealing themselves into the project. Crosby took his problem to the Justice Department where he met Robert Peloquin.

Peloquin launched a Justice Department probe of the Bahamian gamblers whom Crosby saw as a threat; shortly thereafter a series of exposés of their ties to the Mob appeared in the American press. A Royal Commission of Inquiry was convened to study the matter, and Peloquin saw that it received the full cooperation of the U.S. Department of Justice. (The Commission was chaired by Sir Ranulph Bacon, the former Scotland Yard chief who later became an Intertel director.) The Commission's probe exposed the casino corruption, put a serious dent in the power of the local gamblers, and even led to the expulsion of one of the most troublesome of Crosby's competitors.

As the resort and casino were erected, Hog Island was renamed Paradise Island, and the Mary Carter Paint Company was reorganized into Resorts International, Inc. A bridge spanning the channel between Paradise and Nassau was constructed, and a security firm, Paradise Enterprises, Inc., was formed to police the casino. Peloquin, who had resigned from the Justice Department, became president of Paradise Enterprises, and William G. Hundley, formerly of the Justice Department's Internal Security Division, became the company's secretary and general counsel.

Paradise Island flourished, and in 1969, little more than a year after the casino opened, Resort International's stock had climbed from $5 to $60 per share. The company's profits were intact because Peloquin and his staff had succeeded in keeping the Mob off Paradise Island. Resorts International realized that the same expertise would be worth a great deal of money to other businesses threatened by organized crime. To tap this growing market, the Paradise Island entrepreneurs formed Intertel.

One of the private intelligence agency's first customers was Howard Hughes, who was heavily invested in legalized gambling in Las Vegas and was beginning to eye the Bahamas as a place to expand his casino operations. In fact, Hughes was planning to move to the Bahamas and abandon his quarters on the top floor of Las Vegas's Desert Inn. For the billionaire recluse, such a relocation was fraught with threats of everything from microbes to Mafiosi, so Intertel was hired to make the arrangements.

The Intertel staff was busy working up an operational plan to rival the Normandy landings when, on Thanksgiving eve 1970, the Hughes organization called Intertel to say the boss wanted to make the move that very night. The meticulous plan was scrapped and every available Intertel agent headed for Las Vegas. Hughes was bundled aboard a private jet and whisked away to the Bahamas with such speed and confusion that the impression was left with many observers that Intertel had kid-napped the billionaire.

The kidnapping theory was further fueled when Intertel took over operation of Hughes's casinos and fired Robert Maheu, Hughes's long-time executive officer. (Maheu is the former FBI agent who procured the cooperation of Mafia figures Sam Giancana and John Roselli to carry out assassination attempts against Fidel Castro on behalf of the CIA.) Maheu hired the private detective firm of Investigators, Inc., to go to Nassau and find out if his former boss was being held prisoner on Paradise Island. The team of eight agents sent on the mission did not ar-rive in the Bahamas unnoticed; their hotel rooms were bugged, their telephones tapped, their mail opened, and their incoming messages in-tercepted. The detectives could only report that Intertel's countersur-veillance had been so thorough that they hadn't been able to learn any-thing of the billionaire's situation.

But apparently Hughes was in complete control of matters and Inter-tel, rather than being his jailer, was his servant. About a year after the Thanksgiving journey, Hughes assigned Peloquin the task of proving that Clifford Irving's forthcoming "autobiography" of Hughes was a fraud. Intertel did this job so well that Irving and his wife ended up in prison.

When the authenticity of the Irving manuscript was called into ques-tion, the publisher, McGraw-Hill, produced three cancelled checks to-talling $650,000 made out to and endorsed by "H. R. Hughes." Hand-writing experts confirmed that the endorsements were in the handwriting of Howard Hughes, a claim that later proved untrue. Pel-oquin wanted to get a look at the checks to learn where they had been deposited, in the hope that he could trace the transaction back to Irving. McGraw-Hill refused to let Peloquin see them.

As the controversy deepened, a representative of the publisher ap-peared on the "Today" show and exhibited the three checks before the television cameras. Peloquin obtained a tape of the show and had a blow-up made of the shot showing the checks. The photo revealed that the checks had been deposited in the Zurich branch of Credit Suisse, a Swiss bank.

Peloquin flew to Zurich and visited the bank, where he learned that

"H. R. Hughes" was a woman. He called his Washington office and arranged to have a photograph of Irving's wife, Edith, sent to him. He showed the photo to the teller who handled the transaction and she identified it as the woman who had deposited the checks. Peloquin reported his discovery to Hughes's lawyers who turned it over to the U.S. attorney in New York. Irving and his wife were subsequently arrested and pleaded guilty to the fraud.

Within the small world of the Private Sector, Intertel soon acquired the reputation of being "Howard Hughes's private CIA." Such was not exactly the case, however, for the firm had several other major clients. One of these was ITT, a link that involved Intertel in the Dita Beard Memorandum Affair, one of the mini-scandals of the early Nixon administration that presaged Watergate.

The two-page memorandum that became the center of a political vortex was written by Dita Beard, ITT's Washington lobbyist, to William Merriam, head of the company's Washington office. It concerned a secret ITT contribution of $400,000 to the Republican Party for the purpose of buying off a Justice Department anti-trust action against the company. The memo implicated President Nixon, his aide Bob Haldeman, California Lieutenant-Governor Ed Reinecke, and Attorney-General John Mitchell in the payment. It was written in June 1971; nine months later columnist Jack Anderson received and published a copy of the document.

The ITT–White House strategy for troubleshooting the situation involved disavowing the memorandum as a forgery. The company brought in specialists from Intertel to determine whether the memo could be proved authentic. The Intertel document examiners reported that the memorandum had almost certainly been prepared on a typewriter in Dita Beard's office, but added it would be virtually impossible to prove it. Armed with the latter assurance, the company and the White House set out to brand the memo a forgery. Jack Anderson reports that ITT also assigned Intertel the task of discrediting him. If so, it was one of Intertel's failures; ITT and the White House suffered a serious loss of credibility from the affair, but Anderson's reputation emerged unscathed.

Intertel's ties to the Nixon administration actually antedated the Dita

Beard Affair by several years. Resorts International president James M. Crosby happened to be a close friend and business associate of Nixon chum Bebe Rebozo and during the 1968 presidential race Crosby donated $100,000 to Nixon's campaign. Crosby lent Nixon his yacht and was an occasional visitor at the White House after the candidate was elected. As a favor to the president, Crosby hired James O. Golden, a former Secret Service agent who had served as the Nixon campaign's chief of security. (Golden became an Intertel vice-president before moving on to become security director of the Hughes Tool Company.)

Given this affinity of Intertel's proprietors for the Nixon administration, it might seem surprising that the firm inspired the deepest fear and suspicion among the president's advisors. Jack Caulfield, the retired New York cop who handled Nixon's most sensitive security problems, was especially mistrustful of Intertel, which employs many Justice Department veterans who served under Attorney-General Robert Kennedy and are loyalists of the Kennedy family. Considering Intertel's intimate involvement in the affairs of Howard Hughes, Caulfield feared some of the Kennedy people in the firm might learn details of the long and shady relationship between Hughes and Nixon, and turn the information over to the Democrats for use in the 1972 elections. Caulfield went so far as to propose Operation Sand Wedge, a plan for establishing "a Republican Intertel," to be called the Security Consulting Group, Inc. The idea was dropped and the White House Plumbers were formed instead.

Apparently Caulfield's fears of Intertel were unfounded; the firm seems to have steered clear of both sides in the 1972 election. Intertel is, after all, not a conventional private detective agency, but a creature of the world of multinational corporations and international finance. The entrepreneurs who operate in that rarefied atmosphere know there is more to be gained in influencing politicians than in trying to influence elections. Backing one candidate against another is an unnecessary gamble; winners are natural allies, and whoever emerges victorious in the political arena can be expected to share one basic tenet with the conquerors of the international marketplace: ideology is abstract, but wealth and power are tangible. So Intertel leaves the dirty tricks to the political cowboys of the Private Sector and keeps its eye on the profit-and-loss statement.

The men who run Intertel are not simply ex-cops embarked on a second career in mid-life. You'll find no telltale bulge beneath the shoulders of their tailored, three-piece business suits, and their slim attaché cases are more likely to contain pages of computer printout than brass knuckles or handcuffs. Their clients are not retail merchants or jealous spouses, but giant international enterprises that do business under the crazy-quilt pattern formed by the laws of a dozen nations.

The world has grown more complex in the last quarter-century, and business has become more sophisticated and international. Jesse James, Butch Cassidy, and the other desperados of the past are dusty tintypes in the files of Pinkerton's and the other old Private Sector giants. The supercriminals of today are white-collar crooks who pull off massive swindles in the international marketplace, and the Private Sector sleuths hired to catch them must be able to follow a computer audit trail through an accounting system as easily as their predecessors tracked train robbers through the towns and wilderness of nineteenth-century America. The Private Sector constantly reshapes itself to meet the changing needs of its principal client—big business.

The more traditional types of private eyes and rent-a-cops are still with us, of course, and promise to be around in increasing numbers for the foreseeable future. And well into our third century of nationhood we can expect the hired police of the Private Sector to continue to be an influence on our history, our literature, and even our folklore.

3

Company Cops and Corporate Counterspies

Panama City is a quiet coastal town in the Florida panhandle. Its long, white beaches and clear Gulf waters attract vacationers throughout the Southeast during the summer months. But the town is too far north to share the year-round warmth of southern Florida, so the local residents were surprised to see a sudden influx of strangers in early March 1976. Even more remarkable was the vanguard of grim-faced men, each with a gun and shoulder holster beneath his jacket, that arrived four days before the main party. The armed contingent set up shop at the Bay Point Yacht and Country Club and established a security perimeter around the beachside resort, where one hundred rooms had been reserved for a ten-day period. The local police made no objection; they had been briefed by a man from the State Department who asked their cooperation. Very important people were going to be staying at the Club, they were told. The armed men were there to guard them. They were the private police force of the Arabian-American Oil Co.

Aramco, as the oil company is more commonly known, is a consortium formed by Texaco, Mobil, Exxon, and Standard Oil of California. It has an exclusive concession to drill within Saudi Arabia, which sits atop 138 billion barrels of oil, more than the combined reserves of the United States, the Soviet Union, and China. The purpose of the Panama

City meeting was to negotiate the nationalization of the company by the Saudi Arabian government. A central figure in the negotiations would be the Arabian oil minister, Sheik Ahmed Yamani. Barely four months earlier, Sheik Yamani and scores of other OPEC officials were taken hostage by Palestinian terrorists who invaded a meeting in Vienna. The gun-toting Aramco security men were in Panama City to make sure it didn't happen again.

If the local police viewed the Aramco men as rent-a-cops or some other kind of unprofessional Private Sector muscle, they were mistaken. The Aramco force is headed by George W. Ryan, a former FBI agent, and the private cops were trained at the Agency for International Development's International Police Academy in Washington, D.C., at the expense of the Saudi Arabian government. The oil company's police probably equaled or surpassed the Panama City cops in their professionalism, an estimate apparently shared by the terrorists; the Aramco talks took place without incident.

Aramco is not unique in raising its own private police force. From big multinational corporations to small research and development "think-tanks," business is increasingly taking the matter of industrial security into its own hands. General Motors has a force of 4200 plant guards, which makes its corporate police force larger than the municipal police departments of all but five American cities. And the Ford Motor Company has twenty-four ex-FBI agents on its payroll to counter threats ranging from dishonest employees to industrial spies. The business world seems to believe that law enforcement is too important a matter to be left to the police.

Company cops are not a new invention; they've been around since the mid-nineteenth century. Railroads, coal mines, and steel mills had their own police, who were often deputized with full police powers. Like the private detectives of the day, the company cops spent much of their time in labor spying, strikebreaking, and other anti-union activities. In the 1920s and 1930s, the Ford Motor Company organized its "Service Department," which was really a company police force composed of former boxers, bouncers, football players, and FBI agents. The Department became well-known for its anti-labor work, which climaxed in 1937 with a brutal attack on demonstrators near a Ford plant. UAW leader

Walter Reuther was among the victims of the assault, as were several newsmen and photographers covering the demonstration. The incident resulted in some very bad publicity for Ford, and helped bring an end to the use of Private Sector cops against organized labor.

Today, the immediate concern of the company cops is not strikes, but terrorism. At home and abroad, big business has become a target for bombings, kidnappings, and even assassinations. Tension seems to be highest among those firms doing business in Argentina.

In 1972, the People's Revolutionary Army kidnapped Oberdan Sallustro, an executive of the Fiat automobile company in Buenos Aires. The kidnappers demanded that Fiat reinstate 250 workers fired in a labor dispute at an Argentine Fiat plant, and contribute $1 million worth of exercise books, shoes, pencils, and other items to needy schoolchildren throughout the country. They also demanded that the Argentine government release fifty jailed guerrillas and fly them to Algeria. Fiat accepted the ransom demand, but before it could act, the government cut off the arrangements by threatening the company with prosecution for ''illicit associations'' with the kidnappers. The police tracked down the abductors, but Sallustro was shot to death when they stormed the hideout.

About a year later, Anthony DaCruz, an American citizen and technical operations manager for Eastman Kodak in Argentina, was driving in a Buenos Aires suburb when his car was rammed by a pickup truck. DaCruz was forced into another car at gunpoint and taken away. His kidnappers delivered him to Kodak safe and sound for a ransom of $1.5 million.

A few weeks later, the People's Revolutionary Army tried to grab a Ford Motor Company executive as he left a company plant in Buenos Aires. When company police tried to intervene, the terrorists opened fire, wounding the businessman and another Ford employee. The two recovered, but the company received a demand for a $1 million contribution to Argentine charities to forestall a repeat attempt. Ford paid.

Less than a month afterward, it was Firestone Tire and Rubber Company's turn. John R. Thompson, president of Firestone's Argentine subsidiary, was riding in a chauffeur-driven limousine when it was intercepted by a squadron of five terrorist vehicles. The guerrillas smashed in the car's windows, grabbed Thompson, knocked the driver into a roadside ditch, and fired a fusillade into the air before driving off with their captive. Thompson was kept in a tent inside a room somewhere in Buenos Aires while his abductors worked out the details of a $3 million ransom, to be paid in Argentine pesos. The kidnappers picked up the huge pile of peso notes in an armored car. Three days later—presumably the time required to count the ransom—Thompson was released unharmed.

More recently, companies have become reluctant to release the details of such incidents, or even to acknowledge that they have taken place. However, corporate security consultant Fred Rayne reports that there have been about 170 kidnappings in Argentina in recent years, and more than $100 million has been paid in ransom. Rayne says that one company, which he doesn't identify, paid $14,200,000 to kidnappers for the life of one senior executive. In other Latin American countries, the threat of kidnapping is less severe, but present nonetheless. Businessmen have learned to live looking over their shoulders, and to rely on the company cops for their well-being. The problem is worse than the business establishment is willing to admit.

The growing popularity south of the border of snatching an American businessman and then selling him back to his employers has resulted in a number of Private Sector developments. One of these is the new type of driving school which instructs company chauffeurs in such exotica as how to keep from being forced off the road by an overtaking vehicle, how to avoid being boxed in fore and aft by the bad guys, and how to execute a 180-degree turn while skidding to a stop at a terrorist roadblock. Such training is predicated on the principle that a company official is most vulnerable to kidnapping during his daily routine while on the road.

The BSR Counter-Terrorist Driving School offers this kind of training at its two-mile road-racing course at Summit Point, West Virginia. The course is conducted by Bill Scott, a former U.S. and European road-racing champion, who also trains racing drivers at the same location. The curriculum includes films and lectures, high-speed driving, and such escape maneuvers as ''bootleg turns, J-turns, off-road recovery, and barricade breaching.'' Among the first students to take the four-day, $1295 course was Joe Battle, chauffeur for FBI Director Clarence Kelley.

The popularity of kidnapping has also brought about a boom in the bodyguard business. Guardsmark, Inc., a professional bodyguard outfit, estimates there were 20,000 bodyguards in 1975, and projects a figure of 70,000 for 1979. Wackenhut Corporation recently observed a 22-percent annual growth in its bodyguard business. Unlike the $2-per-hour rent-a-cops who are often nothing more than a warm body in a uniform, professional bodyguards, who wear plainclothes, are highly trained in defensive techniques and earn upwards of $20,000 per year.

Yet another gimmick inspired by the kidnapping craze is kidnap ransom insurance. No insurance company will admit writing a policy that reimburses a client company for its losses in ransoming a kidnapped employee, since such a disclosure would be an open invitation to terrorists. Many such policies contain a clause cancelling the insurance if the insured company discloses its existence. Premiums for this kind of coverage can run as high as $40,000 per year, and the deductible amount that must be paid by the insured in the event of a ransom may be as much as a half-million dollars.

Businessmen who forgo overseas travel are not necessarily proof against kidnapping. In 1974, for example, the K-Mart retail chain was the target of a rash of abductions. On four occasions, K-Mart store managers or their families were grabbed and the company was forced to dip into the till to obtain their release. Campbell's Soup installed electronic tracking devices in their executive's automobiles in case any of them are kidnapped.

But the most popular kind of anti-business terrorism within the United States seems to be bombing. According to the government's National Bomb Data Center, there were 2074 actual or attempted bombings during 1975; 69 people were killed and 326 injured, and more than $27 million worth of property was destroyed. While only a few hundred of the bombs were aimed at commercial or industrial targets, those bombings represent most of the property damage. In company mailrooms across the country, x-ray equipment scans incoming envelopes for letter bombs.

A CIA study predicts an increase in terrorist activities within the United States, partly due to increased contact and cooperation between foreign and U.S. terrorist groups. The CIA analysis also forecasts the list of terrorist targets may be extended to include such things as off-shore drilling rigs, nuclear reactor sites, the computer that controls the Bay Area Rapid Transit system in San Francisco, and pipelines.

Most company police forces respond to such alarming predictions simply by beefing up conventional security: more guards, metal detectors, fences, lights, and dogs trained to sniff out explosives. However, at least one company has devised a comprehensive program for dealing with the threat of terrorism; IBM has gone beyond the idea of a company police force and worked out a plan for a central intelligence service within the computer company.

In 1974, the *Berkeley Barb,* a California underground newspaper, managed to obtain a copy of a master plan for counterterrorism developed by IBM with the help of the International Association of Chiefs of Police. The plan, in the form of an eighteen-page booklet, was reportedly used as the text for a two-week course taught at the company's training school in Glen Cove, New York.

In a preamble, the authors of the plan noted IBM's relative good fortune to date in not having experienced the kidnapping or murder of any of its employees. This good luck is attributed to the computer maker's "low profile in some of the overseas areas where major terrorist groups currently operate." But, the authors warn, such good fortune cannot be counted on to continue, even in the United States. "For the domestic radical extremists," they write, "IBM remains as a symbol of post-industrial technological oppression, which is vulnerable both because of its general role in technology and because it is a strong, relatively self-contained organization which has successfully resisted unionization."

The plan reviews the various shades of political extremism, granting the largest share of attention to the radical left. However, the authors note in passing what they call "restorationist extremists," meaning groups on the far right, such as the Ku Klux Klan and the American Nazi Party. "For the domestic restorationist extremist, IBM is only rarely likely to be a target," they write. "Main line American restorationists are likely to be proud of IBM as a symbol of American strength, although Minutemen and Birchers will be alarmed at evidences of IBM's dealing with Soviet Bloc countries and the People's Republic of China." Less doctrinaire "restorationists" presumably understand that, while waving the flag is patriotic, business, after all, is business.

The remedy prescribed by the plan's authors is to develop a corporate intelligence system which will keep track of the terrorists. The plan is quite specific regarding the structure of the system and its role in the corporation. In fact, the language could easily have come directly from an internal CIA working paper:

An intelligence system on terrorists and extremists should allow rapid acquisition, analysis, and dissemination of current data from a specially constituted, specially skilled group, which exists in close liaison with top management. . . .

The group would be equipped to issue periodic as well as special intelligence alerts, and should be staffed to provide analytic support in developing immediate countermeasures for specific situations. It should thus be in close relation to those who must make the actual response. . . .

Corporate countermeasures should be under the control of an "action directorate," which can function both at CHQ [corporate headquarters] level and as a flexible resource to sites [local IBM installations]. It should have an inventory of both policies and systems, for the range of likely response situations. It should be in continuing coordination with similar directorates in other organizations, in recognition of the fact that terrorists seek to exploit vulnerabilities of not only specific organizations, but vulnerabilities created by the failure of organized communities to plan and act in concert.

The IBM plan was nothing less than the design for an international intelligence directorate to operate inside the company.

Publication of the plan by the *Berkeley Barb* caused excruciating embarrassment to IBM, which immediately disavowed the document through a statement from the company's chairman and chief executive, Frank T. Cary. Cary said the plan was "totally repugnant" to IBM, that it had been allowed to be used in an IBM training course "through a series of errors," and that it would be withdrawn and never used again.

Why IBM was so self-conscious about the plan is not obvious. Although it was rather elaborate and couched in such pseudo-military terms as "action directorate," "countermeasures," and "intelligence alert," it was in essence a design for a system that could be used to anticipate terrorist attacks and coordinate efforts to head them off. One might expect IBM to assert this much as a minimum of what it was entitled to do to protect itself. Whatever potential abuses were inherent in the IBM plan, they were trivial in comparison to what another computer manufacturer had already been doing for several years.

Honeywell, Inc., is a Minneapolis-based company and one of the hundred largest industrial corporations in the world. In addition to computers, Honeywell's $2.5 billion in annual sales include a wide variety of other items; if you look closely at the thermostat in your home or office, for example, you will probably see that it was made by Honeywell. Also on the list of Honeywell's products are some particularly nasty fragmentation bombs. The weapons were designed for use against troops, but in Southeast Asia they were inevitably used on civilians. Because of its role in supplying such weapons to the Vietnam War, Honeywell became a particular target for antiwar demonstrations and other protests. One tactic of the protesters was to buy Honeywell stock, which gained them admission to the company's annual stockholders' meetings; in 1970, the meeting had to be adjourned after only fourteen minutes due to a protest demonstration.

The tactics of the Honeywell protesters were nonviolent and generally within the law—there was no threat of terrorism to the company. But the FBI turned its attention to the anti-Honeywell groups anyway, apparently at the request of Honeywell's company cops. The Bureau's tactics included infiltrating paid informers into the protest groups to get information about planned demonstrations. The information was turned over directly to Honeywell, Inc., for use by the company's cops. The arrangement amounted to employing the FBI as an extension of Honeywell's private police force. The fact that both the president of Honeywell, Inc., as well as the chief of Honeywell's company cops, are both members of the Society of Former Special Agents of the FBI may have had something to do with facilitating this cozy arrangement.

Terrorist attacks and political demonstrations are certainly not the only concerns of the company cops. There are, of course, such problems as employee pilferage, vandalism, and professional burglary. But in a number of highly competitive industries, such as computers, pharmaceuticals, chemicals, cosmetics, fashion, and automobile manufacturing, there is another major threat: industrial espionage.

In order to survive and flourish in the marketplace, many companies need much more information about their competitors than the rival firms are willing to give out. The businessman wants to know everything he can find out about the competition's new products, advertising campaigns, price policies, expansion plans, management structure, staff changes, investments, wage negotiations, employee morale, and even company gossip. Collecting such information is referred to variously as "commercial analysis," "market research," or "competitive intelligence." Depending on the lengths to which a company goes to acquire the data, it may also be called industrial espionage.

Espionage is usually involved when a company seeks a certain kind of competitive information known as a "trade secret." Many formulas, processes, devices, or other technical procedures cannot be patented; the Patent Office rejects about 20 percent of the patent applications it receives on the grounds that the idea doesn't meet the rigid legal definition of what may be protected by a patent. But such a discovery, when it has been developed at considerable effort and expense, and when it provides the developer with a definite commercial advantage, is considered in law to be a trade secret. The law recognizes the trade secret as a kind of property which belongs exclusively to its owner, but it offers little in the way of real legal protection of such information. For the holder of a trade secret, the best means of protecting it remain the lock, the fence, and the company cop.

Rarely do businessmen bent on stealing the competition's trade secrets resort to anything so crude as illegal entry or safecracking; often a much easier and perfectly legal alternative is available. To learn a rival's trade secrets, the business spy contacts an executive recruiter, or an employment agency, or he merely puts an ad in the Help Wanted column of the newspaper. The mobile employee is the business equivalent of the defector in international espionage. Hiring away a competitor's employees is probably the most widely practiced technique of industrial espionage. Valuable information about a rival company can often be obtained simply through the technique of interviewing applicants currently employed by the firm in question; often the openings the applicant thinks he's being considered for don't even exist, and the interview is staged merely for the purpose of picking his brain.

In a variation of the gambit, an enterprising employee may forgo the step of offering his inside knowledge to a competitor and go into business for himself, using his former employer's proprietary know-how. Analogic Corporation, a Massachusetts electronics firm, charged in 1976 that this is exactly what two of its former employees did. The company succeeded in obtaining an injunction ordering the rival firm to stop manufacturing a device that appeared to be a duplicate of one developed by Analogic.

Some dishonest employees who resort to do-it-yourself industrial espionage use a more direct approach: they take the company secrets and try to sell them to competitors. Often this trick backfires, however, when the potential customer proves too honest and blows the whistle on the thief. In 1976, for example, an engineer working for the NALCO Chemical Company in Illinois tried to peddle $16 million worth of the firm's secret chemical formulas to competitors. They called the cops, and the engineer received a $2000 fine and two years' probation for his trouble. Also in 1976, an employee of Coulter Electronics, Inc., a small New York electronic firm, grabbed the plans for a new laboratory blood-analysis instrument that the company had developed at a cost of $1 million, and for which a $100-million market had been projected. When an accomplice tried to sell the design to the rival Technicon Corporation, that firm's president immediately called the head of Coulter and helped bait a trap to catch the thief. The two electronics outfits not only bugged the hotel room where the sale was to take place, but they installed a hidden, closed-circuit television camera in the room's TV. When marked money changed hands, the police, who watched the transaction from an adjacent room, charged in and arrested the would-be seller. Of course, as in international espionage, one only hears of the failures, for the successes, per se, never make the headlines.

Stealing and trafficking in trade secrets is most common among small and moderate-sized businesses. Large corporations also engage in industrial espionage, of course, but lately their methods tend to be much more sophisticated and circumspect. The December 1975 issue of *Business Horizons,* a publication of the Indiana University Graduate School of Business, contained a paper entitled "Competitive Business Intelligence Systems," by David I. Cleland and William R. King, which offered a revealing insight into how the game is played in the plush boardrooms of the *Fortune* 500. The authors are faculty members at the University of Pittsburgh, but their paper clearly demonstrates a thoroughly professional understanding of the principles of intelligence.

Cleland and King offer their readers an abstract model of a business intelligence system. Basic to their design is the understanding that useful intelligence rarely arrives in the form of a microfilm roll or a coded message. Strategically important information exists in a multitude of bits and pieces, most of which are openly available for the taking, but all of which must be carefully fitted together into a massive jigsaw puzzle before it begins to make sense. (This is true in both international espionage and industrial spying.)

The local chamber of commerce in a town where a competitor has a plant, for example, can tell you all about the size of the facility, the number of employees, and the products manufactured there. Subscribe to the local newspaper, the authors advise; it often contains news of promotions, business expansions, and other useful data. Find a broker who has sold the competitor's stock; he may have investigated the company's strength and weaknesses, and he'll probably be willing to tell you about them. Buy a share of the company's stock; it will entitle you to go to the annual stockholders' meeting and ask some very pointed questions. You'll also find a wealth of information in stock prospectuses and annual reports. Check with your own purchasing department; you and your competitor may share a common supplier, who might be persuaded to tell you what, and how much, the competition is buying. Professional associations and trade conventions offer plenty of opportunities to pick up information about the competition. And your own sales people can be a bountiful source of information about the competition, picked up in contacts with customers and other sales people.

"Reverse engineering" is a legal way of getting a look at a competitor's technology: you buy his product and take it apart to see how it works. You can get a picture of his research program by examining his patent applications, which are available to the public for inspection. (Be careful—many companies deliberately patent their failures to mislead the competition, but the astute business spy may be able to second-guess such tricks.)

Of course, none of these perfectly legal techniques for collecting business intelligence would preclude a company from also resorting to illegal or unethical measures, but information gleaned from a talkative job-seeker, a disgruntled employee, or even an illegal bug, becomes much more revealing when it is fitted into the larger context established through ethical collection techniques.

The Cleland and King paper was not merely an exercise in abstract theorizing about business intelligence operations; many, if not most, large corporations actually have such a function hidden away somewhere in their organization. For example, IBM, which only went to the planning stage with its counterterrorist intelligence system, has had an efficient business intelligence system in operation for many years. Buried in the organization chart of its Data Processing Division is something called the "Commercial Analysis Department," which compiles reports from branch offices on competitors' products and activities. And Citicorp, the banking conglomerate, has an executive whose title candidly describes his function: "Manager of Competitive Intelligence."

Banks are especially sophisticated in acquiring commercial intelligence. Accurate forecasts of foreign political and economic developments are as essential to the making of loans as they are to the making of foreign policy. In fact, the information collected by some large banks seems to be more accurate than the intelligence available to the federal government. For example, in February and early March 1977, Chase Manhattan and Citibank correctly predicted the collapse of the Strategic Arms Limitation Talks with the Soviet Union, a development that came as a distinct shock to the Carter administration. The bankers also accurately forecast the $2 to $3 billion increase in the Defense Department budget that was proposed in the wake of the SALT failure. Hundreds of overseas branches, contacts among the powerful at home and abroad, and firsthand knowledge of what the smart money was doing, all contributed to the bankers' intelligence breakthrough.

Not all business spies have traded in their trenchcoats for three-piece pin-stripe suits, however. The rough-and-tumble school of industrial snooping may be out of fashion in the world of multinational commerce, but it is alive and well among smaller companies. Nothing could better illustrate this than a case that erupted into the headlines in 1975.

The story actually began on the evening of January 3, 1973, in Santa

Monica, California, where a fire destroyed the main plant of Keronix, Inc., a small electronics firm. Fire investigators found that the blaze had been deliberately set. The arsonists had taken a typewriter, an adding machine, and a six-pack of Seven-Up from the Keronix offices before starting fires in two locations in the plant. Other valuable equipment had been stored in the offices, but, curiously, nothing else was missing.

The Keronix officials began to suspect the theft was a ruse to mask the true reason for the fire—industrial sabotage. They hired the Continental Investigative Agency, a Los Angeles private detective firm, to investigate. The agency assigned Herbert Atkin, its vice-president, to work on the case. After a two-year investigation by Atkin, Keronix filed a suit against a competitor, Data General Corporation of Southboro, Massachusetts, charging, among other things, that it was responsible for the fire.

Both Keronix and Data General are manufacturers of minicomputers, small-scale data processing systems that have become increasingly popular in business, industry, and government during the last few years. Data General is relatively a giant of the minicomputer industry; its 10-percent share of the worldwide market puts it number two in the field. Keronix, on the other hand, is a tiny competitor in the minicomputer field. Nonetheless, Keronix charged Data General with trying to put it out of business.

According to the Keronix suit, Data General hired Boston private eye Dan Sullivan to spy on its operations, and Sullivan, in turn, hired some California detectives to tap Keronix's telephones. Failing to tap the phones, the suit alleges, the detectives posed as Keronix employees to obtain copies of Keronix's long-distance telephone calls, in an effort to learn the identity of Keronix's customers.

Data General admits hiring Sullivan, but denies he or his associates were doing anything illegal. The company accuses Keronix of pirating its trade secrets, and says Sullivan was hired to learn if any Data General employees were responsible for leaking them to the competitor. Sullivan reportedly gave the Data General staff a clean bill of health and concluded that Keronix had acquired the proprietary information by purchasing Data General equipment and software and employing "reverse engineering" to work back to the underlying trade secrets.

Meanwhile, the Los Angeles County sheriff's office turned up the typewriter stolen during the Keronix fire. It was traced to a local man named Ralph A. Zoebish. Zoebish, who was on probation on another stolen property charge, worked in the shipping department of a company next door to Keronix. He told the police he had been hired by one of Data General's private detectives for a fee of $500 to set fire to the Keronix plant. Data General denied any connection with Zoebish and hired the prestigious investigative firm, Intertel, to discredit the man's story. At the same time, the company filed a countersuit against Keronix.

Data General's countersuit charged Keronix with the illegal use of its trade secrets, and it also accused Herbert Atkin—Keronix's private detective—of falsifying the evidence on which Keronix based its suit. Legal papers filed in Santa Monica by Data General's lawyers in support of their accusations against Atkin described him as "an admitted associate of known underworld figures." The documents stated that "Atkin" was not the man's true name; the private detective's real name was Herbert Itkin.

Until Data General's lawyers unearthed his name, Herbert Itkin did not exist. He vanished from the world in September 1972 through the good offices of the FBI and the Justice Department's Witness Relocation program. For four years prior to his disappearance, Itkin lived in a guarded hideout on Governor's Island in New York Harbor, leaving his sanctuary only occasionally to testify as the government's star witness in a series of labor racketeering and political corruption trials. His testimony helped put away Tammany Hall leader Carmine deSapio, New York City Water Commissioner James L. Marcus, and sixteen other persons involved in organized crime. For twenty years Itkin had worked as an undercover informant for both the FBI and the CIA, in Southeast Asia, the Caribbean, and, finally, New York City. The Data General lawyers' charge that Itkin had associated with underworld figures was certainly true, but that association was on behalf of the U.S. government.

In 1972, the government gave Itkin a new identity and moved him, his wife, and four children to Southern California. Because all ties to his past life were severed, he was limited in the choice of jobs available to him. He decided to work as a private investigator, and joined the Continental Investigative Agency. For three years he lived as Herbert Atkin, Continental's vice-president, until the Data General case led to his unmasking.

In July 1975, *Business Week* carried a long story on the Keronix–Data General dispute. The article recounted Itkin's involvement, but carefully omitted Itkin's new name, or the name of the Continental agency. Reporter John Berry felt those details were unimportant to the story, and that their publication might conceivably put Itkin and his family in danger. The *New York Times* was not so responsible, however; a few days after the *Business Week* article appeared, the *Times* printed a rehash of Berry's story—without attribution—but included Itkin's new name, and identified the Continental Investigative Agency. As though this might not be enough information for a Mob hit man, the *Times* also ran a full-face photograph of Itkin with the story.

When Data General's lawyers learned of Itkin's true identity, they must also have learned of his former status as a government undercover agent. It is unclear, then, why they chose to expose him and raise the issue of his being "an admitted associate of known underworld figures," since those associations were part of his honorable service to government law enforcement agencies. Also something of a mystery was the means Data General's lawyers used to learn the true identity of the private detective.

Several of the New York corruption trials in which Itkin was the government's witness were prosecuted by Robert Morvillo, head of the frauds section in the U.S. attorney's office. Morvillo also helped relocate Itkin and his family and create the "Atkin" identity. In 1973, Morvillo left the government and went into private practice. One of his first clients was Data General, which hired him when a Los Angeles grand jury began investigating the Keronix fire. Morvillo denied he had given Itkin's true identity to Data General, and the electronics company also claims he was not the source. No one, however, has been able to explain the extraordinary coincidence.

The Data General–Keronix lawsuits were due to take years dragging through the courts. But for Herbert Itkin the case was closed. There remained only the problem of insuring the safety of his family and himself in the wake of the exposure by Data General. And he must have felt a new sense of the treachery that threatens those who fight the secret corporate wars. For in twenty years of undercover work for the FBI and the CIA, Itkin had never been burned so badly as when he ventured into the world of the company cops and the business spies.

4

The Telephone Cops

There is a crime so heinous that merely to be suspected of it is legal grounds for the wiretapping of your telephone without a warrant. Your every telephone conversation will be tape-recorded for as long as it takes to establish your guilt or innocence. If no evidence against you is overheard, you will never know that your privacy was violated. If your telephone conversations indicate you are guilty of this crime, there will be a knock on your door. It won't be the police, the FBI, the CIA, or any official law enforcement agency, for the law does not grant them this kind of power over a person suspected of this crime. The men on the other side of the door will be from one of the most powerful private police forces in the country—the telephone company cops. And the crime they are empowered by law to investigate through wholesale warrantless wiretapping is not murder, kidnapping, espionage, or treason; it is telephone fraud—cheating Ma Bell out of a dime.

Title III of the Omnibus Crime Control and Safe Streets Act of 1968—the federal wiretapping law—gives the telephone company carte blanche to eavesdrop on its customers, so long as such listening can be fitted under either of the broad headings "rendition of telephone service" or "protection of the rights or property" of the telephone company. The definition of those terms is left entirely to the telephone cops, since there is no legal requirement even to notify the courts or the official police that such a tap has been installed. If you suspected the telephone company or anyone else of cheating you, and you went out and tried a little wiretapping to see if you could prove it, you would be subject to a $10,000 fine and five years in the slammer. But if the telephone cops think you may be trying to fiddle a few free phone calls, they have the legal right to stick their ears into every facet of your private life you may happen to discuss on the phone. That tells you a little about the difference between you and Ma Bell.

There are more than 1800 telephone companies in the United States, some with homey American names like the Farmer's Mutual Cooperative Telephone Company, the Yell County Telephone Company, and the William Butts Telephone Company. But 83 percent of the national telephone system is owned by the Bell System, the twenty-four affiliates and subsidiary companies of the American Telephone and Telegraph Company—Ma Bell. AT&T is a government-sanctioned monopoly that does $30 billion worth of business annually. It provides its customers with the best telephone service in the world.

Just because it works so well, Americans take for granted a degree of efficiency and reliability in their telephone system that is unknown throughout most of the world. Even in much of Europe the phone service is sluggish and uncertain, while in most of Asia and Latin America the telephone systems resemble a pair of tin cans and a piece of string, compared to our domestic product. Within the United States there are over 120 million telephones spread out among the fifty states, and any one of them can be connected to any other in a matter of seconds, and at a reasonable price. Few of the goodies that come from the cornucopia of American industry can claim to offer such unalloyed blessings to the consumer as the telephone. It doesn't pollute the environment, waste energy, give you cancer, rot your teeth, or weaken your mind. It is an indispensible comfort to the old person who must live alone and the lovers who must live apart. They know they can depend on it, and even if they are among Ma Bell's harshest critics, they have to admit she must be doing something right. Unfortunately, she has lately been caught doing quite a few things wrong, and all of them involve, in one way or another, the telephone cops.

There is no question that the telephone company needs its own security force; any business that has to leave boxes full of money unattended on streetcorners has special problems in this department. Ripping off pay telephones may seem like a nickle-and-dime racket, but some professional thieves specialize in it, learning to pick coinbox locks swiftly and unobtrusively. They set up phony laundromat and vending machine businesses to turn the silver into long green without attracting suspicion from bank tellers. An experienced coinbox artist who works steadily and doesn't get caught can collect $100,000 per year.

Beyond safeguarding the billions of dollars in company assets sprinkled around the country, the telephone cops are also charged with protecting telephone customers. A wide assortment of baddies, ranging from extortionists to perverts, use the telephone to prey on the public, and the telephone cops do a necessary job in helping the official police catch them. But the telephone cops also have the task of protecting the telephone customer from wiretappers, and this is a circumstance of exquisite irony; if your telephone has ever been tapped, the odds are well over a thousand to one that it was the telephone cops who tapped it.

While no one knows how many illegal wiretaps are placed by suspicious spouses, industrial spies, or political dirty tricksters, telephone repairmen turn up about 200 of them each year in the normal course of maintaining the lines, or in response to an annual deluge of 10,000 complaints from suspicious telephone subscribers. Another 500–600 wiretaps are annually installed by federal, state, or local police armed with legitimate court orders. But the telephone cops, during the only five-year period for which statistics are available, listened in without a single warrant on 1.8 *million* telephone conversations, ostensibly for the purpose of catching toll cheats.

Telephone toll cheating, for those who may not know, is a species of electronic larceny invented some years ago by a group of people who call themselves "phone phreaks." The phone phreaks discovered that the Bell System was converting to a network of electronic switching exchanges. The new exchanges operate through a set of audible tones transmitted over the telephone lines. The phreaks' key discovery was that one particular tone—2600 cycles per second—can be used to get access to the long-distance lines without leaving any record that might result in a toll charge. The phreaks devised a little instrument that became known as ''the blue box'' to take advantage of this fact. The device, which is about the size of a small transistor radio and has a set of buttons similar to a push-button telephone, is used to produce the series of tones necessary to make a toll-free call to almost any telephone in the world. Less common, but still very popular among phone phreaks, is ''the black box,'' a device that can be attached to one's phone to permit incoming toll calls to be received without charge to the calling party— a sort of do-it-yourself WATS line.

The phone phreaks' underground is comprised of individuals, mostly young, possessed of two distinctly American traits: technical ingenuity and a loathing of the telephone company. Banded together as ''the Technological American Party,'' they publish their own technical journal, *TAP,* full of how-to-do-it information, and hold an annual convention in New York. The convention is well attended by the telephone cops, as well as the phreaks; the former bring along cameras and the latter bring along masks.

William Caming, attorney for AT&T, last year told a House subcommittee that toll fraud has cost the Bell System about $1 million since the blue and black boxes were first introduced back in the 1960s. But to whatever extent this figure includes long-distance dialing by the phone phreaks, it is deceptively inflated. Electronic toll fraud doesn't take money out of Ma Bell's pockets, it just avoids putting any in. The typical phone phreak toll call is not one he would have made and paid for anyway, even if he didn't have his blue box. Phone phreaks call the U.S. Embassy in Moscow to ask ''What's happening?'' or the guard shack outside Buckingham Palace to inquire ''How's the weather over there?'' If a phone phreak calls an acquaintance in Sydney, Australia, he usually has only one thing to say to him: ''I just ripped off Ma Bell!''

The real problem for the phone company is not the phone phreak, but the heavy toll-user who invests in a blue or black box to reduce the size of his phone bill. The telephone cops say it happens all the time; recently they have accused singer Lanie Kazan, actor Robert Cummings, and international wheeler-dealer Bernie Cornfeld of blue box violations.

To trap the toll cheats, the telephone cops have come up with a new electronic gadget of their own. The device scans telephone lines in search of the telltale 2600-cycle tone the blue box uses to sneak into the long-distance lines. Whenever that frequency is heard by the device, the telephone line is automatically tapped—the telephone cops prefer the word "monitored"—and the conversation is tape-recorded. However, 2600 cycles is well within the range of human speech, and the telephone cops' electronic tap often snaps shut on the fully paid-up conversations of solid citizens. Of the 1.8 million calls taped by the device during a five-year period, it is certain that 700,000 did not involve fraud. In fact, in less than 2 percent of the conversations the telephone cops eavesdropped on was there legal proof that a blue or black box was in use.

Last year AT&T attorney William Caming appeared before the National Wiretap Commission, a panel appointed by Congress and the president to review the effectiveness of the federal wiretapping laws. The telephone company lawyer resisted the suggestion of some Justice Department officials that the law be changed to require telephone cops to obtain court orders before tapping someone's phone, just like every other police force. That wouldn't work, he testified, for the simple reason that in most cases of suspected toll fraud, the telephone cops wouldn't have enough evidence to get a warrant if they needed one. In other words, the telephone cops wouldn't be able to do their job if they were forced to play according to the rules, and the telephone company's right to collect its dimes transcends the right of thousands of innocent telephone subscribers to converse in private. The Commission went along with the telephone company and made no recommendation that the law be changed.

The telephone cops' "no big deal" attitude toward warrantless wiretapping is only a reflection of Ma Bell's generally blasé approach to customer privacy. Telephone company employees are no more scandalized by the prospect of listening in on someone's private chat than the groundskeeper at a nudist camp would be shocked by the sight of naked flesh. Christina Huggins, a former Pacific Telephone Company operator, recently revealed that company technicians working in telephone switching centers search the lines until they find an interesting conversation—especially one in which the subject is sex—and switch it to the loudspeaker for the enjoyment of their fellow employees. One woman employee, Mrs. Cheryl Crouse, heard the voice of her husband on the loudspeaker making a date with another woman. The company fired her when she began to listen in on her spouse on a regular basis; he may have been cheating on her, but he wasn't cheating Ma Bell, so the poor man was entitled to *some* privacy.

More than 10 percent of Ma Bell's customers pay a monthly charge to the telephone company to keep it from listing or otherwise giving out their telephone numbers. But a small newspaper, the *Los Angeles Vanguard,* recently discovered that Pacific Telephone and Telegraph— a Bell System company—routinely handed over unlisted numbers to the IRS, the FBI, the CIA, the armed services, the police, the governor's office, and a host of other agencies, including the U.S. Fish and Wild-life Service. Two California telephone customers have filed a class-action suit, demanding that the company refund the unlisted number charges to the 1.3 million customers who mistakenly thought they could pay Ma Bell to respect their privacy.

The privacy of telephone customers' toll records is another area in which the telephone company is sometimes less than scrupulous. The detailed list of the numbers you call, the date and time you called them, and how long you talked, form a revealing index of who you know and what you're up to. Reporters who do most of their information-gathering on the telephone have especially fascinating toll records, and the FBI, the IRS, and other government agencies show a keen interest in getting a look at them when hunting whistle-blowers or unauthorized leakers among the ranks of federal government employees. Toll records are not covered by federal wiretapping laws or other statutes, so telephone company employees are free to hand them over to any cop who asks for them, which is what they often did until recently. Since 1974, it has been Bell System policy to require a subpoena, except in the case of the FBI, which is still given the records on the strength of a simple written request signed by the FBI director.

Advances in surveillance technology have reduced the need for the police to go to the phone company for toll records. A device known as a "telephone decoder," or "pen register," collects the same information when it's attached to the customer's telephone line. The instrument makes a paper-tape record of the number you call, the date and time you called it, and the length of the call, and it does this for local calls as well as the long-distance calls that would show up on your toll record. One model of the telephone decoder manufactured by a company called Voice Identification, Inc., seems to have been designed for use by the telephone cops; the paper tape also shows whether the 2600-cycle blue-box tone was overheard during the call. Because the device does not actually record the telephone conversation, it is not covered by the federal wiretap laws, and can be used by official and private police without a court order. The telephone cops, of course, would not need a warrant to use it, even if the device were considered to be a wiretap.

The unrestricted power of the telephone cops to wiretap puts them in a position to do favors for official policemen who want to tap someone's phone but can't quite establish "probable cause" to obtain a court order. The telephone company often recruits its security agents from among the ranks of retired policemen and former FBI agents, so if a police officer doesn't know a telephone cop personally, he probably knows another policeman who does. The smooth operation of this Old Boy Network is illustrated by the March 1975 disclosure of an association between the Chesapeake and Potomac Telephone Company's Security Office and the Baltimore Police Department's Vice Squad.

Whenever a Vice Squad officer suspected a house or apartment was being used for illegal gambling, he would get the telephone number of the residence and turn it over to a retired police officer, identified only as "Captain Burns," who worked for the telephone company. According to the testimony of former Vice Squad officer George Guest, the former cop would arrange to have the telephone cops tap the line and listen in for a few days. Afterward he would get back to the officer and let him know if anything had been heard on the line to confirm his suspicions. If so, the officer would apply for a search warrant, listing "a reliable informant" as the source of his information. One imaginative officer dreamed up a more elaborate explanation of how he came to learn of the illegal gambling. He claimed that the suspect was sitting next to him on a park bench when a dog jumped into the man's lap, knocking to the ground a bag full of lottery slips he was carrying. One officer later testified, "Some of the Vice affidavits were like reading *Grimm's Fairy Tales.*"

James H. Ashley, a former official of Southwestern Bell, recently revealed that "In the past 10 years, the Bell System has upgraded its security force, doubling it in size and hiring FBI types who are used to using wiretaps." But the telephone cops don't all belong to a single, giant police force. All Bell System companies and a few of the larger independent telephone companies have their own security departments. The unifying organization that unofficially links most of these security forces is the Society of Former Special Agents of the Federal Bureau of Investigation, the FBI agents' alumni organization. The Society, which has been described by one former agent as "Hoover's Loyal Legion," consists of some 6600 gung-ho ex-agents, about half of the total number of former FBI agents living. The telephone company security departments are particularly well represented in the organization.

Of the 665 security officers who work for Bell System telephone companies, at least 76 are former FBI agents, and most of these ex-agents are in management positions. Joseph Doherty, AT&T's Corporate Security director and architect of the massive wiretapping program that recorded 1.8 million private telephone conversations, is a member of the Society. Senior security executives of New England Telephone and Telegraph, Bell Telephone of Pennsylvania, Northwest Bell, Mountain States Telephone and Telegraph, Pacific Northwest Bell, and Pacific Telephone and Telegraph are also members of Hoover's Loyal Legion. South Central Bell's security manager for the State of Alabama is one of three ex-agents who hold senior posts in that Bell System subsidiary. Thirteen Society members work for Southern Bell, including two General Security managers, two Division Security supervisors, and the security manager for the State of Tennessee. Southwestern Bell also boasts thirteen Society members, all with the title of security manager or security supervisor, and scattered throughout Texas, Oklahoma, Missouri, Arkansas, and Kansas.

The independent telephone companies are not completely lacking in representation in the Society of Former Special Agents. General Telephone and Electronics—which controls ten million of the seventeen million telephones outside the Bell System—employs twenty-eight Loyal Legionnaires, including the security directors of its subsidiaries in California, Florida, Indiana, Kentucky, Michigan, Ohio, Pennsylvania, and General Telephone of the Southwest. United Telephone—with 2.5 million non-Bell phones—claims only two, its security directors in Florida and the Midwest.

To suggest that the high concentration of ex-FBI agents among the telephone cops represents a conscious plan to facilitate illegal wiretapping by the Bureau might earn one the title of "conspiracy theorist." Let's just say it's an interesting coincidence that, in the words of one former FBI eavesdropping specialist, FBI wiretappers "find convenient."

The line separating the telephone cops from the official police is nowhere thinner than in Texas, where Southwestern Bell's security department seems to be the local headquarters of the police Old Boy Network. Of the forty-four security agents in the department, fifteen are former FBI agents. Until recently, six of the ex-agents and three other telephone cops held commissions as Special Texas Rangers, giving them almost the same arrest and firearms powers as the regular Rangers. In Houston, Southwestern Bell hired 300 local policemen to moonlight as security guards at telephone company buildings in the area. Bell also hired Deputy Police Chief W. L. Williams and M. L. "Joe" Singleton, the head of the Police Department's Criminal Intelligence Division, to work part-time managing the off-duty cops.

Southwestern Bell's telephone cops set up a special service called "Law Enforcement Liaison," which hands over to the police information about telephone subscribers. The service does a brisk business answering 10,000 police inquiries annually. Many of these requests simply involve matching a customer's name and address to a telephone number turned up by a police investigation, but Law Enforcement Liaison also releases unlisted numbers and toll record information to the cops. In the face of considerable evidence to the contrary, Southwestern Bell denies that the service also gives the cops "cable-and-pair" data, information that is almost essential to installing an illegal wiretap.

The cord running from your telephone to the wall contains a pair of wires that connect the instrument to the central exchange, which may be several miles away. After it leaves the immediate vicinity of your house, apartment, or office, the wire pair converges with others coming from neighboring telephones. Hundreds of wire pairs are carried within a cable through underground ducts and over telephone poles until they finally terminate in the local exchange switching equipment.

The wireman who wants to put an illegal tap on your telephone prefers to avoid the immediate vicinity of your home or office if possible, for fear of attracting attention and discovery (although some wiretappers disguise themselves as telephone repairmen and pretend to be working on the lines). He cannot put on the tap at the local telephone exchange; even if he could get into the building, the tap would soon be detected by one of the many maintenance technicians working there. That leaves one alternative: tapping into your wire pair in the cable somewhere between your home or office and the telephone exchange. But which cable-and-pair among the hundreds or thousands filling the underground ducts and festooning the telephone poles? That information can only come from someone with access to the telephone company's wiring plans, someone like a telephone cop.

The fact that it is often almost impossible to place an illegal wiretap without receiving cable-and-pair information from someone in the telephone company was very much in the mind of Houston police chief Carroll M. Lynn during his recent probe of illegal tapping by officers in his department. Chief Lynn was appointed by the new liberal city administration of Mayor Fred Hofheinz in 1973. Soon after he took office, he discovered the department had carried out a ten-year program of political spying under his predecessor. The Criminal Intelligence Division had compiled thousands of dossiers on citizens having no criminal records or associates. Most of the individuals spied upon were political activists of one coloration or another. The spy files were full of personal information, often including sexual gossip, and much of the data could only have been acquired through wiretapping.

Police in Texas are forbidden to wiretap in any circumstances; court orders cannot be issued to legalize wiretapping by the local cops. This curious state of affairs in one of the country's leading law-and-order states results from Texas's lack of any state law to regulate wiretapping, a situation that made the state a happy hunting ground for wiretappers until 1968, when Congress passed the Omnibus Crime Control and Safe Streets Act. Under the new federal law, local police cannot wiretap unless there is a state law to regulate their electronic eavesdropping; otherwise, wiretapping in such states is reserved exclusively to federal agents with federal court orders. Texas will probably remedy this situation soon by passing its own wiretap law, but at the time the Houston cops were compiling their spy files, any wiretapping on their part would have been a federal crime. Chief Lynn launched an internal investigation to learn how the intelligence information had been obtained.

The probe disclosed that sixty-two Houston police officers had conducted more than a thousand illegal wiretaps during a seven-year period. Chief Lynn charged that some 200 employees of Southwestern Bell had cooperated with the police in the illegal tapping. Many police officers in Houston and other Texas cities confirmed the charge that the telephone company was very cooperative in placing illegal taps. A Southwestern Bell spokesman said the company could not deny that some of its 14,000 employees might have been involved in the illegal wiretapping, but stressed that this would be a violation of company policy and grounds for immediate dismissal.

In practice, however, there is little risk to the telephone cop who helps the police install an illegal wiretap because of the security force's autonomy within Southwestern Bell. In a wire service interview, the chief telephone security agent in Houston revealed that he can demand cable-and-pair information from other telephone company employees on the strength of his simple assertion that a court order for wiretapping exists. He doesn't have to show anyone the warrant, and there is no system to check his statement. The cable-and-pair information is given to him over the phone, so apparently there is no written record of the request. According to one Southwestern Bell telephone cop, misuse of this power is prevented by "my integrity and the integrity of those with whom I work."

The telephone cops' denials that they had cooperated in the illegal tapping were not borne out by later developments in the case. Several of the Houston cops named by Chief Lynn were indicted by a federal grand jury, and the testimony given in their trials confirmed the police chief's charges that Southwestern Bell had aided in the tapping. Anthony V.

Zavala, one of the indicted officers, testified that he had received cable-and-pair information from the telephone cops on a half-dozen occasions, and that Southwestern Bell had also handed over customer toll records to him without a court order.

While several Houston police officers were indicted and convicted of wiretapping, none of the Southwestern Bell telephone cops was brought up on related charges, a fact later cited by Southwestern Bell vice-president Charles Marshall as proof that the charges against the telephone company were unfounded. But the absence of prosecution of telephone cops seems to have been a result of the FBI's lack of enthusiasm for pursuing the matter; Anthony J. P. Farris, a former federal prosecutor in Houston, says he had a lot of trouble getting the local FBI field office to take any interest in the case. When he finally put his demands for action in writing in a letter to the Bureau, the field office assigned one agent to the case, a sleuth whose investigative reports consisted mostly of photocopies of newspaper clippings reporting on Chief Lynn's probe.

The listlessness of the FBI probe of the telephone cops may have been caused by the fact that those Southwestern Bell security officers with the greatest responsibility for any illegal taps were themselves alumni of the Bureau. Perhaps more important was the knowledge that any thorough probe of the illegal wiretapping in Texas would soon lead back to the Bureau itself; according to the testimony of several Houston cops, the local FBI office was one of the chief consumers of the information gleaned from the taps. And ex-officer Zavala revealed that the FBI field office had its own illegal taps, presumably installed through the cooperation of the telephone cops. The Houston police had to take the fall all by themselves.

Not all of the indicted cops were convicted, however. Nine officers were acquitted by jurors who later told the press, "We did not think these were evil men. Most of us felt we want the police force, and that they were hampered enough as it is," and "I sincerely believe that they had no evil intentions or a bad purpose in anything they did." Which may have been a particularly bitter pill for Chief Carroll Lynn. His resolve that the Houston police should obey the law made him the target of a harassment campaign by the Houston Police Officers Association.

In June 1975, the cops took out a full-page newspaper advertisement attacking him, and the resultant public pressure forced him to resign. And that development should have cheered the telephone cops, for it was Chief Lynn who first accused them of involvement in the illegal wiretapping.

Investigating individuals who make "false allegations" against Southwestern Bell is yet another task of the telephone cops, according to Jerry L. Slaughter, Southwestern Bell's chief security man in Houston, and a former FBI agent and Special Texas Ranger. Slaughter, in a wire service interview, cited as examples of such "false allegations" recent charges by some Southwestern Bell executives that the company had been engaged in unfair rate-setting, political slush-funding, and yet more illegal wiretapping. Many of the accusations were spelled out by one Bell official in a suicide note which concluded with the warning, "Watergate is a gnat compared to the Bell System."

The Southwestern Bell executive who took his own life was T. O. Gravitt, the $90,000-per-year vice-president in charge of Texas operations. Shortly after he took over that job in 1973, Gravitt was contacted by his old friend James H. Ashley, then Southwestern Bell's general commercial manager. Texas was then the only state in the union without a public service commission, so it was Ashley's job to press for telephone rate increases in negotiations with the city councils in 200 Texas cities. He told Gravitt that Southwestern Bell was using deceptive accounting practices to justify its demands for inflated telephone rates.

Gravitt and Ashley began to work for reform of Texas rate-setting practices within Southwestern Bell. They raised the issue with higher officials in the company, but their efforts were cut short by the telephone cops, who suddenly began to investigate "allegations of impropriety" on the part of the two executives.

"Practically every security man in Southwestern Bell was on our case," Ashley later said. "I was told the investigation was aimed at Gravitt and nothing would happen to me if I cooperated. Gravitt was told it was an investigation of Ashley."

In fact, the telephone cops seemed out to get as much dirt as possible on both men. Gravitt learned that more than 150 company employees had been asked whether he had solicited gifts from them, made passes at women workers, or asked his subordinates to "fix him up" with female companions. On October 17, 1974, convinced that both his reputation and career were ruined, Gravitt started his car inside the closed garage of his Dallas home, climbed behind the wheel, and went to sleep.

After Gravitt's body was discovered, Southwestern Bell officials descended on the dead executive's home and rifled through his papers. A telephone company man tried to make off with one of the documents, but was caught in the act by one of Gravitt's sons. It was Gravitt's suicide note, and it was dynamite. The note charged Southwestern Bell with creating a $100,000 slush fund by raising the salaries of telephone company executives who then "voluntarily" contributed the additional money to the fund. The note said the slush fund was used for political contributions and other payoffs to officials who control Southwestern Bell's telephone rates.

Gravitt's charges were further elaborated by James Ashley, who was fired by Southwestern Bell shortly after his friend's death. Ashley said the telephone company operates a secret wiretapping system to collect financial information about some of its largest customers in Houston, San Antonio, Dallas, Fort Worth, and Lubbock. He further charged that Southwestern Bell used its telephone cops to eavesdrop on the city officials who have the power to approve or deny the company's rate requests.

"When I went to a city to negotiate a rate increase," Ashley said, "I knew everything there was to know about the officials who would lower the rates. How much they owed, who they were sleeping with, if they could be gotten to."

If a city councilman was in financial trouble, the telephone company would throw some business his way as a favor; if that didn't work, they would pressure him through the banks he had borrowed from.

"If a city official was having an affair with some woman," Ashley said, "we didn't have to spell it out for him to get his cooperation. All we had to do was ask him how Mrs. So and so was getting along. . . . If we didn't have information on the councilman the company would just tap a few telephones. Pretty soon we'd know everything we needed to know."

Spokesmen for the Bell System quickly denied the charges against Southwestern Bell, but similar stories were unfolding in several other states. After reading of Gravitt's suicide, in October 1974, John J. Ryan, a former vice-president in charge of Southern Bell's operations in North Carolina, said he had administered a political slush fund along the same lines as the one described by Gravitt and Ashley; some of the money was contributed to congressional and gubernatorial candidates in the 1972 election. William R. Clark, a member and former chairman of the Missouri Public Service Commission, resigned after the April 1975 disclosure that he had been a guest of Southwestern Bell on a Texas hunting trip; the company maintained an 11,000-acre hunting preserve near Uvalde in south-central Texas where public officials were invited to shoot deer and pheasant from padded swivel chairs in carpeted shooting blinds. In Kansas, two members of the state Corporation Commission, Dale E. Saffels and Vernon Stroberg, admitted they had taken an expense-paid trip to Las Vegas, courtesy of Southwestern Bell; it was later disclosed that all members of the Commission held special toll-free telephone credit cards issued by the company. Similar revelations of slush-funding and entertaining public service commissioners by Bell System executives were made in South Carolina, Georgia, Florida, Alabama, Mississippi, Louisiana, Oklahoma, Arkansas, Tennessee, Kentucky, and Illinois.

Southwestern Bell continues to deny the charges made by Gravitt and Ashley, and the company will eventually have its day in court; a $29-million slander and libel suit by James Ashley and the family of T. O. Gravitt against the telephone company is pending. However, the Texas Senate Subcommittee on Consumer Affairs carried out its own investigation of Southwestern Bell and found that the telephone cops had cooperated with the official police in illegal wiretapping; that the company had used deceptive accounting practices to seek inflated telephone rates; and that the company had improperly influenced Texas public officials through a program of political contributions and other favors. In its report, the subcommittee wrote: "The company has squandered time, energy and brainpower on a continual quest for political influence, when it might have better employed such energies in economizing its own operations."

But the Texas Senate subcommittee seems to have missed the point; the problem with the Bell System is not that it hasn't spent a wealth of time, energy, and brainpower on improving its efficiency. The telephone company is a marvel of efficiency, and that, ultimately, is the root of the problem.

AT&T is a well-oiled machine built to do two things: make money and provide telephone service. Because it does those things so well, it is the largest company in the world. If the Bell System were as sluggish and inefficient as, say, the postal service, we would never grant it a monopoly to control 83 percent of our telephone service. We would never indulge it by letting it raise a small army of former federal agents. And we would never grant it a legal license to conduct wholesale wiretapping.

Back in the 1920s and 1930s, some people used to say in defense of the Italian dictator Benito Mussolini that he got the trains to run on time. That may have been so, but history showed the Italians they would have been better off making Mussolini head of the railroads instead of head of their country. When things get too efficient, freedom has to adjourn to the mountains.

The telephone cops are the shock troops of the Bell System, the intelligence service of a mammoth commercial enterprise. It costs a lot to run a private police force, and you can be sure the telephone cops earn their keep. They are merely another instrument of Ma Bell's awesome efficiency.

Ma Bell says the telephone cops are saving us money, too; if they didn't catch those toll cheats, you and I would have to make up the difference through larger phone bills. But aren't the telephone cops themselves responsible for larger phone bills when they compile blackmail files on public officials who set telephone rates? And how much are they supposed to be saving us, anyway? How much have we been paid to surrender our privacy to them?

But Ma Bell says, "Don't worry your head about those things." She says, "Pick up your telephone and call somebody." She says, "It's oh, so good to hear you smile."

5

The Secret Listeners

Thomas Kiernan surveyed the shambles of his three-room Manhattan apartment and wondered whether his telephone was tapped. The thieves picked the one evening when he and his wife and baby daughter would be away for several hours. They broke the locks on the front door and thoroughly ransacked the place. But Kiernan knew it was not just another New York City burglary.

The intruders passed up several valuable paintings, a stereo, a television set, and a box of expensive jewelry as they systematically ransacked every room. They were looking for some items in particular and they found them: a stack of letters and documents, sixteen tape recordings, and a 382-page handwritten manuscript—all materials for a book which Kiernan, a freelance author, was writing. Nothing else was taken.

Kiernan's book was to have been an investigative study of Richard Nixon's longtime friend and associate, Charles G. ''Bebe'' Rebozo. The day before the break-in, the writer phoned a professional stenographer to say that his manuscript was complete and ready for typing. He made other telephone calls that day, calls which, if overheard, would have revealed the family's plans to be out of the apartment between the hours of 3 and 10 P.M. that November day in 1975. And Kiernan recalled something else: several times in recent days his telephone would ring once, then stop. When he picked up the receiver, no one was on the line. Had the burglars tapped Kiernan's telephone to learn the opportune time for the break-in?

The New York Telephone Company said no. Ma Bell said professional wiretappers never do anything to interfere with their victims' normal telephone service and arouse suspicion. The explanation is true, so far as it goes, but it stretches coincidence to the breaking point. Somebody knew Kiernan's manuscript was complete; somebody knew it was still in Kiernan's apartment; and somebody knew when Kiernan and his family would be out. All of which makes for pretty good odds that Kiernan's telephone was tapped, simply because there are more wiretappers around than there are successful clairvoyants.

The fallacy of the telephone company's explanation is the assumption that all wiretappers are "professionals." It is true that federal wiremen learn their craft in the government's own electronic eavesdropping schools, where they are taught to tap telephones discreetly, without creating telltale rings, clicks, or other suspicious sounds. But federal agents also learn to pick locks, something the intruders who tore open Kiernan's front door obviously couldn't do. The fact is that there are a great many unskilled operators in the Private Sector, and one or more of them seem to have found employment with whoever wanted to prevent publication of the Rebozo exposé.

No one knows the full extent of wiretapping by the Private Sector; private detectives who conduct electronic eavesdropping are breaking federal law and can be punished by a $10,000 fine and up to five years in prison, so they are understandably reluctant to respond to surveys. But there are strong indications that wiretapping and bugging services are a major activity of many Private Sector firms.

A private investigator who specializes in finding and removing electronic listening devices for clients, but who flatly refuses to install them, told me that, on the average, he receives one request per week to do illegal tapping; most of those soliciting taps are either businessmen spying on their competitors or suspicious spouses. Another detective made a virtually identical report to the National Wiretap Commission, a panel appointed by Congress and the president to assess the effectiveness of the federal anti-wiretapping laws. The Commission's investigators also discovered that the sought-for wiretapping services are readily available to anyone prepared to pay the price; they called 115 private detective agencies randomly selected from the Yellow Pages of seven large cities and identified themselves as businessmen who wanted to tap their competitors' telephones. Forty-two of the agencies—more than a third—either offered to install the illegal taps or referred the callers to someone else who would do it. Prices quoted ranged from $30 to $5000. And many of the agencies that refused to install the taps offered to show the callers how they could do it themselves. If, as seems likely, the brisk demand is able to locate the easily available supply, then a very considerable amount of illegal wiretapping goes on in the Private Sector.

For a variety of reasons, federal and state anti-wiretapping laws are difficult to enforce, and relatively few violations by Private (or Public) Sector eavesdroppers are ever punished. Still, the client who hires a Private Sector eavesdropper risks the same criminal prosecution as the wireman who actually installs the tap. And technical expertise is not the only quality sometimes lacking among private tappers; many also seem devoid of simple good judgment, as were the two who tapped Paul Rothermel, former FBI agent and security chief for Texas oil billionaire H. L. Hunt.

The private detectives who placed the tap on Rothermel's Richardson, Texas, home telephone in January 1970 used a device known as an "in-line transmitter," the most common type of Private Sector tap. Unlike the police or federal agents who can obtain the official or unofficial cooperation of the telephone company and install their taps in lines and equipment miles from their victim's telephone, the private tappers were forced to splice into Rothermel's line somewhere between the instrument and the telephone pole outside.

The in-line transmitter is actually a tiny, low-power FM station that broadcasts on a special frequency band not used by commercial stations. It picks up both sides of a telephone conversation and sends a signal out over a distance of a few hundred feet. A special-purpose receiver, together with a voice-activated tape recorder, is concealed somewhere within that range, often in the trunk of a parked automobile. This was the technique used to tap Rothermel.

Despite Rothermel's professional instincts, he might never have noticed the car containing the tapping equipment parked near his home. But Texans are noted for their sportsmanship, and it may have been in some such spirit that the wiremen chose a fire-engine-red fastback for the job. This did attract Mrs. Rothermel's attention; she became curious about the snappy car and the strangers she saw so often sitting inside it. After several days she called the police.

Apparently the tappers hadn't completely worked out their cover story, for when the patrol car arrived they chose a discreet retreat over trying to brazen things out. Peeling rubber and sailing through a corner stop sign, the bright-red car departed the Rothermel environs. The police elected to follow, and, when they overtook the private investigators, their suspicions were thoroughly aroused. They insisted on looking in the bright-red trunk, where they discovered the tapping and recording equipment, plus several tape reels of the Rothermels' telephone conversations. The case was turned over to the federal authorities.

The case against the two detectives was, of course, open and shut, and they were convicted on federal wiretapping charges and sentenced to three years in prison. But the prosecutors also wanted Mr. Big, the person who had hired the tappers. Whoever he was, Mr. Big seemed very big indeed, for Mississippi Senator James O. Eastland, chairman of the Senate Judiciary Committee, had contacted the Federal Parole Board about the possibility of paroling the convicted wiretappers. Meanwhile, the two private detectives, true to the code of their calling, continued to refuse to name their client to the federal prosecutors.

But federal prosecutors have ways of making people talk. Specifically, they hauled the two detectives before a grand jury and gave them immunity from further prosecution in the case, thus cancelling their Fifth Amendment right to refuse to answer, and confronting them with the choice of either naming their client or having additional time tacked onto their sentences. Whatever the two men decided to do in the face of this dilemma remains a secret, as do all grand jury proceedings, but shortly thereafter—in February 1973—the grand jury handed down wiretapping indictments against several people, including two of the richest men in the world: Nelson Bunker Hunt and William Herbert Hunt, the multimillionaire sons of Rothermel's employer, H. L. Hunt.

At their trial, the Hunt brothers testified that they had arranged for the tapping of Rothermel's telephone because they believed the former FBI agent and several other Hunt employees had embezzled millions of dollars from HLH Foods, a family-owned company. They had told their father of their suspicions but H. L. Hunt refused to believe that his most trusted family retainers were cheating him. In order to obtain incontrovertible proof, the Hunts brought in the wiretappers.

In his testimony, Bunker Hunt readily admitted hiring the private detectives to wiretap his father's employees, but he pleaded innocent to the federal charges on the grounds that he didn't know wiretapping was illegal. The claim was entirely plausible, but one not usually considered relevant to guilt or innocence in a court of law, where ignorance of the law is not a valid defense. In any case, the Lubbock, Texas, jury saw things the Hunts' way and acquitted the brothers. Bunker Hunt candidly attributed their acquittal to the huge sums he and his brother spent to hire the best defense team available (unconfirmed reports put the cost of the Hunts' defense at $1 million).

"My heart goes out to ordinary people and poor people who can't afford proper defense," Bunker Hunt told reporters. "If we'd just been ordinary folks, I'm afraid we would have been in trouble."

Undoubtedly, but if the Hunts had just been "ordinary folks," instead of heirs to a Texas oil fortune, they wouldn't have hired the wiretapper in the first place. Still, most Private Sector wiretapping is done by or for very ordinary people, and in the vast majority of such cases neither the tapper nor the tapee is likely to be a millionaire. In a study reported by the National Wiretap Commission, 68 percent of the illegal Private Sector taps uncovered were installed by jealous spouses, and another 11 percent involved other domestic spying, including parents eavesdropping on their offspring. One Texas doctor and his wife had a continuous tap on their daughter's telephone. Between 1967 and 1973 the couple, who suspected their daughter was involved in drug traffic, tape-recorded thousands of hours of her telephone conversations.

The domestic eavesdropper isn't likely ever to feel the full weight of the law for his actions, so long as he keeps them in the family. A thirty-two-year-old Florida man in the midst of a divorce tapped his own telephone to get the goods on his wife for use in a custody battle. The court sentenced him to six months' probation. And the U.S. Fifth Circuit Court of Appeals, in another case, found that a person is entitled to tap his own telephone, even if the tapper's wife or husband is unaware of the tap. In effect, the court placed wiretapping in the same category as sexual intercourse, making it proper when done with benefit of clergy.

Household snooping is not the only Private Sector electronic eavesdropping sanctioned by the courts. In 1973, the security manager of a Macy's department store tapped the store's telephone lines and listened in on the employees' conversations (perhaps to discover what, if anything, they might be telling Gimbel's). Charges were brought against the wiretapper under the federal law, but the court decided that an employer may eavesdrop on his employees' conversations when the calls go through his own switchboard.

Ever wonder whether your own telephone is tapped? Every year about 10,000 people worry about it enough to call in the telephone company for a check. Ma Bell sends out a technician to investigate each complaint; if he finds a tap, and there isn't a court order somewhere to go with it, he'll let you know and also report it to the police. The company says that happens in fewer than 2 percent of the cases. But a really first-class wiretap job is almost impossible to detect, even by the phone company. And if the tapper knows his business, the victim will never hear anything on his phone to make him suspicious in the first place.

If you really think you might be bugged, calling in the telephone company is only a partial approach to the problem anyway. For example, a telephone man wouldn't even have been looking for the device someone used to invade the privacy of an Alexandria, Virginia, couple. One June evening in 1975, the two were preparing to go out to dinner when the husband noticed a loose panel in the bedroom closet. When he removed the panel, he found a microphone. Police officers who were summoned to the apartment discovered the other end of the microphone cord and a tape recorder in the apartment of the resident manager of the apartment complex.

Short of tearing down your home or office, rebuilding it, and posting around-the-clock guards, there is no way to be completely confident you aren't being bugged. But if you've become the target of a Private Sector snoop, rather than someone from an organization like Army Intelligence or the CIA, then you can probably turn up whatever secret little presents he's hidden around your digs by hiring what is known as an "audio countermeasures specialist."

In television and the movies, secret agents discover hidden microphones by looking under tables and inside lampshades, but the real thing is almost never visible to the naked eye. Sniffing out electronic eavesdropping devices is a highly specialized craft whose practitioners have become much in demand in recent years, since the Watergate revelations made the general public especially conscious of bugs and wiretaps. Audio countermeasures people command fifty to one hundred dollars per hour to "sweep" homes, offices, and boardrooms for hidden listening devices, a process that can take anywhere from several hours to a couple of days. For his money, the client buys a sense of security and peace of mind that is often completely unwarranted, for there are few professional services as infested with crooks and incompetents as the audio countermeasures business.

With a small capital investment in some mysterious-looking equipment, and the price of a few newspaper advertisements, the unscrupulous operator can set up shop as an audio countermeasures specialist without fear of challenge; few states or local jurisdictions license or otherwise regulate such services. For his client, there is no easy way to confirm that the countermeasures man is doing his job. In most cases, of course, there is no listening device hidden on the premises, so the client has lost only whatever fee he pays the bogus bug-chaser. A few phony operators with a sense of theater even give their pigeons a thrill by dramatizing the "discovery" of a hidden microphone that they themselves planted. But the client who is actually a target of electronic eavesdropping, and who hires a phony debugger, is not likely ever to learn that he is bugged or that he was ripped off. Bad bug-hunters are like sloppy parachute packers; they are rarely confronted by dissatisfied customers.

One private investigator who offered his clients debugging services invested in a piece of first-class bug-sniffing equipment. After several years he returned it to the manufacturer. He had used it so much, he said, he thought it was probably due for some periodic servicing. A technician examined the instrument and discovered it wasn't working at all; it had no battery. The abashed private eye admitted he never knew it needed one.

Obviously, one way to check up on your countermeasures man is to plant your own bug and see if he finds it. The trouble with this is it's just not practical. You can, of course, buy one of the little wireless microphones advertised in the back of many magazines and plant it behind your bookcase. If your debugger doesn't turn it up, he's not even trying. But even if he finds it, that's no guarantee he has the expertise to locate the more sophisticated equipment actually used by professional buggers. And if you try to buy that kind of gear for your test, you'll find price tags running to the thousands of dollars, and you'll risk five years in jail and a $10,000 fine because simply possessing such equipment happens to be a federal crime.

About the only way for the layman to discriminate between bogus and genuine debuggers is to watch them in action. The phony seems to be putting on a kind of magic show. One egregious fraud described in a National Wiretap Commission report used a little gray box with red and green lights to hunt bugs; the red light was supposed to indicate the presence of a bug, and the green meant no hidden devices in the vicinity. Or, as the bogus technician would chant as he waltzed through his client's premises, "Red, you're dead; green, you're clean."

The real McCoy, on the other hand, gives the impression of someone engaged in hard labor. Let's follow a typical countermeasures man as he conducts a "sweep." His first brawny task commences when you open your door to him and he starts to lug his equipment across your threshold; a fully equipped bug-chaser will typically show up lugging several attaché cases full of heavy electronic equipment. After he sets up his gear, he'll probably begin by sweeping for the most common type of eavesdropping device, the room bug.

For years, entertainers who must move about the stage unencumbered by a microphone cord have used wireless microphones. The device is nothing more than a small microphone hooked up to a miniature FM transmitter. The whole rig is about the size of a cigarette pack, small enough to be concealed beneath the performer's clothing, and the signal it sends out can be picked up by an FM receiver within a few hundred feet, amplified, and channeled into the public address system. If the same device were concealed in the drapes or attached to the underside of a conference table, it would be a room bug. However, this type of wireless mike isn't sensitive enough to pick up conversations across the room, so it must be concealed within a few feet of where the speaker is expected to be. And it's too large to be concealed effectively within so narrow a radius. Our countermeasures man should have no trouble finding it through a simple search, without even using any of his fancy equipment.

Wireless mikes specifically designed for eavesdropping are another matter, of course. The same breakthroughs in electronics that permitted development of the pocket calculator and the electronic digital wristwatch have made possible astonishingly small listening devices. Some ultra-sensitive microphones are no bigger than a match head, and the only limiting factor in miniaturizing such equipment seems to be the size of the battery needed to power it. The smallest bug now in use is an aspirin-sized item that sells for $2000. Its sensitive microphone can pick up sounds from across the room and broadcast them on an FM carrier over distances of up to 800 feet. Somewhat larger bugs are much less expensive; one about the size of a small matchbox goes for only a few hundred dollars.

Such listening devices pose a real challenge for our debugger; they could be hiden anywhere, including inside a martini olive. (But one former government wireman insists that no one has ever bugged a martini olive. People who put olives in martinis, he says, never say anything worth overhearing. More to the point, he adds, people capable of ordering a martini with an olive are equally capable of eating the damn thing while waiting for the next round.)

The countermeasures specialist will try to locate hidden room bugs by tuning in on the FM signal they send out. The bugs broadcast on a remote part of the frequency spectrum, usually in the 30 to 50 megahertz or 70 to 90 megahertz bands, far from the commercial FM broadcast band of 88 through 108 megahertz. Special FM receivers are used by eavesdroppers to listen in on the bugs, and the same equipment is used by the debugger to find hidden transmitters. As the receiver's dial is turned past the frequency the bug is using, a "quiet spot" is encountered amid the background hiss. If the receiver is placed near the bug, turning up the volume control produces the same squeal heard in public address systems when the amplifier is set too high. Countermeasures people call the effect "sing-around," and know it is a sure sign they've found a bug.

In practice, stalking the hidden room bug isn't quite this simple. The tiny transmitters are set to put out the weakest of signals to make detection difficult, and often the countermeasures receiver won't register their presence until it comes within a few inches. Thus the debugger must slowly move his sing-around unit over every square inch of the room, all the while sweeping the FM bands in which the bugs operate. Clearly there is plenty of opportunity for a bug to go unnoticed during such a search. To guard against this possibility, debuggers have devised more elaborate instruments known as spectrum analyzers or spectrum monitors. These devices check a broad range of radio frequencies simultaneously for the telltale presence of a microtransmitter. Some of the latest models can be used to sniff out bugs simply by switching them on and walking through the rooms under investigation.

The bugmakers, too, are constantly refining the state of their art. One of their most diabolical inspirations recently made its appearance on the eavesdropping scene. It's called the subcarrier bug, and it employs the same principle FM stations use to broadcast special background music services or other special programs. The stations send out their regular programming on their FCC-assigned frequency, and simultaneously transmit their special programs on virtually the same frequency, using what is called a "subcarrier" or "sideband." The special programs are not heard on conventional FM radios and must be separated from the main carrier signal by a special receiver.

The sneaky thing about the subcarrier bug is that it can be electronically camouflaged so that our countermeasures man will miss it entirely. When he switches on his spectrum monitor he will, of course, pick up the signals from any local FM stations. He will identify them as such and move on, not realizing the clever eavesdropper has planted a subcarrier bug to operate on the same frequency as one of those local stations. The bugger will, of course, have selected a station that doesn't use its subcarrier channel, so that those sideband frequencies can be used to transmit conversations overheard by the bug. Our debugger, tuning to that frequency, will hear nothing but the local station and will get no sing-around effect. Unless, of course, he is using some of the latest and most sophisticated bug-sniffing equipment designed to turn up subcarrier bugs.

Yet another detection-resistant bug can be turned on and off remotely through a radio-control mechanism operated by the eavesdropper. When he hears the countermeasures man approaching the listening device, he can shut it down until he's sure the debugger is gone. The feature can also be used to conserve battery life by turning off the bug during periods when the premises are known to be vacant. Czech Intelligence tried to bribe a State Department employee to plant such a device in the office of an undersecretary of state a few years ago, but there have been few reports of its use in the Private Sector. Which may mean it works so well it never is detected.

It would be wrong to assume that the contest between eavesdropper and countermeasures technician is merely a matter of equipment; it is also very much a duel of wits. Clever buggers have been known to hide some second-rate devices they're sure will turn up in a countermeasures sweep in the same room where they have concealed a first-class detection-resistant bug. The idea is that the countermeasures man will think his job is done when he finds the junk, then tell his client the place is clean and go home without further sweeping.

When the hunt for telltale radio signals is complete, the debugger's work really begins. The next step will probably be a physical search for concealed listening devices, which could include a ''hard wire'' microphone—a mike connected to a tape recorder or listening post by wire, rather than radio signal. The countermeasures man will have brought along a variety of tools, such as pliers, tweezers, rubber hammers, metal detectors, and perhaps even a portable x-ray machine. The bug-chasers will literally take the place apart: air conditioning vents are removed and ducts inspected; baseboards are pried loose; and the wall-plates covering electrical outlets and switches are removed. Electrical appliances, such as clocks and lamps, are excellent concealment for built-in bugs, which have the added advantage of no batteries to run down; they draw their power from the appliance supply and will go on working indefinitely.

The physical search of a home or office for eavesdropping devices is the most time-consuming and expensive part of a countermeasures sweep, and a client may elect to omit it if he is willing to risk a little security to save money. However, anyone doubting that such searches can turn up items absolutely invisible to electronic sweeping might reflect on the following story.

Anthony Pellicano, the Chicago-based private eye profiled in Chapter 6, is also an accomplished audio countermeasures specialist. On one occasion he was hired by a woman who suspected her husband was spying on her. She brought in Pellicano to sweep their home while the husband was away. In most domestic cases, the countermeasures technician assumes he is not looking for the kind of first-class professional bugging job he might encounter in, say, an industrial counterespionage assignment. But Pellicano knew of the husband's profession, so he brought along his complete set of countermeasures equipment. The husband was an electronic eavesdropping specialist.

After sweeping the house with a spectrum monitor and finding nothing, Pellicano began his physical search, starting with the bedroom, the most likely eavesdropping target in a marital case. When the detective looked under the bed, he found a small, shallow dish filled with milk. Pellicano showed it to his client, who professed to know nothing of what it was doing there or how it got there. Next, Pellicano pulled back the mattress and found, wedged between it and the spring, a lemon.

To most countermeasures men, the discovery would have remained a puzzle, but Pellicano happened to share with the husband of his client an Italian heritage, and he immediately recognized an ancient surveillance technique devised in the Old Country long before Marconi invented the wireless. The lemon had been placed where it would be squeezed beneath the mattress when the bed was in use, and the juice dripping from the lemon would fall into the milk below, curdling it. When the bed was used for the chaste repose of solitary slumber, only a little juice would run, only a little milk would curdle. But when subjected to the buffeting of active amatory engagement, the fruit would squeeze dry and the milk fully coagulate. Whatever the accuracy of the technique, it had one merit the professional eavesdropper surely knew: there is no law against it.

After the countermeasures man has put the premises back together, he will turn his attention to the greatest threat to the client's privacy: the telephone. There are 149 million telephones in the United States, making ours the most highly wired society in the world in both per capita and absolute terms. Annually, the American telephone system carries more than 200 *billion* telephone conversations, a respectable chunk of all the person-to-person communication taking place in America. It is a happy hunting ground for professional eavesdroppers.

When you pick up your telephone to make a call, something happens in a telephone company office which may be around the corner or several miles away. A relay closes, sending you a dial tone and connecting your telephone to a switching computer, which, as you dial, will decide how to route your call through the telephone system. This is your local telephone exchange, and your telephone, as well as every other phone sharing the same three-digit prefix, is connected to it by a pair of wires that may be several miles in length. Someone out to tap your phone can hook into those wires almost anywhere along the way.

The wire pair coming from your telephone leaves your house, office, or apartment and runs to a "junction box," where it converges with the lines from other phones in the same building or neighborhood. Most Private Sector tappers will hook in somewhere between the telephone and the junction box; beyond the box your wire pair is lost amid the bundles of wire pairs from other telephones. Of course, a tapper with a friend in the telephone company may be able to obtain the "cable-and-pair" information that will enable him to climb a pole and locate among the thousands of others the two wires from your telephone.* If so, that's where he'll put the tap, because the farther the tap is from your telephone, the less likely your countermeasures man is to find it.

If the police, FBI, or other law enforcement agency have a court order to tap your telephone legally, they'll probably do it right at the telephone exchange. They'll locate your telephone line at the exchange and hook on a leased line running to their offices, where they operate a centralized listening post covering all the legal taps in town. There is absolutely no way for a countermeasures man to detect such a tap, short

---

* This was the technique used by the Houston police; see Chapter 4.

of gaining access to the telephone exchange and inspecting your line where it terminates there. And only telephone company technicians are permitted to enter the so-called frame rooms, where the exchange switching equipment is located.

Soviet Intelligence has devised a way to tap the American intercity trunk lines that carry long-distance calls. The technique is based on the fact that about 70 percent of long-distance calls in the United States are carried through the air on microwaves, instead of through wires or cables. The calls are sent over chains of microwave relay stations crisscrossing the country. The stations are set about twenty miles apart; each one receives a microwave beam carrying thousands of telephone calls, and retransmits it to the next station, which is just visible on the horizon. However, some of the beam spills past the relay station's antenna and can be picked up by anyone in the vicinity using the same kind of receiving equipment as the telephone company. According to testimony of U.S. intelligence officials before both the Rockefeller Commission and the Senate Intelligence Committee, the Soviet Union uses this technique to spy on long-distance telephone conversations within the United States. Some press reports say the calls are intercepted by the array of antennas mounted on the roof of the Soviet Embassy in Washington, D.C., and that Russian plans to build a new embassy on a higher elevation in the city are prompted, at least in part, by a desire to improve reception of the telephone signals. The Soviets are also reported to be intercepting telephone microwaves at their United Nations offices in New York, their trade consulates in Chicago and San Francisco, and various residences in New York and Maryland.

Of course, any eavesdropper who succeeds in tapping the microwave beam of the telephone company's trunk lines will be flooded by a veritable Niagara of telephone conversations, and the problem of separating the one of interest from the thousands of others pouring in is no small technical hurdle. But according to Thomas C. Reed, the Pentagon's director of communication systems, it is a task well within the power of modern computer technology. Reed warns that "any underworld organization, blackmailer, terrorist, or foreign power" is capable of doing it, so we may assume that a large Private Sector firm with a well-heeled commercial or industrial client could also do it. The technique is expensive, but it's the most risk-free means of wiretapping, since the wireman need never come near his victim's premises or telephone line. And there's virtually no way in the world for a countermeasures man to detect it.*

Returning to the more common forms of wiretapping, our countermeasures man will probably begin by looking for a tap somewhere between the telephone instrument and the junction box, which may be down the hall, in the basement, or on a nearby telephone pole. Most Private Sector taps will be installed somewhere between these two points, because most wiretapping practitioners don't have the entree with the telephone company needed to spring the cable-and-pair information for a tap further along the line. Fortunately, this is also the one zone in which the countermeasures man has anything like a reasonable chance of detecting a tap.

A tap could be either direct or wireless. In the former, a pair of wires is spliced to the telephone line, then run to a nearby home or office where the tapper has placed a tape recorder. A wireless tap is a tiny FM transmitter similar to a room bug, which is wired into the line; a receiver–recorder arrangement planted somewhere within a radius of a few hundred feet picks up the conversations.

Wireless taps are hunted in much the same way as room bugs, by trying to detect the signal they sent out while operating. Direct taps are harder to find; they might be uncovered by checking the electrical current running through the telephone line, but a visual check of the entire line is the only sure way. Still, most Private Sector tappers prefer wireless taps because they're safer. If a direct tap is discovered, the tapper will find the police waiting for him at the other end of the wire when he drops by to put a fresh reel of tape on his recorder.

Suppose your debugger tells you he's checked your telephone line and found no bugs. Does this mean you can call up your partner, lover,

---

* The problem of microwave telephone tapping has been the subject of a secret two-year study by the National Security Council. In July 1977, government sources disclosed that the Carter administration was considering a number of proposals to correct the problem, including the use of underground, high-security telephone cables, as well as electronic scrambling and encoding devices. The drawback to all such proposals, however, is the enormous cost involved.

or co-conspirator and freely exchange your deepest secrets? It certainly does not. About the only thing it does mean is that—apparently—no one has sicced a cut-rate private eye on you to tap your telephone. It is no guarantee that some high-powered industrial spy outfit hasn't tapped your line on a telephone pole six blocks away, or that the Feds aren't doing the same thing down at your local telephone exchange. You don't know that the telephone company itself isn't eavesdropping on you for business or pleasure. And you have no assurance the KGB, the Mafia, or some other organization isn't listening in on your long-distance calls as they bounce across the continent on microwave beams. A competent countermeasures sweep can assure you that there are very probably no bugs within the finite bounds of your home or office, but the telephone system is simply too vast for anyone to guarantee that your telephone conversations are secure. Talk on the telephone as you would in a crowded elevator.

What about voice scramblers? They are devices you attach to your telephone to turn your voice into a electronic jigsaw puzzle as it goes out on the line; an identical unit on another phone puts the puzzle back together. Anyone eavesdropping on the line in between hears nothing but strange and unintelligible sounds. Scramblers can be a great aid to telephone privacy, but they have their limitations.

There are about fifteen companies in the United States presently manufacturing voice scramblers, and the cost of the devices ranges from $260 up to more than $6000. The least expensive scramblers offer little real privacy; they simply invert the frequencies in the human voice to make it unintelligible to the eavesdropper, and a good electronics technician would have little trouble whipping up some circuitry to restore the intercepted sound to clear speech. Worse yet, speech scrambled by the simplest of these cheaper devices can be unscrambled by any identical model built by the same manufacturer. They offer minimal protection against casual nosiness in, say, a radio-telephone system, but they are useless as protection from a dedicated eavesdropper.

For a somewhat larger price tag, more effective scramblers can be had which will encode the scrambled speech according to a key set by the users; the key can be changed periodically to insure security. Some of these devices offer a very high degree of privacy, but no commercially available system can provide absolute security. The only 100-percent secure scrambler systems, if they exist at all, are restricted to government use and are enormously expensive.

Exactly how much security one is buying in any given telephone scrambler system is difficult to estimate. Certainly even the most sophisticated commercially available system can be defeated by a crack cryptanalytical outfit such as the U.S. National Security Agency, or by most other federal intelligence agencies. And it must be presumed that most other large industrialized nations can do the same thing. The possibility that the same code-breaking technology is available in the Private Sector for high-stakes industrial or commercial spying should be taken into consideration by those who must calculate the risks involved in using scramblers to guard corporate secrets. But to your basic freelance wiretapper, a good scrambler system will present an impenetrable obstacle.

There are a few drawbacks to scramblers, however. For one thing, they attract attention. A scrambled telephone conversation advertises itself to anyone who happens to be listening as somebody's secret. A call that might slip through the telephone system unnoticed among the hundreds of thousands of others, if it were held in the clear, may draw the attention of all kinds of people when scrambled. And some of them may know how to unscramble.

Finally, it should be noted that most scramblers put a considerable strain on the ears. The voice on the other end of the line sounds as though it were coming from the bottom of the ocean, and the listener must often ask the speaker to repeat. For anyone who has difficulty hearing on the telephone a scrambler may not be practical.

If you've got a secret to keep, the best word of advice regarding the telephone is to be careful from the moment you pick up the receiver. And an equally valuable word of caution is to continue to be careful after you hang it up, for the telephone in repose can be nearly as treacherous as the telephone in use. To our countermeasures man, the telephone instrument is the one object in the room demanding the most careful attention. And the reason for this is that the familiar little appliance has been a potential room bug of superior quality from the day the telephone installer took it from its carton and connected it to your wall. Finding out whether it's actually being used to spy on you is one of the major tasks of the debugger.

When you hang up your telephone, the weight of the handset pushes down a pair of plastic pegs, called "plungers," set into the cradle. The plungers open a switch—variously known as a hookswitch or a switch-hook—which disconnects the microphone in the mouthpiece from the line linking your telephone with the local exchange. But a simple change in the wiring will shortcircuit the hookswitch and turn your telephone into an open microphone even after it's been hung up. If your phone line is tapped, the eavesdropper will also be able to hear conversations held near the phone when it's not in use. The trick is known as a "hookswitch bypass."

If the eavesdropper is lucky, he won't even have to sneak into your home or office to tamper with your telephone, because many telephones come from the factory with the equivalent of a hookswitch bypass. The unit that rings the bell to signal incoming calls happens to have all the necessary elements of a dynamic microphone; about 5 percent of the ringer mechanisms will actually function as microphones. And since the ringer remains connected to the telephone line even when the receiver is hung up, the effect is identical to a hookswitch bypass, i.e., the telephone is potentially bugged.

Peculiarities in the wiring of some telephones also produces the same effect. In 1970, Governor Marvin Mandel of Maryland discovered the special Civil Defense hot-line telephone in his office was acting like a room bug. Subsequently, several other state governors discovered their hot-line phones—all part of a network called the National Warning System—worked the same way. The Pentagon and AT&T claimed it was merely a wiring error. Arnold "Pete" Preston, a telephone countermeasures man with Dektor Counterintelligence and Security in Virginia, discovered that some special telephones used in commercial and industrial applications are inadvertently designed in such a way as to have the equivalent of a hookswitch bypass. If the code stamped on the bottom of your phone is "500AC" or contains the digits "568," you may have one.

Fortunately, it is easy for a countermeasures man to discover a hookswitch bypass; he simply taps into the telephone line and listens. If he can't hear sounds made near the hung-up phone, he knows the hook-switch is working normally. But he does not know whether someone has installed a harmonica bug in the telephone.

The harmonica bug—also known as the infinity transmitter, or the "listen back"—is an eavesdropping device that must be wired into the telephone. To activate it, the eavesdropper calls the target phone from another telephone; any telephone anywhere will do, so long as it can be used to direct-dial a call to the target phone. Just before the phone begins to ring, the eavesdropper blows into a harmonica, sending a tone over the line to activate the bug. The bug turns itself on and, in effect, answers the telephone, preventing it from ringing. Now the activated bug will pick up conversations in the room and transmit them over the telephone line to the eavesdropper. When he's heard enough, another toot turns the device off and breaks the connection. When the harmonica bug is not in use, the telephone will react normally in a countermeasures check. The device is difficult to detect.

Checking the telephone for bugs and related tampering is one of the most demanding tasks facing the countermeasures man. The job requires the use of a specialized instrument called a telephone analyzer, which tests the internal wiring of the phone for the presence of modifications, and generates harmonica-like tones to activate any harmonica bugs that may be present. For one of the multiple-line phones or call-director units in such wide business use, only the most advanced telephone analyzer instruments will do the job.

The quiet contest between eavesdropping and countermeasures is a technological tug of war. Like living insects, electronic bugs develop a resistance to whatever is used against them. No sooner is one generation of eavesdropping device wiped out by a new countermeasures technique than a hardier strain appears, immune to that particular insecticide. The competition between electronic spies and counterspies has raised the techniques of electronic eavesdropping to a very specialized skill. In fact, the day of the self-taught genius who whips up bugs in his basement is largely over; anyone planning on entering the bugging field these days should resign himself to going back to school.

There are only a few bugging schools. The best is probably the one operated at Fort Holabird, Maryland, by Army Intelligence, which trains students from several government agencies, as well as the Baltimore Police Department and the Maryland State Police. In the Private Sector, bugging schools are run by two of the largest manufacturers of electronic surveillance equipment. One of these companies is the well-known maker of home-movie equipment, Bell and Howell.

Bell and Howell Communications Company, a Waltham, Massachusetts, subsidiary of the camera maker, has long been one of the leading Private Sector suppliers of bugging equipment. Since 1970, the company's Special Operations Group has conducted quarterly "Intelligence Officers Training Seminars," courses in various cities in the United States. At least one instructor is a former CIA eavesdropping specialist. The courses are limited to police officers and other law enforcement personnel having a legitimate interest in the subject, but National Wiretap Commission investigators questioned the enrollment of officers from states in which bugging and wiretapping is forbidden even to the police.

Until recently, for example, the State of Texas has had no state law governing electronic eavesdropping. Under the terms of the federal anti-bugging law, the 1968 Omnibus Crime Control and Safe Streets Act, eavesdropping is denied to the police in such states because there is no legal mechanism for them to obtain a court order. Thus, since 1968, Texas police officers have been forbidden to tap phones or use bugging devices. Still, police from the state have attended the Bell and Howell school. In November 1971, eight officers from the Texas Department of Public Safety—the state police—were sent to the company's seminar in Miami Beach, Florida. The trip and tuition were paid out of federal funds from the Law Enforcement Assistance Administration. The rationale for such training may be those portions of the course dealing with such things as countermeasures, or the use of wireless microphones concealed on the officer's person (a practice permitted by the federal law), but students in the seminars will receive the full curriculum of wiretapping and bugging. It may be no coincidence that Texas police have recently been involved in illegal wiretapping scandals.

Bell and Howell lately has discontinued the manufacture and sale of wiretapping devices, and it has deleted wiretapping techniques from its electronic surveillance courses. The move leaves the National Intelligence Academy of Fort Lauderdale, Florida, as the leading Private Sector bug school in the country.

Despite its official-sounding name, the National Intelligence Academy is a wholly private enterprise. It was started in 1973 by Leo Goodwin, Jr., the millionaire son of the late founder of the Government Employees Insurance Company (GEICO). Tax-exempt funds from the Leo Goodwin Foundation were used to set up NIA as a kind of public service to police everywhere. Goodwin, a police buff in his late fifties, is quoted by the *Fort Lauderdale News* as saying, "We've got public-spirited people out helping to save everything from the sea otter to the yellow-winged butterfly. But who is putting money into saving and helping law enforcement?"

In his fight to save the blue-coated bug-dropper, Goodwin teamed up with Jack N. Holcomb, an experienced wireman and sometime Caribbean adventurer. Using Goodwin's money, Holcomb began by starting Audio Intelligence Devices (AID), a manufacturer of bugging equipment. A few years later the pair formed NIA. According to Goodwin and Holcomb, the school is a completely separate and distinct operation from the manufacturing plant; according to a former employee, the school exists to sell equipment made by AID. Whatever the ultimate objectives of NIA, its close ties to AID are undeniable. The two organizations share opposite ends of the same two-story, concrete-and-glass building on 62nd Street in northwest Fort Lauderdale; George E. Martin, NIA's secretary-treasurer, also serves as personnel director for both NIA and AID. AID president Holcomb serves as a consultant to NIA. And the bugging equipment used in the NIA classrooms is strictly AID gear.

Apprentice buggers pay a $760 tuition fee to enroll in AID's two-week course in electronic surveillance. According to school rules, enrollment is limited to career law enforcement officers with a minimum of two years' experience working narcotics, vice, intelligence, organized crime or criminal investigation, or internal security. The applicant is supposed to submit fingerprint cards in triplicate, mug shots in duplicate, and a signed authorization from his or her commanding officer. But a former NIA employee says none of these credentials is ever checked, and sometimes the requirement for them is waived. The ex-

NIA man also says the school accepts students from every state, including those in which the police are not permitted to bug or wiretap, and no effort is made to determine whether the techniques taught to the student at the academy happen to be illegal back home.

NIA does not totally ignore questions of legality, however. The first hour of the eighty-hour bugging course consists of a lecture by the NIA attorney on the subject of electronic eavesdropping and the law. With that preliminary out of the way, the student snoopers settle into two solid weeks of bugs, taps, and the other paraphernalia of electronic surveillance. In the past, NIA has employed instructors with CIA and other federal government backgrounds. More recently, however, the ex-Feds have left, and the faculty is composed largely of former Florida police officers.

The bugging course includes field trips to the other end of the building where AID workers assemble the tiny listening devices the students will use in their work. But the curriculum isn't entirely academic. The students learn to carry out such practical exercises as concealing a bug within a room in less than five minutes (under the watchful eye of an instructor observing by means of closed circuit television), and how to deal with suspicious telephone company personnel.

The high point of the two-week course comes when the instructor opens a door normally kept locked, and leads the students into Classroom D. Classroom D is the sensitive core of NIA, and one of the few areas of the school not shown to most visitors. The room contains sample installations of just about every telephone, junction box, aerial and underground telephone cable, and any other access point where a wiretapper might hook in. The equipment is linked to form a miniature working telephone system, which the students can use to carry out such training exercises as tapping into a line while a conversation is in progress without alerting the speakers.

Students who successfully complete the NIA course are awarded certificates endorsed by the State of Florida's Commission on Police Officer Standards and Training, a regulatory board that certifies the school and its faculty. In November 1975, NIA reported to the National Wiretap Commission that it had trained more than 300 city, county, state, and federal law enforcement officers. Inevitably, through retirement, resignations, or layoffs, many of the NIA graduates will eventually migrate to the Private Sector, bringing their training and expertise with them. Most will take the high road, working as audio countermeasures specialists; but a few will choose the low road, illegally selling their eavesdropping skills to the highest bidder.

Despite the laws against it, electronic snooping seems to have become a permanent part of the American scene. We think of it as a space age phenomenon, an artifact of the 1960s and 1970s; in fact, it is somewhat older. Bugging and wiretapping have been around long enough to be considered an American tradition.

Consider this: Private detectives stage a midnight break-in at the offices of a prominent law firm. They search the files, tap the telephones, and plant a bug. Later, when they're caught, they claim they were trying to trace the source of a leak. When the matter is probed further, the involvement of a highly placed public official is disclosed. The politician involved in the affair attempts a cover-up by invoking ''national security.''

It sounds like yesterday's headlines, but the story unfolded in the New York newspapers in 1916.

The private eye who led the break-in was William J. Burns, the legendary founder of the detective agency that still bears his name. Burns's client was millionaire J. P. Morgan, the Howard Hughes of his day. Morgan sent Burns to burgle the offices of Seymour and Seymour, a law firm that, like Morgan, was involved in selling munitions to Great Britain and France (the First World War had entered its second year, although the United States was not yet involved).

Burns installed in the Seymour firm's offices a detectophone, a crude predecessor of today's room bug. The detectophone was a concealed microphone which could be linked by a hidden wire to some nearby listening post. Burns rented an adjacent office from which to monitor the device. With the help of the New York City police, Burns also installed wiretaps on the Seymour telephones.

The operation went sour when a disgruntled ex-employee of Burns's went to the district attorney and blew the whistle. Burns claimed the bugging of the Seymour offices was entirely proper because its purpose was to obtain evidence of a crime. The crime in question was the alleged leaking by a Morgan employee of the financier's business secrets to someone in the Seymour offices.

Meanwhile, revelations that Morgan had used the New York police as his own private cops to help tap the Seymour telephones embarrassed the mayor, who tried to cover up the affair with the mantle of "national security." When a state senate investigating committee began to take an interest in the case, the mayor pronounced this warning: "I want to say one thing, that anybody who has been warned that vital interests of the United States as a Government were involved, and who, knowingly, deliberately jeopardizes those interests, while he may not be guilty under any statute of treason to the United States, is a traitor to his country at heart."

The mayor later enriched the plot by hinting darkly at a conspiracy to supply arms to Pancho Villa in Mexico, but in the end no evidence was offered to suggest that the affair was anything but simple business espionage on the part of J. P. Morgan. Burns was convicted of illegal entry and fined $100. The matter quickly faded from the headlines.

The Seymour wiretapping was a routine matter for the New York Police Department, which operated a five-man wiretapping squad out of an office at 50 Church Street, from which vantage point the officers could tap any telephone in New York City. During a two-year period ending in 1916, the squad tapped 350 telephones. Wiretapping by the New York police, which was done at the discretion of the police commission and without court order, dates back to at least 1895.

The detectophone used by Burns to bug the lawyers' offices was by no means a new invention in 1916. Recently, the Nick Harris Detective Agency of Los Angeles discovered it owned an antique device similar to the one Burns employed. The device, which is the size and shape of a suitcase, dates from 1907, nearly a decade before the Seymour bugging. Sales literature found with the instrument proclaimed: "Hears even a whisper . . . perfect crime detector . . . endorsed by the International Association of Chiefs of Police, District Attorneys, Sheriffs, Government Officials, and Private Detective Agencies . . . its evidence has been admitted by the highest courts. . . . the old method of trying to force statements and confessions by the famous third degree has been supplemented by the more humane and accurate method. . . .''

How long has it been going on? Take a look at the first patent for a telephone scrambler, issued to a twenty-five-year-old inventor named James Harris Rogers. The patent is dated December 20, 1881, just five years after the telephone itself was patented. A cynic might suspect that the first wiretap was installed the day after the first telephone was connected. He would be wrong; there was a massive wiretapping operation going on in 1867, nine years *before* the telephone was invented.

The wiretap ring included some Western Union telegraph operators and a Wall Street stock broker. The ring would intercept telegraph dispatches sent to Eastern newspapers by their correspondents in the West. The intercepted messages would be replaced by counterfeit ones reporting bankruptcies and other disasters supposedly befalling companies whose stock was traded on the New York exchange. When the news they invented drove down the price, the wiretappers would buy up their victims' stock. The ring was broken by private eye Allan Pinkerton, who, in a letter to the president of Western Union, may have been the first to suggest a federal anti-wiretapping law: ''The lines must be protected by Congress so that a man who stole communications from the wires was equally guilty as the man who stole letters out of the mail and opened them. . . .''

Congress finally got around to passing such a law in 1968. Meanwhile, the Private Sector's secret listeners got 101 years' head start. They are still going strong.

6

Four Private Eyes

Newspaper feature writers seem to have a fund of cherished clichés to draw from on slow news days. One of the most serviceable is the private detective story, in which the reporter selects a few local gumshoes from the Yellow Pages, calls them up, and asks, "How do the fictional private eyes of books, movies, and television compare to their real-life counterparts?" Invariably the real-life counterparts give the same disillusioning answer: Life in a trenchcoat is nothing like the whodunit writer supposes.

Pressed to elaborate, the real-life PIs (private investigators) usually begin by complaining that the job doesn't offer the sexual fringe benefits—usually designated by the code word "blonds"—enjoyed by the fictional sleuths. And there is a scarcity of the sort of well-heeled client who says things like "Money is no object, Mr. Spade." Unattainable to the real private eye are those familiar trappings of the TV detective's success: the plush office, the beautiful and efficient secretary, and the luxury car complete with telephone; the job just doesn't pay well enough to make those things affordable. And the real PIs say they envy the kind of cases the fictional detectives are asked to solve; exciting and interesting jobs rarely come their way.

It's true. For the typical practitioner of the private detective profession, the job is dreary and poorly paying. The tasks he is most often handed are: preemployment background checks of job applicants, background checks of insurance and credit applicants, undercover work in retail stores to catch shoplifters or dishonest employees, and investigation of insurance and workmen's compensation claims. Occasionally a client hires him to tail an errant spouse for evidence in a divorce case, or to undertake the quasi-legal kidnapping of children in a custody case. The job ranges from dull to sleazy, and it pays a hundred or so per day plus expenses when the PI works, which is by no means all the time.

But there are exceptions to this dreary rule, an elite handful of private detectives whose careers rival the most famous of fictional sleuths. Some of them cultivate a deliberate flamboyance, most of them are expensive, but all of them turn up regularly in whatever high-stakes cases happen to be around.

Lake Headley is neither a swashbuckler nor particularly high-priced. A spare, mustachioed man in his mid-forties, Headley might be a blackjack dealer or a deputy sheriff, two jobs he held while living in Las Vegas. The son of the chief of police of Goshen, Indiana, he spent seven years as a noncom in the Indiana National Guard and the U.S. Army, before moving to Vegas. Headley worked several years as an intelligence officer in the Clark County, Nevada, Sheriff's Department, then resigned to open his own private detective agency. He supplemented his private detective work with stints as a ''21'' dealer at the Horseshoe Casino, until he finally moved his business to Los Angeles in 1970. In L.A. he went to work for Luke McKissack, noted civil rights attorney, and he gradually became a thorn in the side of the law enforcement establishment he once belonged to.

Headley helped bring about the acquittal of many of McKissack's clients, including the first black GI court-martialed by the army in a Vietnam ''fragging'' incident, and a Los Angeles man charged with first-degree murder. In 1973, Headley made history by becoming probably the first person on record to make a citizen's arrest of an FBI agent.

The incident happened in Rapid City, South Dakota, where American Indian Movement leaders Russell Means and Dennis Banks were standing trial on charges growing out of the seventy-one-day occupation of the Wounded Knee village on the Oglala Sioux reservation in South Dakota. Luke McKissack, attorney and assassination investigator Mark Lane, Headley, and some twenty-five other lawyers and investigators had formed the Wounded Knee Defense/Offense Committee. The Committee opened an office in Rapid City and defended the AIM members free of charge.

The FBI mounted a rather ostentatious surveillance operation against the Committee, apparently intended as harassment. All visitors to the Committee's office were photographed by FBI agents. Late one evening, Headley and two of his investigators discovered five automobiles full of FBI agents parked outside the Committee offices. When the detectives jotted down the license numbers, the agents sped away. The next day, Headley's assistants, a young man and woman, were arrested and charged with "tampering" with the Bureau's automobiles. A Committee member was beaten and another, a woman, was knocked down a flight of stairs while trying to photograph some of the agents.

Headley discovered that the FBI agents had purchased several thousand dollars worth of electronic gear from a local Radio Shack store, equipment that could be used for the purpose of electronic surveillance. The agents took the equipment and quietly moved into the College Inn Motor Hotel, an establishment that happened to be just next door to the offices of the Wounded Knee Defense/Offense Committee offices. Headley and Mark Lane paid a visit to the motel to question the desk clerk and see what they could find out about their new neighbors. As Headley entered the lobby, one agent grabbed him and tried to throw him out onto the street.

Headley disengaged himself from the man's grip, then informed him he was under arrest. A citizen's arrest, Headley told him, and the charge was assault. Headley asked the desk clerk to call the police, then waited in the motel lobby with the dumbfounded FBI man. Mark Lane, who had been watching the incident from the sidelines, quipped, "I think you can let him keep his belt and shoelaces, Lake; he doesn't look suicidal to me."

By the time the Rapid City police arrived, Headley and some of the other Committee members had arrested three more FBI agents. The confused police officers took everyone off to the county jail, where

Headley swore out complaints against the four federal agents. One of the glowering men told Headley, "I'll be seeing you again sometime," but this never came to pass. When the police later tried to locate the agent, the FBI informed them he had left Rapid City and the Bureau couldn't locate him. Charges against the remaining three agents were dropped, and there has been no report of whether the FBI ever found its wandering employee. Headley and the Committee continued their work on behalf of the AIM leaders, and the government's case was eventually dismissed, largely because of the FBI's heavy-handed methods.

Back in California, the primary topic of conversation was Patty Hearst, who had just been kidnapped from her Berkeley apartment by a group calling itself the Symbionese Liberation Army. Headley had heard some intriguing rumors about the case and became interested in the background of Donald DeFreeze, the self-styled "General Field Marshal Cinque," leader of the SLA. DeFreeze had run afoul of the law several times in California, and Headley decided to take a look at his court records in the Los Angeles County Clerk's office.

"He had been on probation in three different places," says Headley. "He kept getting arrested for things like robbery, burglary, bombs, automatic weapons and the like, but he was always allowed to go free."

DeFreeze had been caught on the roof of a Cleveland bank carrying two handguns, a set of burglar tools, a knife, and a hand grenade. He was released on $5000 bond and returned to Los Angeles. He was only put away after a parking lot shootout with a pair of bank security guards and several Los Angeles police officers. Even under a permissive criminal justice system, DeFreeze's ability to stay out of jail seemed remarkable. Headley began to suspect that he may have been a police informer, a theory bolstered by one name he kept running across in DeFreeze's file in the County Clerk's office, an intelligence officer in the Los Angeles Police Department. The file was thick, and examining it required several visits. Headley noticed that with each succeeding visit the file seemed to shrink a little; items here today were gone tomorrow. His suspicions fully aroused, Headley telephoned the intelligence officer named in the file. The officer was reluctant to discuss DeFreeze, but finally admitted that the SLA leader had once worked as his informer.

"I had to cut him loose," he said, "because I knew he was psychologically dead." The intelligence officer added ominously, "He's going to be killed."

The conversation took place on May 2, 1974. Eight days later Headley and author-researcher Donald Freed disclosed the results of their investigation of DeFreeze to a San Francisco press conference, and warned that DeFreeze and his SLA companions may have been marked for death by the police. Seven days later, on May 17, DeFreeze and five other SLA members died in a blazing shootout with members of the LAPD's SWAT team in a house in the Watts section of Los Angeles.

The circumstances of the siege of the SLA hideout aroused some public suspicion that the police had no intention of taking the fugitives alive. It was charged that the SLA members were given little time to consider the SWAT team's "come on out or else" ultimatum before the police laid down a withering barrage of some 6000 rounds of rifle and automatic weapons fire that ignited the building, turning it into an inferno. The police responded by saying the gunfire had been initiated by the occupants of the house. Suspicion was heightened when it was later disclosed that the police had not attempted to call the fugitives on the functioning telephone located in the house.

One man who was especially skeptical of the official explanations was Dr. L. S. Wolfe of Emmaus, Pennsylvania, father of Willie Wolfe, who died along with DeFreeze and the other SLA members in the shootout. At the time of the siege, there were no arrest warrants out on Willie Wolfe, and it seemed hard to believe that, given the chance, he wouldn't have walked out of the house before the shooting began. Determined to know the truth about his son's death, Dr. Wolfe hired Headley, Donald Freed, and a young private detective named Rusty Rhodes to investigate the case.

The trio began by probing the prison career of DeFreeze, which began after his conviction in the 1969 bank shootout in Los Angeles. DeFreeze was given a five-years-to-life sentence and sent to the California Medical Facility at Vacaville, a state correctional institution where some very controversial experiments in prisoner behavior modification have been carried out. Some critics of the Vacaville program have charged that the prison is used by the CIA to experiment with mind-altering drugs, a charge that sounded like bizarre West Coast paranoia until a recent Freedom of Information Act suit by John Marks of the Center for National Security Studies brought about the release of CIA documents proving that it was perfectly true. DeFreeze reportedly was given some behavior-modifying drugs while at Vacaville; a fellow inmate recalls that the SLA leader would pop pills into his mouth "like candy."

During his three years in Vacaville, DeFreeze became secretary of a prison project called the Black Cultural Association. The group met twice weekly and was presided over by an instructor from the Afro-American Studies program at the University of California at Berkeley. The instructor, Colston Westbrook, encouraged some of his Berkeley students to attend the Vacaville meetings, and it was in this way that DeFreeze met Willie Wolfe and some of the other middle-class whites who later joined him in the SLA. Headley believes that Patricia Hearst, then a Berkeley student, attended some of the BCA Vacaville meetings under an assumed name, and thus knew DeFreeze long before her February 1974 kidnapping by the SLA.

Late in 1972, DeFreeze was transferred from Vacaville to the prison at Solidad. A few months later he was moved to a minimum security section of the institution, from which he immediately escaped. According to official accounts, this was the last anyone heard of DeFreeze until after the Patricia Hearst kidnapping, when the authorities received a taped message which began, "My name is Cinque. . . ."

But Lake Headley has pieced together a somewhat different story. He located Wayne M. Lewis, a former FBI informant, who says he was in official contact with DeFreeze in July 1973 after his escape from Solidad. Lewis claims his "handler"—Special Agent Donald L. Gray, purportedly a nephew of former FBI Director L. Patrick Gray—told him DeFreeze was an informer not only for the LAPD but for the FBI as well. Lewis says Gray described DeFreeze as having become "uncontrollable," and had to be disposed of. He says he was being groomed to move into the SLA and replace DeFreeze when his cover was blown and the operation had to be abandoned. While Lewis can only offer his own word in support of most of this story, he has proof of at least one part of it: a letter over the signature of FBI Director Clarence Kelley acknowledging that Lewis was a paid Bureau informant from November 1972 until June 1974.

Headley also points out that Colston Westbrook, the Berkeley Black Studies instructor who introduced DeFreeze to Willie Wolfe and some of the other SLA members, served for almost four years in various spots around the globe as an employee of Pacific Architects and Engineers, Inc., a firm generally regarded as a CIA proprietary company. This item, taken together with Lewis's story and the recent revelation of CIA involvement in the Vacaville drug and behavior-modification experiments, forms the chilling outline of a circumstantial case that the federal government was somehow involved with the SLA.

"It's possible," says Headley, "that this was a kind of Plumbers operation run from inside the Nixon White House and aimed at infiltrating some of the activists groups in California. When Watergate came along there would have been no way to call up DeFreeze and tell him to halt the project; he was on the loose with guns, money, and who knows what else. He became a Frankenstein's monster, so he had to be eliminated.

"But that's only a theory," Headley added.

It's a theory that would explain the reactions of the police and the FBI to Headley's investigations, however. After he became involved in the case, the cops and the Feds stuck to him like flypaper for a while, then resorted to concocting and leaking a falsified intelligence report charging him with being almost everything from a Mafia hit man to a heroin addict. Perhaps Lake Headley did not discover the true story of the SLA and the Hearst kidnapping. But somewhere along the way he seems to have touched a very sensitive nerve.

Wallyne Parker hadn't seen her daughter in thirteen years, not since the day in 1958 when her husband left her in Illinois, taking along five-year-old Patty Jean. Later Mrs. Parker learned he had taken their daughter back to his hometown in Texas and there succeeded in obtaining a divorce and custody of Patty Jean. After that they seemed to have vanished. Mrs. Parker remarried (Parker is her present name) and had three other children, but she never forgot her first child. In hope of being reunited with her, she often placed advertisements in the personal columns, but she never received any reply.

In 1971, Mrs. Parker asked the *Chicago Daily News* to help her find her daughter. The newspaper brought in a private detective who soon picked up the long-cold trail of Mrs. Parker's ex-husband and daughter. The man had brought the child back to Illinois and given her up for adoption, claiming the little girl's mother was dead. Patty Jean became Cynthia Ann, grew to womanhood in the home of her adoptive parents, and had recently gotten married. The detective found her and arranged a tearful but joyous reunion in suburban Chicago.

Like Patty Jean/Cynthia Ann, David Garland was an adopted child. He was raised by Philip and Lee Garland, an Oak Park, Illinois, couple. After Mr. Garland died, David's adoptive mother told him the story. His original name was Ryerson, she said. Beyond that, she knew nothing of his life before she found him in an orphanage at the age of four. But David Garland was determined to find out.

The young man could not afford to pay for the search, so, like Mrs. Parker, he asked the help of the *Chicago Daily News*. Again the newspaper brought in a private detective, who soon brought the case to a happy conclusion. David was the son of Elmer and Nora Ryerson, a Chicago dockworker and his wife. In 1952, family difficulties forced the Ryersons to place their one-year-old son Elmer, Jr., in an orphanage, where he remained for three years until he was adopted by the Garlands. Mrs. Ryerson says she and her husband never gave their permission to offer Elmer/David for adoption, and that she protested in vain when she discovered her son was gone. She was not told who had adopted him. The sixty-year-old woman was overcome with emotion when she met the young man her one-year-old Elmer had become, in the Chicago offices of the private detective.

David Garland's parents and Wallyne Parker's daughter were both located by the same missing persons specialist, a Chicago private eye named Anthony Joseph Pellicano. Tony Pellicano has been asked to find more than 4000 missing persons, hasn't failed yet, and doesn't expect to. He is the best in the business, as he will readily tell you himself. Pellicano, who sometimes goes by the name Tony Fortune, has the perceptiveness of Sherlock Holmes, the tenacity of the Royal Canadian Mounted Police, and the modesty of Muhammed Ali.

Pellicano started out working for a Chicago department store as a skip tracer, someone who tracks down people who move away without paying their bills or leaving forwarding addresses. He discovered he had a remarkable talent for locating missing persons, including the kind that don't consider themselves missing, and he decided to go into business for himself. Fifteen years and several thousand cases later, the thirty-two-year-old Pellicano is one of the leading people-finders in the country. His services don't come cheap, at $500 per day plus expenses, a $1500 minimum, adding up to a typical charge of several thousand dollars to find someone. If he were to fail he wouldn't charge anything; but, he says, that's never happened.

Pellicano doesn't apologize for his high fees, but he admits they're made necessary in part by a high-overhead operation; he is one private eye who lives up to the image of the TV detective—a plush office, a beautiful and intelligent secretary, and a luxury car complete with telephone. Sometimes Pellicano's fee is dwarfed by the financial stakes involved, as in the case of "Aggie the Cat Lady," an old woman who supported herself by selling shoelaces and razor blades on street corners. The detective tracked her down for one of his clients and gave her some welcome news: she was the heiress to a half-million-dollar estate.

Much of Pellicano's business consists of tracing runaway husbands or children, although the number of runaway wives he is asked to find sharply increased a few years ago, a phenomenon he attributes in part to the women's liberation movement. Most of the fugitive wives are in their twenties, and locating them is often more difficult than finding a runaway husband. A woman can change her name through a marriage of convenience and her appearance through a trip to the beauty parlor.

"People who try to disappear usually forget one thing," says Pellicano. "They don't change their birthday. That's how I find a lot of them."

But that's just one ploy in Pellicano's bag of tricks. Much of the tracer's art is simple psychology.

"I have to know everything about a person, including why they ran," he says. "I have to learn to think and act like, and, in a sense, become that person. Actually, I'm not looking for the missing person, but for the one person who knows where he is."

Sometimes that person is a friend or relative of the object of Pellicano's search. Or it might be a clerk in a motor vehicle bureau who can look up the name and address that goes with a particular license plate number. Or a telephone company supervisor who has control of unlisted telephone numbers or customer toll records. Or the sergeant on duty in the local police records department. In other words, it could be any of hundreds of people who are not going to cooperate with a private detective who says he's working on a missing person case. Don't worry, Pellicano has ways of making them talk.

Lon Chaney, Sr., the silent screen star and master of theatrical makeup, called himself "The Man of a Thousand Faces." Tony Pellicano, who does much of his tracing by telephone, is a man of a thousand voices. He is blessed with a sharp ear and the uncanny ability to duplicate the myriad ways in which different regions, races, and ethnic groups speak the English language. He is also endowed with a fine audacity, without which the other two talents would go to waste.

"The most important thing in this business," says Pellicano, "is to have a lot of self-confidence." To the records sergeant in the New Orleans Police Department, he is Sergeant Breen of the New York P.D., trading some gossip and cop talk before asking for an item from somebody's rap sheet. Switching to a southern falsetto, he is an elderly woman complaining to the telephone business office about some toll charges on her bill, learning in the process of a collect call from a phone booth in Berkeley, California. Next he is an urban black, then a Texas newspaper reporter. Like someone possessed by a host of demons, Pellicano lends his voice box to a score of different personalities, each invented by the resourceful people-finder. Each pretext telephone call turns up some morsel that can be used to make the next call seem more authentic. The information snowballs as Pellicano zeros in on his quarry. The final phone call is for a cab to take him to the airport; the last act is to be played in person.

A day or two later the case is closed and Pellicano is back in his movie-set offices in the Chicago suburb of Westchester. The wall is hung with shields, samurai swords, and nunchukas, the Oriental wood-and-chain fighting sticks, but the weapons are there to be seen, not used; Pellicano relies on his master's rating in Gung Fu to get him out of difficult situations. In an adjoining room, a small fortune in electronic debugging gear is assembled, for the private detective is also a specialist in audio surveillance countermeasures and has an impressive list of corporate clients who regularly call him in to sweep their offices and boardrooms for wiretaps and hidden microphones. Pellicano hunts them with the same tenacity he brings to his missing persons cases, but they are arid things of copper and Bakelite, a far cry from his flesh-and-blood quarry.

The door opens and his secretary ushers in a sad-eyed young woman. Pellicano leans forward slightly and steeples his fingers as she tells her story. Two years ago she was divorced, the court granting her custody of her two children: a five-year-old son, a three-year-old daughter. A few months later their father took them from a schoolyard playground. She has spent the past eighteen months in Florida, Texas, and California trying to find the little boy and girl, but father and children seem to have vanished from the face of the earth. Will Pellicano take the case? He'll see what he can do, he says.

After the woman has gone, Pellicano sits and stares at the notes he took while questioning the woman about her husband. Hunter becomes quarry. He is angry and resentful, hurt by his wife and robbed of his own flesh and blood by the courts. He is ready to take the law into his own hands, but where can he run to? How will he support himself and his children without leaving a trail for his wife to follow? Most important of all, who can he confide in? After a long while, Pellicano turns and picks up the telephone. The game, as Holmes used to say, is afoot.

Remember Harry Caul? He was the master wireman played by Gene Hackman in Francis Ford Coppola's film *The Conversation*. Caul became obsessed with his hidden microphones and tape recorders, and finally fell victim to the same paranoia he inspired in others. The word in some quarters is that Caul was modeled on Harold Lipset, the famous San Francisco detective. I asked Lipset if it was so.

"I've heard that before," he replied, smiling slightly. "I guess I'd rather not think that I was the inspiration."

Lipset did serve as technical advisor for the film, and even played a small cameo role in it, all of which may have inspired the rumor. But Hal Lipset would be the most logical choice for the Caul model, not because he is paranoid—he's not—but because he probably has done more bugging and wiretapping than any other private detective. In San Francisco, where he pioneered the use of electronic eavesdropping, Lipset became known as "The Private Ear."

He's a mild-mannered, balding man of fifty-seven, with no obvious sharp edges. He does not cultivate flamboyance. He's been around for a long time and he's not out to prove anything, except on behalf of a client. Lipset got his start in investigative work with the army during World War II. He enlisted before Pearl Harbor, went through Officer Candidate School, then on to a criminal investigation course taught by the near-legendary FBI agent, Melvin Purvis. After the war, he returned to San Francisco and, in order to support himself, his wife, and his newborn child, he went to work as a government investigator, first probing housing fraud for the Office of Price Administration, then working undercover for the Veterans Administration. Finally he took out a California private detective's license and went into business for himself. Sometime during those postwar years he met Ralph Bertsche; it was the beginning of a historic friendship.

Bertsche is an electronics engineer and veteran of the army's Signal Corps. After his discharge from the service, he began to build and experiment with a then unfamiliar type of electronic equipment—audio surveillance devices. He had developed some pretty good eavesdropping gadgets, but the world was not yet beating a path to his door.

Electronic surveillance was still considered an exotic technique to be left to the FBI, the CIA, and similar outfits. Private detectives stuck to the familiar tried-and-true techniques. A PI working a divorce case, for example, might slip a motel desk clerk ten dollars for a look at the register, kick down a door, and snap a few flash pictures of his quarry *in flagrante delicto,* but he would never think to bribe the room service waiter to let him put a tiny wireless microphone in the champagne bucket so that he could tape-record the intimate pillow talk of the errant couple. But when Lipset saw Bertsche's gadgets, he knew he was looking at the future.

Bertsche and his electronic listening devices became an integral part of Lipset's private detective business. At the time—the late 1950s— there was little in the way of legal restraint to electronic eavesdropping; the Federal Communications Act of 1934 placed some obstacles in the way of wiretapping telephones, but Bertsche's tiny microphone–transmitters were a completely new idea, so there was no law to restrict their use in any way. Lipset found that using them brought him better, quicker, and cheaper results than the conventional gumshoe tactics of his competition. Business flourished.

Soon Lipset and Bertsche had a host of imitators across the country as the techniques they pioneered were adopted by private detectives everywhere. But the electronic eavesdropping explosion was beginning to make people nervous, including the lawmakers on Capitol Hill. Lipset was asked to come to Washington and testify before congressional committees as an expert on the state of the art of bugging. Discovering an unsuspected strain of showmanship in himself, the detective demonstrated the ease with which eavesdropping can be accomplished by concealing a bug near one committee chairman and pointing it out to him part-way through his testimony. Lipset also chose this moment in the limelight to disclose one of Bertsche's latest gadgets, the bugged martini olive, which immediately became the consummate symbol of electronic snooping. But the expert witness had made his point too well; it was the beginning of the end of the unfettered bugging that Lipset had built his business upon. Within three years both the federal government and the State of California passed stiff anti-bugging laws. Not at all dismayed, Lipset found a new way to trade on his bugging expertise, yet stay within the law. On the theory that it takes a thief to catch one, he now sweeps his clients' premises for the bugs that may have been planted by some of his thousands of imitators.

But Lipset doesn't specialize in electronic countermeasures. In recent years he has worked increasingly for defense attorneys representing clients such as Angela Davis, Huey Newton, and Bobby Seale. In indigent cases in which the state pays for the defense counsel, the state now also pays for private investigators to assist in the defense, and Lipset is much in demand because of his impressive record of turning up the very fact needed to acquit the defendant.

"I'd like to specialize in cases involving stolen diamonds worth over half a million dollars, beautiful women, foreign travel, with some success at the end of the road," he says. "I had one like that once, but if I sat around waiting for another like it, I'd starve to death.

"I don't specialize in anything but getting answers."

"Right now the frightening thing is that there is no one controlling the CIA. I mean *nobody*. If the CIA really has infiltrated this country to the extent I think it has, we ain't got a country left."

The speaker was not a left-wing radical. He was Charles Colson, one-time White House aide, famous for his declaration that he would walk over his own grandmother to keep Richard Nixon in the White House. The time was May 1974 and Colson was sitting beside a plush backyard swimming pool in a Virginia suburb of Washington, D.C. He had an audience of one, his host, the prominent Washington private detective, Richard Bast.

Nixon was still in the White House, although impeachment now seemed inevitable; Colson was preparing to plead guilty to a charge of obstruction of justice and go to prison. Colson told Bast the CIA had been deeply involved in the Watergate break-in, that President Nixon knew this, wanted to fire CIA Director Colby and bring things out in the open, but was afraid to. Colson said Nixon and Bebe Rebozo had taken a $100,000 campaign contribution from Howard Hughes and used it for personal expenses, that Hughes was closely associated with the CIA, and that the CIA was using Hughes to blackmail Nixon into silence.

"Hughes can blow the whistle on him," said Colson.

Colson visited Bast to ask the private eye to investigate the CIA's role in Watergate. He hoped the investigator might turn up evidence proving that the Agency, and not the White House Plumbers, had planned the Watergate break-in for the purpose of discrediting White House advisors such as himself. Bast said he'd take the case if Nixon would agree to appoint a special prosecutor to probe the matter, and give Bast full presidential backing and grand jury subpoena power. It was more than Colson could swing, so the subject was dropped.

Colson agreed that Bast would be free to reveal the substance of their conversations after the former presidential aide was sentenced. The question of CIA involvement in the Watergate affair was raised repeatedly during the Senate hearings but had never been pinned down; Bast felt Colson's suspicions should be given a public airing. Colson was sentenced a few months later and Bast gave the story to the *Washington Post*.

When asked to comment, Colson told the *Post* his talks with Bast had merely been "to explore theories . . . in a very offhand fashion." He specifically denied Bast's report that Colson had told him Nixon had considered firing William Colby. But those familiar with both Bast and Colson believed the private detective, who has a reputation for truthfulness. And if Colson had known Bast better, he would never have bothered to deny the report. The detective had concealed a microphone in the flowers beside his swimming pool and tape-recorded every word of his conversations with Colson.

In choosing Richard Bast to lead the proposed investigation of the CIA, Colson came to the right man. Now in his mid-forties, Bast has been working cases in the nation's capital for the past twenty years and has an unrivaled reputation for honesty and effectiveness. And while many private detectives would find themselves compromised in such an assignment by ties of friendship or former association with people in the federal intelligence establishment, Bast would have no conflict of interest problems. He has been waging a one-man war against stupidity and dishonesty in government investigative agencies during most of his career.

Bast is tough, smart, and gutsy, and has a rigid either–or code of right and wrong. He started out working for John J. O'Brien, the late dean of Washington divorce lawyers, and isn't the least ashamed to admit that much of his business has been divorce cases.

Barbara Howar, Washington journalist, TV personality, and White House insider during the Johnson years, recalled in her recently published memoirs becoming the object of Bast's professional attentions. Without naming him, she describes a "wild-eyed fanatic, a man who was to haunt me for years both in nightmares and in reality." Bast is a little kinder in his recollection of Howar. She was very smart, he remembers, and it was no easy job to tail her. Bast had been hired by Howar's husband to get evidence for a divorce action and to recover a small fortune in diamonds he had presented to her in happier days. Howar and her lover had discreetly booked two rooms in a plush Montego Bay hotel, but planned to use only one of the accommodations. Bast got to Jamaica ahead of the couple, made his arrangements with the hotel staff, and bugged both rooms. Howar and her companion arrived and checked in, and the private detective spent the first two nights tape-recording their pillow talk. After the two had retired on the third night, Bast and several assistants burst in on them armed with flash cameras. Howar recalls ruefully that Bast bore no resemblance to Sam Spade, a claim not entirely justifiable: Bast's line as he crashed through the hotel door could have been written for Humphrey Bogart: "Come on, baby, gimme the diamonds."

During the course of his career Bast has made some powerful enemies, including the Federal Bureau of Investigation. The private detective keeps sticking his nose into cases that often end up reflecting unfavorably on the competence and even the integrity of FBI personnel. A few years ago the Bureau responded by trying to nail Bast on a violation of the federal anti-bugging law.

The FBI charged Bast with violation of a section of the law that prohibits advertising bugging devices. Bast, who was selling electronic gear as a sideline, had distributed a catalog offering among other things a shirt-pocket-sized tape recorder that could be used for clandestine recording of face-to-face conversations. Such taping is permitted by the federal law if at least one party to the conversation is aware of it, which is exactly the way in which Bast's advertisement suggested the tiny recorder be used. In fact, professional police journals such as *Law and Order* or *Law Enforcement Communications* regularly carry similar advertisements.

Violation of the advertising clause in the anti-bugging law carries a $10,000 fine and a five-year prison term, but there was never any real prospect of convicting Bast. The private detective was acquitted, but he was still penalized by the thousands of dollars he had to pay in legal fees to defend himself. He tried to sue the FBI to recover the damages done him in the case, but was brought up short by a recent Supreme Court decision that makes police officials immune from such litigation, even where it can be demonstrated that the prosecution was frivolous or malicious.

Had the FBI been satisfied with simply shafting Richard Bast, they might have come out ahead in this skirmish. However, the Bureau chose the occasion to raid Bast's office and poke through his files. The agents took away several tape recordings that had no bearing on his alleged illicit advertisement. Here the Bureau made a bad mistake.

On the grounds that the tapes had been seized illegally by the FBI,

Bast obtained a court order forcing the Bureau to return the tapes and the transcripts made from them. Bast inspected the FBI transcripts and noticed some interesting discrepancies. Perfectly audible passages on the tapes had turned up hopelessly scrambled in the FBI's official transcript of it.

"Yeah, I called him" had become "Yeah, cold ham." "Bag man" turned into "bad man," and "shylocking" became "Skylocking." Bast found 248 errors on one page. Bugged room conversations, where the audio can be of poor quality, averaged about fifty errors per page, but even the transcripts of clear telephone tape recordings ran about thirty goofs per page.

The errors often had the effect of completely demolishing the sense of what the speaker said. "De Klotz ain't doing nothing" was translated as "the clock says he hasn't done nothing"; while "a witness bond to appear at Paul Coppola's trial" was transmogrified into "up to Kichenape to appear in front of a Polish trial."

The transcripts were not rough working drafts that could be corrected later; each bore the stamp "EVIDENCE, FEDERAL BUREAU OF INVESTIGATION." They were a representative sample of the kind of documentary evidence the FBI daily turns over to prosecutors for use in criminal and civil cases. Bast showed the transcripts to his friend Les Whitten, a reporter and associate of columnist Jack Anderson. Whitten succeeded in obtaining other FBI tapes and transcripts for comparison. Bast and Whitten found 30,000 errors in 150,000 words of tape transcripts, but they discovered something even more significant: many of the "errors" appeared to have been deliberate.

In one conversation, a Mafia man is asked by a Customs agent if the FBI had been informed of a certain payoff. The mobster's audible reply, "Yes, yeah," had been transcribed as "No." A Mafia courier's reference to smuggling explosives under the very noses of FBI agents assigned to watch him was omitted. Another hood's account of a postal law violation was dropped. In one tape interview, a federal agent quotes a State Department employee as saying "everybody at every level is taking their cut" of American aid to Vietnam; the FBI transcribed the statement as "everybody never knows who's taking a cut." Repeatedly, references to crimes the FBI should have investigated were completely dropped from the Bureau's transcripts.

Whitten and Jack Anderson publicized the transcript inaccuracies in their syndicated column and attracted the attention of the House Intelligence Committee. Chairman Otis Pike assigned two staff lawyers to look into the matter. Meanwhile, Bast and Anderson tried to learn if any scrambled documents had been used to help convict anyone. They didn't have to look far before learning that the answer was yes.

Former Oklahoma Governor David Hall was convicted, along with co-defendent W. W. (Doc) Taylor, of attempting to bribe John Rogers, the Oklahoma secretary of state. One FBI transcript entered as evidence in the case has Hall saying to Rogers, "I want you to do something that will help us both and . . . (inaudible)." But Bast and the other investigators played the tape from which the FBI made the transcript and heard Hall say, "I want you to do something that will help us both and won't have anything to do with the state," a clear implication that bribery was not being proposed. Someone in the Bureau either lost or found his nerve at this blatent doctoring of evidence, because the FBI itself filed a corrected transcript of this tape during the trial. But such was not the case with other tape transcripts used to convict Hall and Taylor. One principal in the case described Taylor as "most concerned and pretty much shook up" at the prospect of bribery, but the FBI transcribers rendered it "less concerned and pretty much sure" to pay the bribe. The speaker, who is accused of acting as a middleman in the case, says at one point "I can't" pay the bribe. The FBI transcribed that as "All right now." The U.S. attorney who prosecuted Hall and Taylor has admitted the transcripts he used contained numerous errors. The convictions are being appealed.

In another recent incident, Bast took on the FBI, the Justice Department, and the CIA all at once and managed to spread a large measure of grief throughout all three agencies. For Bast, the affair began when private investigator Robert Peters, the disgruntled former employee of one of Bast's competitors, came to him with a story of wrongdoing by his ex-boss. Peters had been fired by Don Uffinger, a quick-fisted and flamboyant private eye who does about 40 percent of his business in divorce cases. Peters told Bast of one case he had worked on with Uffinger.

Uffinger's client was the wife of a CIA official. She suspected her husband of being unfaithful; specifically, she believed he was having a homosexual affair with his boss. According to Peters, Uffinger gave the woman a small wireless microphone and instructed her in how to plant it in her home, which she did. Peters says that he, Uffinger, and the woman monitored the bug from a parked car and overheard the two CIA men in what sounded like a homosexual act. Wife and private eyes charged into the house and photographed the two, and Uffinger decked one of the intelligence officials when he grabbed for the camera.

Armed with the photographs, the wife successfully sued for divorce. The two CIA men reported the incident to the Agency's Office of Security, probably precipitating a sudden demand for smelling salts in the antiseptic corridors of the CIA's Langley, Virginia, headquarters. The CIA security officers quietly arranged for one of the men to resign, the other to retire, and, apparently, for the court records of the divorce action to disappear. The messy business had been thoroughly tidied up until Uffinger fired Peters and Peters blabbed to Bast.

In admitting that they had bugged the CIA man, Peters was accusing Uffinger and himself with a clear violation of the federal anti-bugging law. In any circumstances Bast would have been obliged to report the incident to the Justice Department, but we may assume a special enthusiasm for this duty on the part of the private detective, for Uffinger is a highly valued FBI informant. Bast may have viewed the situation with the same relish as a nonbeliever contemplating a Christian Scientist with a case of appendicitis. And it didn't matter if Peters denied telling the story to Bast; the reels of Bast's hidden tape recorder had been silently turning during their little chat.

Bast reported the matter to U.S. Attorney David Hopkins, who turned it over to the FBI for investigation. The FBI, however, already knew of the incident; Special Agent Charles Harvey had received a report from one of his informants—private eye Don Uffinger. The Bureau assigned another agent to look into the case. Uffinger claimed that Peters was lying, that he and Peters had peeked in the CIA man's window, not bugged him, in order to know when to rush in with the camera. The wife, who would have been an accessory in any illegal bugging, confirmed Uffinger's story. For his part, Peters denied telling the story to Bast, even though Bast had the proof on tape. The FBI and the Justice Department dropped the case for lack of evidence. After Jack

Anderson publicized the incident in his column, the Justice Department promised a new investigation. That was in October 1974, but nothing has been heard of the matter since.

Richard Bast is all but retired from the private eye business these days. He has found trading in commodity futures to be an easier and better paying line of work. As I interviewed him in his Washington office, he often turned to a computer terminal behind his desk where reports from commodity, currency, and stock exchanges flashed on a video screen.

"Soy beans are up," he noted. "So's the German mark. So far I've made $4000 today.

It was not yet noon.

He still takes on an occasional case, but only if it interests him, and his fee is $1500 per day, plus expenses. But as long as he continues to make good money in buying and selling, there's really no reason to go back to detective work. I hear that over at the Bureau they're praying for a bull market.

7

Private Clubs, Secret Societies, and Vigilance Committees

The FBI said it was sorry it broke the law. In May 1976, the Senate Intelligence Committee released a report detailing decades of illegal break-ins, wiretaps, and assorted dirty tricks carried out by the Bureau. The next day FBI Director Clarence Kelley made a public act of contrition to the American people on behalf of his agency. There had been abuses, Kelley acknowledged. "Some of these activities were clearly wrong and quite indefensible," he said, adding, "We are truly sorry."

The FBI director had apologized. Five days later he apologized for the apology.

In a letter to the Society of Former Special Agents of the FBI, Kelley explained the reason for his speech. For several months the Bureau had been receiving some unfriendly attention from Congress and the news media, he said. Congress was seriously considering legislation that would severely restrict the activities of the FBI. Kelley said he had "carefully reviewed the situation and decided the time had come to make certain admissions . . . because I believe this action might well prevent or at least somewhat retard the proliferation of highly restrictive legislation."

Kelley's public apology for the Bureau's abuses apparently had irritated some of the members of the former agents society and prompted the organization's president to write Kelley asking for "clarification." The FBI director felt compelled to disavow the sincerity of his speech in order to placate the ex-agents, and admit publicly that his apology was merely a public relations maneuver to keep the legislators' hands off the Bureau. The incident was an eloquent illustration of the power of the Private Sector.

There is no single voice that speaks for the hundreds of thousands of private cops, former cops, and would-be cops who make up the Private Sector. The collective power of the American private police subculture surges through a wide variety of groups—professional organizations, private clubs, cliques, and Old Boy Networks. Guard services, corporate security staff, and police technology manufacturers are represented by the American Society for Industrial Security. Private investigators band together in the World Association of Detectives. Military intelligence officers and some of their civilian admirers have formed The National Military Intelligence Association, with the Pentagon's blessing. Veterans of the Secret Service can join the Association of Former Agents of the U.S. Secret Service, while many former employees of the Central Intelligence Agency, the Defense Intelligence Agency, the National Security Agency, and other federal intelligence agencies are eligible for membership in the recently formed Association of Retired Intelligence Officers. But by far the most powerful of the Private Sector clubs is the Society of Former Special Agents of the Federal Bureau of Investigation.

The Society was founded in 1937 and has grown over the years along with the number of living FBI alumni; the 6600 members comprise roughly half of the surviving Bureau veterans—the half whose devotion to the myth of J. Edgar Hoover demands expression through something midway between a fan club and an organized religion. As a Society president put it some years ago, "The amalgam that binds the agents of the FBI to the bureau is Mr. Hoover and his leadership. He is also the amalgam that binds the . . . members of our organization together in our devotion to each other, to the Federal Bureau of Investigation, and to Mr. Hoover, whose life is the fulfillment of the motto of the FBI: fidelity, bravery, integrity."

The Society sells a desk-top bust of Hoover, copies of his writings, and other sacred objects. It publishes a monthly newsletter, *Grapevine*, holds a convention every October, and maintains a small full-time office staff in New York City. But it is far more than a cult for the worship of the late FBI director.

The Society is not a collection of superannuated federal pensioners; a glance at the group's roster shows a great many of the members served less than ten years with the FBI, many less than three years, and a few only one year. For them a tour with the Bureau was a kind of internship, a career step, but not a career. Most employers try to hire long-term workers and avoid the expense of training a large number of short-timers, but the FBI seems to encourage a certain amount of turnover. The reason may be that a loyal alumnus on the outside can often be more useful in achieving the Bureau's goals than a special agent on active duty with the FBI. The Society appears to be an instrument of this policy—its Executive Services Committee is a placement bureau aimed at populating the most powerful security positions in both the public and private sectors with former FBI agents.

Society members—or, as they call themselves, Exes—hold senior security executive positions with almost every major private sector employer in America. In the automobile industry, five Exes work for General Motors, nine for Chrysler, and twenty-four for the Ford Motor Company, which sponsored "The FBI" series on television. American Motors employs only one Ex, its director of corporate security.

The Society is well represented among major airlines. American employs eleven Exes, United nine, Eastern and Pan American four each, and TWA three. The security directors of Continental Airlines, Hughes Airwest, and Western Airlines also belong to the FBI alumni group.

In the money industry, Merrill, Lynch, Pierce, Fenner, and Smith employs eleven Exes, including its vice-president in charge of security. American Express's vice-president for corporate security is an Ex, as are the directors of security of Manufacturer's Hanover Bank and the brokerage firm of Paine, Webber, Jackson, and Curtis. The assistant security officer of Riggs National Bank is a former agent, and the FBI has at least two friends at Chase Manhattan, including a vice-president of the bank.

Fifteen major oil companies employ Society members in senior security positions. Atlantic Richfield has six, Continental Oil five; five work
for Gulf, and seven each for Mobil and Texaco. Large contingents of
ex-agents work in the insurance and chemical industries, and many can
be found on the security staffs of retail chains. A small army of Exes
serves in the security departments of Bell System subsidiaries and other
telephone companies.

One of the largest concentrations of Society members is in the aerospace and electronics industry, where virtually every major company
has one or more Exes. Boeing has seven, Hughes Tool eighteen; fifteen
work for ITT, nine for Motorola, sixteen for North American Rockwell,
twelve for Westinghouse, and twenty-three for Lockheed Aircraft, to
name only a few.

Nonindustrial employers also hire ex-agents. The security directors
of Brandeis, Cornell, Harvard, and Southern Illinois Universities, and
Rider and Union Colleges, are Exes, as are the security chiefs of the National Basketball Association, the National Football League, and the
National Hockey League. The director of security for Playboy Enterprises is a six-year veteran of the FBI.

Many ex-agents find the FBI training and image marketable assets in
the rent-a-cop and private investigative business; the Society's roster
lists members who work for detective firms with such names as Special
Agent Consultants, Special Agent Investigators, Special Agents Research, and Special Agent Systems. The most successful private security entrepreneur among the alumni is George Wackenhut, founder and
president of the Wackenhut Corporation, the third-largest supplier of
contract guard and investigative services in the United States. Wackenhut employs eighteen of his fellow Society members in executive positions in his company. Some of Wackenhut's rent-a-cop competitors also
employ ex-agents; Pinkerton's has three Exes, while Burns has seven.
Vincent W. Gillen, the private detective hired by General Motors to spy
on Ralph Nader during the 1960s, is a Society member, and his company, Fidelifacts, Inc., provides employment for eight other alumni.
Another member, William F. Mitchell, is president of the small, but
highly respected detective agency, Mitchell Reports.

Many former agents can be found in top public sector police positions. Five Exes now work for the New York State Police, one for the Chicago Police Department, and two in the Los Angeles City Attorney's office. E. Wilson Purdy, the sheriff of Dade County, Florida, is an Ex, as is Henry Wade, the Dallas, Texas, district attorney. Former agent Evelle Younger is attorney-general of California. In past years, members of the Society have included a Boston police commissioner, a New York City deputy police commissioner, a New York State police superintendent, and the directors of the Secret Service, the Defense Intelligence Agency, and the National Security Agency.

One Ex, W. Donald Stewart, is a fourteen-year veteran of the FBI who left the Bureau in 1965 to join the little-known Defense Investigative Service, a group that has earned the nickname "The Pentagon Plumbers." Stewart rose to the rank of inspector-general of the Pentagon group that took part in some of the investigations of press leaks launched by White House Plumber David Young. Stewart was assigned the task of finding and plugging the leaks in the Pentagon that were furnishing information to columnist Jack Anderson. Some Pentagon employees who became the targets of Stewart's investigation are critical of his interrogation style, which, they say, includes hysterical desk pounding and screaming obscenities. Stewart denies this and says he is always a proper gentleman when questioning a suspect. He also denies a newspaper report that he tried to blackmail his way into the directorship of the FBI after the resignation of L. Patrick Gray, although he does recall having filed an application for the job. Stewart recently left the government for the private sector and formed his own firm, Stewart Security Services.

Stewart would probably have been a very acceptable director to the old-timers from the Hoover era who still occupy the second echelon of the FBI. A member of the loyal alumni could be relied on to see things their way. In general, the Bureau likes to see Exes get ahead for the purely pragmatic reason that a friendly former agent in a powerful position can be an asset to the FBI. Take the case of Arthur Hanes.

Hanes served in the Bureau from 1948 through 1951. He also seems to have had some contact with the CIA, for at the time of the Bay of Pigs invasion in 1961, Hanes was security officer for the Hayes Aircraft Corporation of Birmingham, Alabama, an outfit that was secretly supplying bombers and pilots to the CIA-backed Cubans. When four of the Hayes aircrewmen were killed in the invasion, Arthur Hanes was given the job of covering up the matter.

Hanes was the attorney who defended the Ku Klux Klansmen accused of the 1965 murder of civil rights worker Viola Liuzzo, and he was also the lawyer sent for by James Earl Ray when he was arrested for the murder of Dr. Martin Luther King, Jr. The former FBI agent was mayor of Birmingham in 1963 when his police chief, Bull Connor, used cattle prods and police dogs on the civil rights marchers, and it was recently disclosed that Hanes was elected to that post with the help of the FBI.

Former FBI informant Gary Rowe, who infiltrated the Klan in the early 1960s, recently testified before the Senate Intelligence Committee about his activities during the 1961 mayoral race in Birmingham. Hanes was running against J. Thomas King, whom Hanes called "the candidate of the NAACP bloc vote." Anti-civil rights feelings were running high in Alabama and Hanes's victory was helped by the Birmingham Mothers' Day Riot, in which a mob of Klansmen beat a group of freedom riders who had just arrived in town by bus. But Rowe had learned of the plans for the attack from the Birmingham police three weeks before it happened. He reported this discovery to his FBI contact, but, strangely, no steps were taken to avert the riot. Rowe also testified that his FBI contacts instructed him to collect political information that would be helpful to Society member Hanes in getting elected.

The Senate Intelligence Committee heard a great deal of testimony from other witnesses concerning such FBI activities as illegal wiretapping, illegal entries, and illegal mail-opening. In January 1976, one member of the Committee, Senator Robert Morgan, a conservative Democrat from North Carolina, told an Ashville Chamber of Commerce breakfast that he felt the FBI had become a threat to individual liberties. After reports of his speech appeared in the press, Senator Morgan began to receive letters from former FBI agents denouncing him as a malicious and dangerous liar. The FBI veterans sent similar letters to North Carolina newspapers, and Morgan believes the letter-writing campaign was orchestrated by the North Carolina chapter of the Society of Former FBI Agents.

Senator Morgan also began to receive special attention from the FBI, which sent his staff reports of his out-of-town speeches to small groups—a subtle notice that the senator was being watched. When Morgan complained in public of the campaign against him by the FBI and the Society, the FBI issued the following statement: "Director Kelley categorically denies the allegations of Senator Morgan that the FBI is surveilling him or harassing him in any manner. With regard to allegations concerning the Society of Former Special Agents, Director Kelley points out that this is an organization completely independent of the FBI and the FBI is in no way responsible for the actions of the society."

But the line separating the FBI from the Society is not as clearly defined as Director Kelley said. In the wake of the Senate disclosures of FBI lawbreaking, the Justice Department's civil rights division began to investigate the long series of illegal break-ins carried out by FBI agents in the New York offices of the Socialist Workers' party. When it became clear that the Justice Department's probe was in earnest, the Society undertook to provide legal defense to the agents involved in the burglaries. The Society hired one of its own members, Edward P. Morgan, a Washington lawyer who once represented the late Mafia boss John Roselli, to defend the agents and created a fund to help pay their legal expenses. In an unprecedented move, Kelley permitted the Society to solicit for the fund inside the Bureau's fifty-nine field offices, where even the Girl Scouts have been forbidden to sell their cookies. Kelley sent a letter to the special-agent-in-charge at each field office urging him to remind his agents about the fund drive. Some agents have anonymously complained to the press that the situation creates a conflict of interest, placing some federal law enforcement officers in the position of subsidizing the defense of individuals being prosecuted by other federal law enforcement officers.

The FBI may claim that the Society is a private group, completely separate from the Bureau and having no special status, but the organization actually is, in effect, a civilian auxiliary of the FBI. There is, for example, a long-standing arrangement between the Bureau and the Society in which selected Exes would be deputized to help out in the event the Bureau decides to round up the tens of thousands of persons on the FBI's Security Index under a proposed FBI program called DetCom (Detention of Communists).

Discipline within the Society is as tight as the Bureau's. When former special agent Joseph Schott published his fond but somewhat irreverent memoir of twenty-three years in the Bureau, *No Left Turns,* the Society promptly drummed him out. Bernard F. Connors was kicked out because of his novel, *Don't Embarrass the Bureau,* a *roman à clef* which had a senior Bureau official turn out to be a female transvestite, an insinuation which definitely embarrassed the Bureau. Norman Ollestad was expelled for his critical study *Inside the FBI.* New Orleans district attorney Jim Garrison was tossed out for challenging the FBI's investigation of the assassination of President Kennedy and for turning up evidence that a fellow Ex, the late W. Guy Banister, was involved in the assassination conspiracy.

This continuous process of ideological purification makes the Society membership nearly unanimous in their views on the FBI and the late J. Edgar Hoover. One exception may be former FBI assistant director Quinn Tamm, who quit the Bureau after a falling out with Hoover. Tamm's dispute with Hoover might have kept him out of the Society had he not become executive director of the International Association of Chiefs of Police, an organization with power and prestige comparable to that of the Society.

The IACP was founded in 1893 in response to the growing need for coordination among separate municipal and state police forces in the United States. Although its members are sworn police officers, the organization is private and has no official powers. In practical terms, however, it has a very considerable influence on police policy matters at both the federal and local levels.

The IACP established the first national clearinghouse for identification records in 1897. After the FBI was formed in 1924, this operation was turned over to the Bureau and became the nucleus of the FBI's Central Fingerprint File. The Association has led the way in establishing standards for police personnel selection and training, crime reporting procedures, and highway safety. It set up the International Police Academy for the State Department, a school for the training of foreign police under a program of the Agency for International Development.

The Association provides management-consulting services to police departments, including advice in such areas as organization, administration, manpower deployment, and personnel. It also serves as an executive recruiting agency for state and local governments, helping them select candidates to fill senior police department vacancies, a function which lends the Association special power and prestige among police officers.

The Association lays claim to the word "international" in its name through the participation of the police forces of sixty-two foreign countries. However, the overwhelming majority of the Association's 10,500 members are American police chiefs; most, of course, head small-town police departments.

Through its publication, *Police Chief,* its research and public information programs, and its lobbying to influence federal anti-crime legislation, the IACP has sought to become—to use the Association's motto—"the professional voice of law enforcement." It has succeeded in this to a large degree, and until recently has remained unchallenged in its chosen role.

In April 1976, Boston police commissioner Robert J. diGrazia delivered a blistering attack on the IACP members, describing them as "the underlings of American municipal government, somewhat as pet rocks, unable to move, grow, change, or innovate." DiGrazia characterized the police chiefs as time-servers, avoiding controversy and acquiescing to politicians who exploit the law-and-order issue and ignore the social ills that cause most violent crime. Criticizing the IACP's small-town cop outlook, diGrazia called for a new organization to represent the country's 500 largest city police departments. Three months later, he and several other big-city police chiefs announced the formation of the Police Executive Research Forum as an alternative to the IACP.

Organizations like the International Association of Chiefs of Police and the newly formed Police Executive Research Forum are made up almost entirely of sworn police officers and thus are not part of the private police industry. But they are private aggregations of police power and influence beyond the control of elected officials, and so constitute a social force similar to that of the hired police. To a lesser extent, police unions like the Fraternal Order of Police, the Patrolmen's Benevolent Associations, and the International Brotherhood of Police Officers share the same characteristics, but these groups are primarily concerned with such things as police pay and benefits, rather than with questions of public police policy.* They are more likely to affect a citizen's pocketbook than his freedom, safety, or privacy.

The same cannot be said of the little-known organization that links the intelligence squads of almost every major police force in the United States and Canada. Although its members are sworn police officers who work for state and city governments, the organization is a private club, not answerable to voters, taxpayers, or elected officials. It cuts across the vertical lines of authority of local government, for its members hold certain allegiances to the group that cannot be countermanded by a mayor, a county manager, or even a state governor.

The organization forms a vast network of police intelligence squads that exchange dossiers and conduct investigations on a reciprocal basis. Several of the police departments belonging to the group have recently been caught in illegal wiretapping, burglary, and spying on the private lives of ordinary citizens. The organization is, in effect, a huge, private domestic intelligence agency. It's called the Law Enforcement Intelligence Unit and almost no one has ever heard of it.

"The LEIU is not a secret organization," says Lt. Ray Henry, chief of intelligence for the Long Beach, California, Police Department, and a former national chairman of the organization.

"The LEIU is so secret that, until recently, even its existence was usually denied," says Douglass Durham, a former Des Moines police officer who claims to have worked as an undercover investigator for the group.

* However, the Fraternal Order of Police may be on its way to becoming an exception to this. In June 1977 the president of the 135,000-member police union told the group's convention in Flagstaff, Arizona, that four members of the Carter administration were "registered Communists." The FOP leader declined to name the individuals he meant, but he predicted "the only thing that's going to stand between this country and a complete takeover by the Communists is the people who wear the badge and the gun."

If the LEIU is not a secret society, it might as well be. Several Washington, D.C., lawyers who specialize in personal privacy and civil liberties cases told me they never heard of the organization. Even among many police officers the LEIU is something of a mystery. One former California cop thought the name referred to the Los Angeles Police Department's intelligence squad. And an investigator for a California district attorney's office described the LEIU as "extremely hush-hush, extremely low-profile."

The LEIU's low profile succeeded in keeping the organization out of public view for twenty years. The group was founded in March 1956 at a secret meeting called by Captain James E. Hamilton, then commander of the Los Angeles Police Department's intelligence squad, and several other senior California police officials. Representatives from twenty-six police and sheriff's departments in seven Western states attended and became charter members. By 1967, the organization had grown to include seventy police forces across the United States, and by 1975 more than 225 law enforcement agencies were involved, including six in Canada.

"The thing is a monster network," says Lake Headley, a former Las Vegas deputy sheriff who belonged to the LEIU in the early 1960s. "It was Captain Hamilton's brainchild. He wanted to take police intelligence away from the FBI. Police departments do the street-level work to collect information, and Hamilton didn't like the idea of turning it over to the FBI and making them the monitor, so he formed the LEIU to circumvent the FBI's network. It was established to form an intelligence network independent of any federal agency. The LEIU is a combination fraternal organization and functioning intelligence agency."

The LEIU is divided into four geographic zones: Eastern, Central, Northwestern, and Southwestern. Each zone is governed by a chairman and a vice-chairman. Nationally there are also a general chairman, a general vice-chairman, a secretary, and a treasurer. The national and zone officers comprise a twelve-member executive board which governs the organization. The LEIU holds national and regional conventions every year. Lake Headley describes the conventions as "big club meetings."

It's not easy to join the LEIU. When a police force applies for membership, it must be sponsored by another agency already in the LEIU, and must be endorsed by three others. All members are notified of the application, and the LEIU carries out a thorough investigation of the applicant agency and the officers working for it who will take part in LEIU activities. Finally, the executive board votes on the application.

"It's a very selective, very elitist sort of thing," says former member Lake Headley. "In a local intelligence squad you kind of look to the LEIU man to jump into a phone booth and come dashing out in a superman suit."

The protective cloak of obscurity shielding the LEIU from public view was lifted briefly in 1975 when the Houston, Texas, Police Department left the organization. Houston police officials announced that their department was resigning from the LEIU after receiving requests from other member agencies for information on the private lives of people with absolutely no criminal connections. In one instance cited by the Houston officials, a California police department asked for a full-scale investigation of a highly respected Houston businessman who was buying a chain of grocery stores in California. The inquiry reportedly included a request for information about the man's investments, business associates, family life, and even his sex habits.

Former LEIU national chairman Ray Henry denies the allegation, describing it as "a bunch of sour grapes." The Houston Police Department didn't quit the LEIU, according to Lt. Henry. "They were kicked out by me because they had something like 200 officers indicted for illegal wiretapping. We're not going to put up with that kind of crap." Lt. Henry said he had a postal registration receipt to prove the Houston Police Department was expelled from the LEIU prior to its announced resignation, and added that the present Houston chief of police had denied the earlier charges by his subordinates of LEIU's spying on noncriminal subjects.

The self-proclaimed sensitivity of the Houston cops to the privacy of ordinary citizens does seem a bit implausible in view of the Department's own record which has recently come to light. Houston has been the scene of one of the major police spying scandals of recent years, involving the Department's Criminal Intelligence Division, the FBI, and the Southwestern Bell Telephone Company.* The affair probably was the cause of Houston's expulsion from the LEIU, although Lt. Henry's pious condemnation of the Department's illegal wiretapping serves to mask what is probably the LEIU's true reason for kicking the Texas cops out.

In 1973, Houston elected liberal Democrat Fred Hofheinz as mayor. Hofheinz promptly made good his campaign promise to replace Houston's hard-line law-and-order police chief, whose department had frequently been charged with brutality to blacks. Hofheinz's new chief, Carroll M. Lynn, soon discovered the police department had carried out a ten-year program of political spying under his predecessor. The Criminal Intelligence Division had amassed dossiers on thousands of noncriminal subjects. Most of the individuals spied upon were liberals, black activists, or civil libertarians, although the cops had also taken an interest in some conservatives. Chief Lynn found dossiers on liberal Congresswoman Barbara Jordan and conservative Congressman Bob Casey. There was also a thick file under the name of Fred Hofheinz, the new mayor.

The police spy files were chock full of personal information, often including sexual gossip, and much of the data could only have been acquired through illegal wiretapping. Chief Lynn launched an internal investigation to determine how the information in the files had been obtained. The probe disclosed that the Houston police had conducted more than a thousand illegal wiretaps during a seven-year period.

The files of the Houston Criminal Intelligence Division were sequestered on the order of a federal judge and turned over to a federal grand jury investigating the affair. The sequestered files included not only the standard CID dossiers, but also one full set of the special files of the LEIU, the complete assortment of intelligence information that Captain Hamilton and his successor had succeeded in keeping out of the hands of the federal authorities for almost twenty years. In the words of Lt. Ray Henry, the Houston cops had permitted the LEIU files to be "seized by civilians," and it is this surrender, rather than the telephone tapping, that seems the more plausible explanation for Houston's expulsion from the LEIU.

---

* For details, see Chapter 4, "The Telephone Cops."

Custody of the LEIU's files is the most sacred trust the organization bestows upon its individual members. The LEIU not only withholds its files from the FBI and other federal authorities, it flatly refuses to show them to anyone who is not an LEIU member. Lake Headley recalls that access to the locked LEIU file cabinets could not be shared by two officers working on the same case unless both were LEIU members. (Today, all officers assigned full-time to the intelligence squad of a regular member agency are considered LEIU members and have full access to the files.) In some instances, a police officer is designated as an "affiliate member" of the LEIU, meaning that he, but not the police department he works for, belongs to the LEIU; he is the only person in the entire department who may look at the LEIU files. Even a request by the chief of police or the police commissioner would have to be refused.

Both regular and affiliate LEIU members are forbidden to show the organization's secret dossiers to "civilians." It makes no difference that the chief of police is appointed by the mayor or city council and serves at their pleasure, he cannot obey any order to make the LEIU files available to them.

"We've had numerous cases where some political figure has tried to gain access," Lt. Henry told me. "We had an agency not so long ago where our members voluntarily resigned from LEIU and returned the files because they weren't sure they could keep their mayor away from them. Nonmembers don't have the need to know or the right to know."

Freedom of information and privacy laws enacted by the federal government and several of the states give every citizen the right to know what is in government files, especially dossiers that may have his own name on them, but the LEIU is completely exempt from such laws. The LEIU is a private club and therefore not subject to freedom of information or privacy laws. That makes the LEIU files more secret than those of the CIA or the FBI.

Any LEIU member can open a file on an individual simply by filling out a form and getting the approval of the local LEIU regional chairman. The form is forwarded to the California Bureau of Criminal Identification and Investigation in Sacramento, a part of the State's Division of Law Enforcement that voluntarily acts as a central coordinating agency for the LEIU. (The LEIU's private status has not prevented it from receiving generous support from state and federal government agencies.) The Bureau of Criminal Identification and Investigation's Special Services Section summarizes all the information provided on the individual and puts it on a five-by-eight-inch card, along with a photograph, if one is available. Copies of the card are sent to all LEIU members to be kept under lock and key in the special LEIU file cabinets.

Some of the LEIU files have been entered into the Interstate Organized Crime Index, a computerized file system developed and operated by the LEIU under a $1.3 million grant from the federal Law Enforcement Assistance Administration. The IOCI system is an international network of computer terminals linked by telecommunications lines to a central computer run by the Michigan State Police in East Lansing, Michigan. In 1975 the LEAA abruptly cut off all funds for the IOCI system.

"The Justice Department put it on ice," said Lt. Henry, blaming the cut-off on public concern over domestic spying. "They decided not to fund anything that uses the word 'intelligence' until the hue and cry dies down. But they just recently called us up and said the pressure is off," he added, "so we may be back on again in a few months."

Pressure on the LEIU resulted from the Houston police charges and from the statements of a former Des Moines police officer who told investigators for the Senate Select Committee on Intelligence that he had served as an undercover agent for the LEIU and was assigned to spy on noncriminal subjects. Douglass Durham, an accomplished pilot, safecracker, photographer, scuba diver, and electronic eavesdropping specialist, said he was part of an LEIU-sponsored exchange program in which undercover officers were traded between police departments in the Midwest. Durham says he was lent by the Des Moines police to work undercover for the police departments of Lincoln, Nebraska, and Cedar Rapids, Iowa. He says some of his assignments involved the surveillance of political dissidents.

Lt. Henry denies that Durham worked for the LEIU; the organization employs no undercover investigators, he says. (But individual LEIU member agencies are committed to conduct undercover investigations, surveillances, and background checks for other member agencies, on request. Durham actually claims only to have worked undercover for the Des Moines Police Department in an exchange program sponsored

by LEIU. The Des Moines, Cedar Rapids, and Lincoln police departments are LEIU members and, presumably, use undercover investigators.) Lt. Henry also denies that the LEIU keeps files on anyone but
people involved in organized crime, adding, ''I hope that story has been
laid to rest, because it's totally false.''

But, when Donald H. Carroll, then LEIU general chairman, testified
before a Senate subcommittee probing criminal justice data banks in
1974, he defined the purpose of the LEIU as ''the gathering, recording,
investigating, and exchange of confidential information not available
through regular police channels on individuals and organizations involved in, *but not necessarily limited to,''* organized crime (emphasis
added). And a 1973 report on the Interstate Organized Crime Index contained this statement: ''The LEIU data base was comprised of persons
of interest to intelligence units other than organized crime subjects.''
Lt. Henry had a copy of the report, and I asked him about the statement.

''I don't understand that statement at all,'' he said. ''I didn't see it, or
it certainly would have been cleared up. There are no subjects in the
LEIU data base except those involved as either principals or associates
in organized crime activities. They don't have to belong to La Cosa
Nostra, but they've got to be involved in some conspiratorial organized
crime activity.''

Would the LEIU's definition of organized crime include radicals or
bombthrowers, I asked.

''No, it certainly does not,'' Lt. Henry replied. ''The LEAA [Law
Enforcement Assistance Administration] has often asked us to include
that kind of individual, and we finally told them to get off the subject.
We're not in that business.''

The 1973 report containing the mysterious statement was written by a
group headed by Charles E. Casey, assistant director of the Organized
Crime and Criminal Intelligence Branch of the California Department of
Justice (an LEIU member agency). I called him and asked what the
statement meant.

''I'm not sure I can explain what it means,'' he replied. ''The LEIU
data base is one hundred percent organized crime, except for a few of
what I would call 'arrested or identified terrorists.' I really couldn't
explain the statement, right off the bat.''

What is an ''identified terrorist,'' and how does he or she differ from the "arrested" variety? The answer is that it's not necessary to have been convicted of any crime, or even arrested, in order to earn oneself an LEIU dossier, according to the 1974 Senate testimony of then LEIU general chairman Donald Carroll. An "identified terrorist" is anyone the LEIU believes to be a terrorist.

Lt. Henry's "no bombthrowers or radicals" claim seems in direct contradiction to Casey's admission that the LEIU files contain "a few terrorists," and neither man offers a very adequate explanation of the "persons other than organized crime subjects" slip appearing in the report of an LEAA-funded study that Casey himself directed. Still, what does it matter if the LEIU has added a few bombers, kidnappers, and hijackers to its collection of loan sharks, pimps, hit men, and gamblers? The disturbing thing about the LEIU files is that the criteria for opening a dossier on someone seem rather vague and subjective. If someone can be deemed a member of organized crime even though he doesn't belong to the Mafia, has never been convicted of anything, and has never been arrested, one is moved to wonder if the LEIU's definition of an "identified terorist" is broad enough to include people who simply disagree with the government.

Lt. J. O. Brannon is a Houston police intelligence officer and the spokesman who first charged the LEIU with spying on law-abiding citizens. I asked him to describe the kinds of noncriminal subjects to be found in the LEIU files. Unfortunately, he could not discuss the specific contents of any of the files seized by the federal court, because of pending legal action against the Houston Police Department by some of the targets of the spying. Yet his general comments served to put the LEIU in better perspective.

Lt. Brannon minimized the importance of the LEIU's special files. He said that the really important information is contained in the full dossiers maintained by each LEIU member agency and made available to every other member agency. Wouldn't those files be exchanged between police forces, even without the LEIU, I wondered. Not necessarily, Lt. Brannon informed me.

Cops can be as suspicious of each other as they are of "civilians." A police intelligence officer who makes a long-distance call to his counterpart in another law enforcement agency may encounter regional or political mistrust, big-city/small-town bias, or any of a variety of other obstacles to an easy exchange of information. For Lt. Brannon, the real value of the LEIU is overcoming this resistance through the regional and national meetings the group holds annually.

"The LEIU meetings are mostly social affairs, but you build up lasting friendships when you go out and have a few drinks with an old boy," Lt. Brannon explained. "Then when he calls you up, you know who you're talking to, because you looked him in the eye just last week—some guy four states away. It's the closeness of the damn thing that I liked. It's just real good."

Brannon said expulsion from the LEIU hadn't made much difference to the Houston police. They still retained the LEIU directory listing the name and phone number of every LEIU contact in the more than 225 member agencies. Houston continues to exchange dossiers with the other LEIU members.

Regarding the current Houston spy scandal, Brannon said, "We spread our wings too far and exceeded what was proper, tapping a few phones and doing a few other things. The damn thing got out of hand here, but I'm reasonably sure they were doing the same thing in every other city. They just didn't get caught at it."

In fact, several other LEIU member agencies did get caught at it during the same general period as the Houston revelations. In Michigan, the State Police and the Detroit Police Department—both LEIU members—were charged with infiltrating and wiretapping a suburban Detroit consumer group at the request of state legislators who had been criticized by the organization.* In New York, a State Supreme Court judge charged New York City's Public Security Unit—the current name for the NYPD red squad, an LEIU member—with carrying out "an open, free-wheeling people-watching mission." And in Washington, D.C., Senators Henry Jackson and Charles Percy asked the General Accounting Office to investigate the use of federal funds by police depart-

---

* In January 1976 a Michigan judge ordered the state police to disband its twenty-nine-man Subversive Activities Unit, or "Red Squad." The ruling was an outcome of a lawsuit filed by the Human Rights Party of Michigan. In his decision, the judge cited evidence that the Red Squad had turned over to the Chrysler Corporation's company cops dossiers on workers who organized health and safety grievances.

ments to carry out illegal spying activities in the nation's ten largest cities. (The police departments of seven of the ten cities are LEIU members.) But the most devastating revelations of police spying came out of Baltimore and Chicago—both LEIU members—where the snooping scandals rivaled that of the Houston department.

The Chicago affair began when the Afro-American Patrolmen's League, which was involved in a discrimination suit against the police department, filed a routine request to subpoena whatever files the local intelligence squad held on the League. It was clear from the records obtained by the court that the police had amassed files on a host of organizations and individuals having no apparent criminal connections. The police department's Subversive Unit—or, as it was generally called, the "Red Squad"—had compiled dossiers on not only the obvious targets of police suspicion, such as political dissidents, but also on such personalities as former Chicago Bears football star Gale Sayers, and local television commentator Len O'Connor. Gaylord Freeman, the chairman of the First National Bank, and Arthur Woods, chairman of Sears, Roebuck and Company, earned themselves dossiers by donating money to a civil rights organization.

Dossiers had also been opened on Father Theodore Hesburgh, the president of Notre Dame University, *Chicago Daily News* columnist Mike Royko, the late Jackie Robinson, Republican mayoral candidate John Hoellen, and an assortment of state and federal legislators. The Red Squad had files on the Chicago Metropolitan Area Housing Alliance, the Organization for a Better Austin (a section of Chicago), and the Citizen's Action Program, a group dedicated to fighting the proposed Crosstown Expressway. A file had been started on a Chicago doctor whose car the police had observed parked in the same neighborhood where the Illinois Communist Party was holding a meeting.

The Red Squad's gumshoes took a few deductive shortcuts in writing up their reports. If your car was parked in the same neighborhood in which some group was holding a meeting, that meant you had attended the meeting. If you attended a group's meeting twice (or if your car was parked nearby twice), then you were a member of the group. Such "facts" were recorded in your dossier and also forwarded to the FBI for inclusion in its files. And the allegation was available to be swapped with any of the 225 other LEIU member agencies.*

In Baltimore, a Maryland State Senate investigating committee probed charges that the Police Department's Inspectional Services Division had spied on politicians, newsmen, and clergymen. They found that the police intelligence squad had also spied on labor unions, colleges and universities, and civic groups concerned with such things as rodent control, highway relocation, and utility rates. In the words of one ISD officer, "If there was a meeting in Baltimore City, we were there."

Baltimore's police commissioner Donald D. Pomerleau was not in the least shy about admitting that he had compiled information on just about everybody. In fact, Pomerleau often boasted of the thickness of his dossiers and told the quaking visitor to his office, "I know where you meet, when you are going to meet before you meet, what you do. . . ." In one case, Pomerleau summoned an individual to his office, showed him his dossier, and watched with despotic satisfaction as the wretch fell to his knees before him and begged the police commissioner not to release the information. It must have been a high point in the 300-year history of Baltimore, the cradle of civil and religious liberties in the New World.

The Maryland Senate investigating committee found that "ISD amassed a data bank containing the names of, and information pertaining to hundreds, perhaps thousands, of citizens of this state, many of whom did nothing more than testify with respect to a particular piece of legislation before the Baltimore City Council, or peaceably walk a

---

* In September 1976 a spokesman for the Civil Service Commission, in testimony before a House subcommittee, disclosed that similar unverified and unreliable information was routinely furnished to the Commission by police intelligence units throughout the country. The spokesman admitted that the reports were kept on file to be used in checking on applicants for federal jobs.

Victims of official police defamation have little in the way of legal recourse available to them. A Louisville, Kentucky, photographer who had been falsely accused, then later acquitted, of a shoplifting charge, discovered that the police had distributed a flyer bearing his mug shot and arrest record to local merchants. The flyer described him as an "active shoplifter." The photographer sued, but in a 1976 decision, the U.S. Supreme Court ruled that a person may not sue a public official for publicly defaming him.

picket line.'' The committee noted that ''the feeling seemed to prevail in ISD that persons who deviated from the norm, who were outspoken or criticized the status quo, members of organized labor, picketers, and protesters, these people were 'potential threats' and society must be protected against them.''

In an interview with the *Chicago Tribune,* a Chicago Red Squad officer declared, ''I believe in the American flag, and I want it to stay American and not turn Pink. The way things are run now, democracy is running wild. Everyone is allowed to do anything they want. I believe the country, the state, and the city come before individual rights.''

A Chicago grandmother who was paid $25 per month by the Red Squad to infiltrate church and community groups told reporters from the *Chicago Daily News,* ''I am a police spy and I am proud of it. I do police spy work because, as far as I'm concerned, God and Country come first. . . . You guys are so busy worrying about constitutional rights, along with the Communists, that they're going to take us over.''

Some might say that such attitudes are typical of the police point of view, but there is little about police intelligence officers that is typical of most policemen. Within a police department the intelligence squad is almost as alien as it is within society as a whole. In Baltimore, many veteran officers were completely unaware of the existence of the Inspectional Services Division. Fewer than forty officers in the department had any idea of the unit's function, and only a small percentage of them were fully briefed on its operation. In fact, the Baltimore cops were themselves targets of ISD spying when they went out on strike in 1974; undercover officers from the unit photographed policemen as they walked picket lines outside their station houses.

In Chicago, too, the Red Squad's activities were shrouded from the rest of the police department. Recruits selected to serve in the unit bypassed training in the police academy so that they couldn't later be identified by former classmates. Senior Chicago police officials claimed to a grand jury that they were ignorant of the Red Squad's activities. But the most bizarre example of the chasm between Red Squad officers and the cop on the beat is presented by one undercover officer who infiltrated a Chicago group and eventually became its president. He admitted to the Cook County grand jury probing police spying activities that he had specifically urged other members of the organization to shoot Chicago policemen, and had even demonstrated the strategic placement of snipers in downtown Chicago which would blow away the greatest number of his fellow officers.

Conspiracy to commit first-degree murder is the worst, but by no means the only case of lawbreaking by police intelligence squads belonging to the LEIU. The Chicago Red Squad, for example, carried out a six-year program of burglary, vandalism, and assault in collaboration with a hoodlum gang masquerading as a patriotic group and calling itself "the Legion of Justice." The Legion was the brainchild of the late right-wing Chicago attorney S. Thomas Sutton, who recruited an unsavory assortment of local thugs with patriotic pretensions to harass peace groups and serve as the unofficial shock troops of the Chicago Red Squad. From 1967 to 1973, the Legion of Justice carried out a series of break-ins, trashings, and assaults on anti-war groups, often under the approving gaze of Chicago police officers parked nearby in their squad cars. In some of the break-ins, especially those in which illegal bugging devices were planted, members of the Red Squad served as lookouts while the Legion hoods did the actual burglary.

The most common type of criminality among LEIU intelligence squads is illegal wiretapping, and this is almost always done with some degree of cooperation from the local telephone company. A former Baltimore vice squad officer told the Maryland Senate investigating committee that the intelligence squad routinely installed illegal telephone taps with the aid of an ex-cop who worked for the Chesapeake and Potomac Telephone Company. A phone company spokesman denied the charge. In Houston, some of the officers who admitted taking part in illegal wiretapping said the taps were placed with the full cooperation of the Southwestern Bell Telephone Company and named some 200 phone company employees as having helped in the illicit eavesdropping.*

Where phone company cooperation cannot be obtained through the police Old Boy Network, other means are employed. Chicago Red Squad officers reportedly obtained the help of four Illinois Bell linemen

* For details, see Chapter 4, "The Telephone Cops."

in placing illegal taps after the men were caught by the police in "compromising positions." The "compromising positions" included drunkenness and sexual misconduct, and the linemen were threatened with arrest and exposure if they refused to cooperate.

Telephone companies are by no means the only part of the private sector that aids LEIU intelligence squads. A police textbook on the subject advises intelligence officers to cultivate contacts in utility companies, airlines, banks, newspapers, bonding companies, private detective agencies, and credit bureaus. The federal Privacy Protection Study Commission recently heard testimony from banks, credit card companies, and hotels, admitting that they routinely surrendered information about their clients and guests to law enforcement officers on a simple oral request, without requiring a court order. However, passage of the 1970 Fair Credit Reporting Act severely restricts the information that a credit agency can release without a subpoena.

Until the May 1971 effectiveness date of the Fair Credit Reporting Act, the Baltimore intelligence squad had received the full cooperation of the Credit Bureau of Baltimore, Inc., a local consumer credit agency, in obtaining full access to the personal information held in its files. After passage of the federal credit law, however, the Baltimore cops found that an important source had suddenly dried up. According to the report of a Maryland Senate investigating committee, several months after the law went into effect, Officer Terry Josephson of the intelligence squad left his $9,000-a-year job with the police department and became vice-president of United Credit Bureaus of America, Inc., one of the largest independent consumer credit agencies in the country, at more than double his old salary.

United Credit Bureaus of America has files on most citizens of Maryland, and Josephson had unlimited access to this information. An intelligence squad officer told the Maryland Senate investigating committee that Josephson supplied some of this data to the police without benefit of court order. The committee's report states that Josephson denied that he was serving as an undercover informant for the Baltimore intelligence squad, but shortly after his role was publicized by a Baltimore newspaper, he resigned his $20,000-plus-a-year job with United Credit Bureaus of America and returned to the police department at his old salary.

In fairness to the LEIU, it should be pointed out that the number of member intelligence squads that have actually been caught breaking the law or spying on noncriminal citizens recently represents less than 5 percent of its membership, although in the opinion of one Houston police official, such practices are much more widespread, and the recent revelations are only the tip of the iceberg. In one sense, it is remarkable that any of the intelligence squads at all were caught, given the inherent difficulty of investigating the police and the unique position they are in to cover up their transgressions. In fact, the probes of the intelligence squads in Houston, Baltimore, and Chicago all encountered the same pattern of police resistance and obstruction.

Baltimore police commissioner Pomerleau tried unsuccessfully to halt a state senate investigation of his department by slapping every member of the investigating committee with a lawsuit. Former Chicago police superintendent James B. Conlisk hamstrung a Cook County special grand jury investigating his department through a variety of delaying tactics. Conlisk insisted on consulting with his lawyer in an adjoining room each time the grand jury asked him a question, including such queries as "When did you become superintendent of the Chicago Police Department?" and, "Did you take an oath to serve and protect the interest of the citizens of the City of Chicago?" During one tiresome three-hour grand jury session, Conlisk made thirty-one trips between the hearing room and the anteroom where his lawyer waited. The grand jury recommended that Conlisk be cited for contempt.

In Houston, the Police Officers Association ran full-page newspaper advertisements to complain about their new chief, Carroll M. Lynn, who had made the initial probe into the intelligence squad's illegal wiretapping. Enough pressure was brought to bear upon Chief Lynn to force his resignation, although the investigation, which had been taken over by a federal grand jury, continued.

Police resistance to the probes also went beyond such legal and public relations maneuvers. In Chicago, a state's attorney investigating the police received a report that his own phone had been tapped. A Baltimore newspaper reporter critical of the police was the target of surveillance and other harassment; on three occasions when he returned to his car parked in the Police Department's parking lot, he found that the tirelugs had been loosened. Police officers called to testify by the state senate committee investigating the Baltimore intelligence squad said they feared for their jobs if it was learned they had cooperated with the committee. In Chicago, many officers called in the grand jury investigation of the Red Squad received the same anonymous telephone message: ''We know you have seen the state's attorney. If you want to stay healthy, you'd better not talk before the grand jury.''

There was a mysterious fire on the eighth floor of Chicago police headquarters during the probe. It seems to have started in one of the filing cabinets holding the Red Squad's files. Other records subpoenaed by the grand jury, such as the Red Squad's electronic surveillance log, had been ''routinely destroyed.'' The Baltimore intelligence squad ''routinely destroyed'' many of its files on political dissidents sometime in 1973. According to Houston police intelligence officer Lt. J. O. Brannon, other LEIU members destroyed their files when it looked as though their political surveillance activities might be investigated.

''After the government seized our files,'' he said, ''guess what Los Angeles did? They burned almost every goddamn thing they had. Some of the other cities did the same thing. They called it 'purging the files.' We should have done the same thing, but we didn't know that's what you're supposed to call it.''

You might also call it destroying evidence of a felony, unless you were merely grateful that such a collection of scurrilous gossip had been consigned once and for all to the flames. But such a celebration of the destruction of police dossiers could be premature. An intelligence officer might be able to state under oath to a grand jury or senate committee that the police department no longer has a dossier on John Doe, but that is no insurance that a copy of John Doe's dossier isn't locked away in the file cabinet of another LEIU member intelligence squad in a city 3000 miles away, or, for that matter, that some 225 copies of the dossier haven't been distributed to every LEIU member agency. And there is also no guarantee that, after the investigators complete their probe of the intelligence squad and turn their attention elsewhere, the squad will not reconstruct its destroyed files from duplicate copies stored elsewhere in the LEIU network. Investigators who look at police intelligence squad lawlessness as a local problem are victims of a shell game. They have never heard of the LEIU, or, if they have, they don't understand what it is.

But whatever the real or potential abuses of the LEIU, it would be a mistake to regard it as simply the sinister apparatus of an incipient police state. The LEIU was formed for a very legitimate purpose, and whatever else it may now be up to, it continues to perform a necessary law enforcement function, the exchange of information on organized crime.

Organized crime is a national enterprise, but the individual police department's jurisdiction ends at the city limits. Loan sharks, narcotics dealers, hit men, and other assorted hoods regularly cross state lines and international boundaries with impunity in pursuit of an illicit buck, and the police force that tries to deal with them as a local law enforcement problem is like a watchdog on a short tether. The cops' basic problem is getting timely and accurate information on the mobile mobsters who may turn up in their town. But providing that kind of information to the local police sounds like the job of the FBI, not some private group like the LEIU. I asked former LEIU general chairman Ray Henry why the Bureau isn't doing it.

"That's a hell of a good question; I wish I knew the answer," he replied. "The FBI has got so many rules and regulations about disseminating information to local law enforcement that you get little or nothing from them. Oh, we exchange information with individual FBI agents, but there is no formal arrangement where information is automatically channeled to all interested agencies by the Bureau. That will never happen through the FBI, but it happens daily through the LEIU."

Lt. Brannon in Houston put it this way: "The FBI is a good organization, but it's useless to us. It prides itself on its files, but do you know where the information in the FBI files comes from? Your local police department. They come over here and have access to everything they want, but when we try to get some information on a suspect from them it's a different story. They pull the guy's file, then sit there holding it and say, 'OK, what do you want to know?' Well, I want to look through the whole file, but they won't allow that. They won't even let us hold it in our hands. It's never going to change because the FBI has this standoffishness. They figure we're a bunch of dumb-dumbs, and we figure they're a bunch of bureaucrats, and it's hard to break down that barrier."

The cops have always said that dealing with the FBI is a one-way street, and many policemen complain that the Bureau is uncooperative and less than zealous in fighting the Mob. And after all the recent revelations of FBI abuses of police power, taking away its monopoly on criminal intelligence information may not seem like a completely bad idea. But the cure could be much worse than the illness; the FBI is, at least in theory, subordinate to the Justice Department and ultimately to the public, while the LEIU is a thoroughly private club. In setting up the LEIU, the cops have created the skeleton of a national police force that is also, in essence, a vigilante organization.*

Beyond the more obvious hazards to civil rights created by a private national police intelligence network, there is also the danger that the LEIU can provide a domestic spying apparatus to federal agencies prohibited from setting up their own surveillance machinery within the borders of the United States. U.S. Army Intelligence, which in the recent past has shown a disturbing propensity for spying on Americans,

---

* As a privately operated police intelligence network, the LEIU appears not to be unique. In May 1977 a group of some 200 law enforcement officers from twelve Western states and Canada met secretly at the Hyatt House Motel in Seattle, Washington. Acting on a tip, members of the local news media contacted the group's organizers and inquired about the purpose of the meeting. They were told by Captain Richard Clark of the Yakima Police Department that the group was called the "Western States Crime Seminar," and that it was holding a three-day meeting to learn "how we can better improve our expertise." Captain Clark denied reports the meetings had anything to do with police intelligence operations. A spokesman also denied reports that the group included representatives of the private police forces of such companies as Exxon and General Telephone.

However, invitations to the meeting signed by Chief Robert L. Hanson of the Seattle Police Department, and Sheriff Lawrence G. Waldt of the King County, Washington, Department of Public Safety referred to the meeting as the "Western States Crime *Intelligence* Seminar" [emphasis added]. A confidential report issued by the Western States Crime Intelligence Seminar after its meeting in Billings, Montana, the year before, contains a list of the participants. Most are from local law enforcement agencies in the Western states, but the list also includes representatives of the FBI, the Secret Service, IRS Intelligence Division, the Treasury Department's Alcohol, Tobacco and Firearms Division, the U.S. Border patrol, the Postal Inspection Service, and the Royal Canadian Mounted Police. The campus police of several local colleges were included, as were Mr. Richard L. Ryman of the General Telephone Company in Edmonds, Washington, and Mr. Tom Strong, a special agent of the Exxon Corporation in Denver, Colorado.

The group's confidential report also contains intelligence information on various individuals, including mug shot, description, and modus operandi. A disclaimer at the beginning of the document denies any liability for misinformation.

is more than a little chummy with the local cops in many cities. The army trained several Baltimore intelligence squad officers in techniques of electronic eavesdropping and surreptitious entry at its Fort Holabird spy school in Maryland. In return, the Baltimore cops passed along many of their intelligence reports to the army. In Chicago, the Red Squad was in daily contact with the army's 113th Military Intelligence Group during the late 1960s and early 1970s, passing along intelligence reports and receiving a variety of technical assistance. The 113th also provided money, tear-gas bombs, MACE, and electronic surveillance equipment to the Legion of Justice thugs whom the Chicago Red Squad turned loose on local anti-war groups. On at least two occasions, the fruits of the Legion's burglaries turned up in army hands. In one case documents stolen from the defense attorneys in the famous Chicago Seven trial growing out of the disturbances at the 1968 Democratic Convention were turned over to the army by the Legion of Justice hoodlums. The Cook County grand jury was unable to discover the full extent of the 113th's involvement with the Chicago Red Squad for a very familiar reason: the army reported that it had destroyed all its records of the liaison.

How extensive the relationship may be between Army Intelligence and other LEIU member agencies is not clear, but the degree of army involvement with local police forces was indicated recently when the army's Criminal Investigation Command applied for funds to buy 324 marble paperweights and 50 walnut wall plaques. The items were to be presented to police chiefs across the country who cooperated with the army's CIC. It would be remarkable if such cooperation did not at least occasionally include access to the files and other assets of the LEIU.

But Army Intelligence is by no means the only federal agency that might find the LEIU's ready-made dossier network to be of value. Coopting the local police in foreign countries is standard operating procedure in the CIA's book of tricks. In the past, the Agency would select foreign police officers for recruitment when they came to Washington, D.C., to study American police methods at the State Department's International Police Academy. When the recruited officers returned to their jobs in their home countries, they would be on the CIA payroll. CIA-watchers familiar with this process were disturbed to learn that the Agency had conducted similar police training courses for police officers from many police departments within the United States. Of course, such training might have been prompted by the purely altruistic motive of disseminating the advanced police technology developed by the Agency for overseas use, but it would be naive to ignore the fact that local police cooperation would be essential to domestic intelligence operations, an area we now know the Agency was involved in from the early 1960s. And given the CIA's Operation Chaos, a program directed at spying on domestic dissidents, it would be doubly naive to suppose the Agency has ignored the LEIU network, which links virtually every major Red Squad on the North American continent.

Douglass Durham, the former Des Moines cop who claims to have worked in an undercover program sponsored by the LEIU, says he heard of a federal government employee who was somehow involved with LEIU.

"I believe his name was Schwartz or Schaeffer," says Durham. "I have no idea of his first name. He was supposedly an employee of the Department of Justice, but I heard rumblings that he was from Central Intelligence. Nobody really wanted to say what the connection was."

Durham is rather vague about the role of this mystery man with regard to the LEIU, and he acknowledges that the report of a CIA connection is only scuttlebutt. However, there is one interesting piece of circumstantial evidence suggesting some sort of interface between the CIA and the LEIU.

There is only one LEIU member agency in the Washington, D.C., metropolitan area, and there is only one LEIU member agency in the entire state of Virginia; it is the same agency, the Fairfax County, Virginia, Police Department. It's a little surprising that the Fairfax County police belong to a network ostensibly dedicated to fighting organized crime, because there is little indication of Mob activity in Fairfax County, a quiet, upper-income bedroom suburb of the nation's capital. In fact, the only enterprise with any known Mafia connections located anywhere in Fairfax County is the 125-acre wooded tract that is CIA headquarters.

Ties between the CIA and the Fairfax County police are, to say the least, close. The Agency has given the Fairfax cops training in electronic surveillance, surreptitious entry, lockpicking, safecracking, and explosives. It has provided equipment and personnel to assist the police department in several of its investigations. The Agency hosted a dinner for one retiring Fairfax police captain who had been particularly helpful to the CIA, and presented him with a $150 watch as a token of its appreciation.

In return for such largesse, the Fairfax police provided the CIA with police badges and identification to be used as cover in domestic investigations. The Fairfax cops have also provided assistance to the Agency in staging the ''arrest'' and interrogation of CIA intelligence officer trainees in order to determine whether they could resist such pressure, prior to assigning them overseas. But the greatest act of fealty to the CIA may have been performed in the early hours of February 19, 1971, when several Fairfax County police officers and CIA agents broke into a photographic studio in Fairfax City, Virginia. The studio was owned by a Cuban refugee whose fiancé was a former CIA file clerk. The Agency was afraid the woman might have taken classified documents and given them to the Cuban, so an illegal entry was mounted in order to search the studio. To insure that everything went smoothly, the break-in expedition was led by the chief of the Fairfax County police. If the Fairfax police were willing to aid and abet the CIA in the commission of felonies, it seems reasonable to assume they would be more than willing to act as a ''cut out'' or interface so that information and influence could pass between the CIA and the LEIU. And it's hard to imagine the CIA passing up that kind of opportunity.

Of course, it's just possible that the LEIU has never been exploited by the CIA, Army Intelligence, or any other federal agency. And maybe, despite the lawlessness and political spying of many of its member agencies, the LEIU is nothing more than a group of policemen dedicated to fighting organized crime. But even granting such a generous benefit of the doubt, the LEIU remains one of the most potentially dangerous threats to freedom in America.

In our society, blackmail has replaced physical force as the currency of political power bokerage. J. Edgar Hoover knew that power lies between the manilla covers of a personal dossier, and he used that knowledge to build and maintain his empire for more than half a century. The

FBI, the CIA, and virtually every other agency given the authority to spy to defend us from foreign or domestic enemies, has sooner or later gone off the reservation and used its power to steal our liberties. *Frankenstein* is an American allegory.

We have been able to save ourselves from the police state—at least thus far—because our form of government is equipped with a system of checks and balances that makes executive agencies ultimately accountable to the people. But there is a powerful dossier subculture in America, a vast Old Boy Network that ties together intelligence agencies, police departments, credit bureaus, private detective agencies, bonding companies, and the many other collectors and compilers of personal information about private citizens. It is an aggregation of police power beyond the direct control of the democratic process.

The LEIU is a part of this subculture, and it is an especially powerful part because it has form, structure, and efficiency. Perhaps it doesn't spy on ordinary citizens, and perhaps it directs its attentions solely toward organized crime, but all that could change with a single meeting of the LEIU's executive board. There is no statutory charter that defines the limits of the LEIU's operations, and so it can be and do whatever its members decide it ought to be and do.

In the meantime, of course, and despite whatever else is on its secret agenda, the LEIU continues to supplement the FBI's uncertain war on organized crime. Perhaps the LEIU plays a vital role, perhaps it performs an indispensable function in our national holding action against La Cosa Nostra.

But somehow there must be a better way.

A quasi-secret police intelligence organization acting without legal authority is only one step removed from that traditional American institution of do-it-yourself law enforcement, the vigilance committee or vigilante society. Vigilantism is older than the Republic; the first American vigilante group—the South Carolina Regulators—was organized in 1767. From then until 1897, eighty-one major vigilante groups were organized in thirty-seven different states, most notably in Texas and California. One thinks of the vigilante as an extinct creature of the Old West, long gone from the American scene. In fact, there has been a resurgence of vigilantism since 1968 and there are now at least 10,000 armed vigilantes in America.

The modern vigilantes belong to an organization called *Posse Comitatus,* the full legal Latin term for what sheriffs of the Old West simply called a posse. (The phrase is translated variously as ''the power of the county,'' and ''to be able to be an attendant.'') The group is also known as the National Christian Posse Association and, sometimes, the White Christian Posse. Posse Comitatus was formed in 1968 by Mike Beach, a retired Portland, Oregon, laundry equipment salesman. Beach sells charters for $21 to local groups who want to start their own chapter, and claims there are now almost half a million members, but the FBI estimates the figure is closer to 10,000. Posse members wear uniforms, badges, carry firearms and official-looking identification cards, and drive around in cars bearing star-shaped decals in imitation of sheriffs' vehicles.

The Posse espouses a sort of right-wing, populist, anti-government philosophy. The group claims that most American government institutions are unconstitutional or illegal, including the income tax, licensing, federal reserve notes, and land-use permits. It says the only legal law enforcement officers in the United States are county sheriffs. Posse members say that one of their major goals is to rid government of corrupt public officials, and Posse founder Mike Beach believes this can best be accomplished through public hangings. Indeed, Posse members in mufti identify themselves with tiny gold nooses worn in their lapels.

The most surprising thing about the Posse members is that they are not kidding. In 1974, a group of them took an IRS agent prisoner. In April 1975, twelve Posse members tried to arrest a county judge in Illinois for attempting ''to break down the sacred family unit''; the judge had found for the ex-wife of one of the vigilantes who was involved in an alimony dispute. In August 1976, seven of the vigilantes took over a potato packing plant in Oregon and held fifteen workers captive in a land dispute; the gang was arrested by the state police. Most of these confrontations end up with the Posse members behind bars, but in February 1976 a vigilante arrested a Washington state trooper for speeding and the charge was upheld and the trooper fined.

Recently police and federal agents in Manitowoc, Wisconsin, raided

a factory in which a group of Posse members were engaged in the manufacture of Laetril, the anti-cancer drug the federal government has
banned as ineffective. The raiders confiscated twelve tons of apricot pits
from which the drug is made, plus 100,000 unfilled drug capsules,
enough raw materials to produce a supply of Laetril for 6000 persons
per day. Proceeds from the illegal drug operation were used by the
Posse to purchase and stockpile caches of guns and ammunition.

The police are not even slightly sympathetic to Posse Comitatus, and
view the group as a dangerous collection of armed screwballs. To date,
there has been no report of actual Posse violence, which could mean either that the vigilantes possess more good sense then they display, or
that they are riding a lucky streak which eventually is going to run out.

The self-deputized ''sheriffs'' of Posse Comitatus belong neither to
the public nor private sectors of law enforcement. They are the image of
the police subculture as seen in a fun-house mirror, but that image is,
nonetheless, still a reflection. If there are cops for hire and cops for rent,
what's wrong with a do-it-yourself cop?

It's not only the vigilantes who distrust established constitutional law
enforcement institutions. Why else the growth of private police forces?
Why else the exploitation of private Old Boy Networks by official
police agencies? Why else the establishment of an unofficial and quasi-
secret intelligence operation by sworn police officers? The Private Sector is flourishing because the public criminal justice system isn't working anymore. Police, both public and private, may condemn the vigilante as a dangerous lunatic, but many are kindred spirits to the Posse
member who summed up his philosophy this way:

''There is no greater law firm than Smith and Wesson, especially if it
is backed up by a 12-gauge injunction.''

8

The Lords of the Files

Harry J. Murphy was very good at his job, which happened to be investigating people for the Central Intelligence Agency. If the CIA was considering you for a career position or a temporary assignment, they'd give your name to Murphy or one of his co-workers in the Agency's Office of Security. When Murphy got through with you, the CIA would know more of your life history than you did yourself.

Murphy knew where to go to find out about you—not just the obvious places like the IRS, the Social Security Administration, or Selective Service, but the truly arcane sources of personal information. If you carved gravestones, for example, Murphy knew your credit rating would be listed in the *Memorial Red Book*. If you raised chickens, he knew there might be a file on you at the Department of Agriculture's Poultry Division. If you sold wine in New Jersey, he knew he could find your photograph and a list of your former employers on your state license application. If you were a doctor, Murphy might start with the *AMA Directory;* if you were a lawyer, he'd turn to the *Martindale–Hubbell Law Directory;* and if you happened to be an Indian chief, that was no problem for Murphy—he knew there was plenty about you on the tribal roll at one of the field offices of the Bureau of Indian Affairs.

Murphy learned all this know-how through experience; after years on the job he was a walking encyclopedia. Most of his expertise was in his head, and the CIA must have realized that when Murphy retired he'd be taking it with him. In 1965, he was given a leave of absence and a federal fellowship to go to the Brookings Institution and write it all down. It took him a year, and the result was a 452-page handbook for government paper-chasers called *Where's What*.

Where's What is the snoop's Baedeker. It's a guidebook for a tour through 6723 different record systems maintained by the federal government, which contain a total of 3.9 billion files, or an average of eighteen files for every man, woman, and child in the United States. And it's also a handbook for the countless dossiers compiled by state, county, and municipal governments. But *Where's What* is by no means limited to information files collected by government; nearly 40 percent of Murphy's catalog of information sources is devoted to personal data depots operated by the Private Sector. Even at that, *Where's What* doesn't begin to do justice to the sheer mass of information maintained by businesses and private agencies on individual Americans.

"There are substantially more records kept by the private, or commercial sector than by the federal government," says David F. Linowes, chairman of the government's Privacy Protection Study Commission. In fact, snooping by private agencies into the lives of Americans rivals government spying on the public, and is in many ways much more insidious. Privacy laws and regulations work somewhat to constrain the bureaucrats' lust for personal data, but private snoops are almost totally unregulated as they amass and exchange the same kind of information. Most Private Sector file fanciers are not the slightest bit reluctant to open their dossiers to police and government investigators, so that which cannot be acquired by government gumshoes through official channels is often readily available through the Old Boy Network. The American dossier subculture has become an entity unto itself, spanning government and the Private Sector. It is almost totally out of control.

Where's What tells how the game is played. Let's say you work for a defense contractor and must apply for a government security clearance. When you come to the point in the questionnaire that asks if you've ever been arrested, you answer truthfully and confidently that you have not.

The government investigator will check with law enforcement sources and confirm your statement. But if he's paid attention to his copy of *Where's What,* he won't stop there.

"There is a little bit of larceny in everybody's heart," the snoop's handbook advises us. Maybe sometime you tried your hand at shoplifting, it suggests. "Unless the article taken is of some value," notes *Where's What,* "a record of shoplifting will not normally find its way into a police file. . . . [But] . . . department stores have their own clearing houses for shoplifting offenses."

Most major department store chains belong to organizations called retail protective associations. Several New York stores, for example, belong to the Stores Mutual Protective Association. Founded in 1918, the Association is reputed to have over half a million files on shoppers or store employees allegedly guilty of theft. Anyone applying for a job in a member store can expect to be rejected if his name is in the Association's files. And the Association's records are reportedly made available to other prospective employers and credit bureaus. Presumably the federal investigator checking your background would have no trouble getting a look at the files of any retail protective association.

No matter how innocent you are of stealing from stores, your name is probably in such a file if you've ever had a run-in with a store's rent-a-cops. Take the case of a young woman, newly hired by a Boston department store, who was fired when her name turned up in a check with Protective Services, Inc. PSI was a private firm that maintained the same kind of blacklist file kept by retail protective associations. The agency's records showed that, five years earlier, the young woman had been suspected of trying to steal three pants suits from another store. The woman denied the charge and the store declined to prosecute her, so there was no arrest record or other official record of the incident. But PSI opened a file on her, and five years later it cost her a job. (The incident was a violation of Massachusetts' Fair Credit Reporting Act, and ultimately led to shutting down PSI.)

Such dossier exchanges present a grotesque caricature of the criminal justice system. The defendant has no rights, while the store's security force acts as police, judge, jury, and executioner. For example, a store employee might be accused of theft and summarily dismissed. The store may have no real case against the individual—he may, in fact, be entirely innocent—and it may choose not to prosecute. Thus, the ex-employee has no forum in which to present his defense, while his former employer is free to brand him "thief," and sentence him to life in the retail protective association's files. The black mark is a time bomb set to go off perhaps years later, when a check into the individual's background turns up the item.

But retail merchants aren't the only people who keep unofficial "rap sheets." Similar to the retail protective associations is a service offered to Nevada gambling casinos by private detective Bob Griffin, a former Las Vegas deputy sheriff. For fees ranging upwards of $1000 per month, Griffin provides the casinos with a four-inch-thick "black book," containing the names, photographs, descriptions, and *modus operandi* of hundreds of people suspected of crooked gambling. If it includes you, you won't even be let inside a casino to gamble, much less apply for a job.

Crooked or honest, if you've ever had anything to do with horse racing beyond the occasional trip to the track or two-dollar bet, there's probably a file on you in the New York City headquarters of the Thoroughbred Racing Protective Bureau. Federal investigators might expect more than average cooperation from the Bureau; about a dozen of its employees are members of the Society of Former Special Agents of the FBI.

Racetrack people are also likely to turn up in the files of the venerable Pinkerton's, Inc., which has been providing security for horse racing since the turn of the century, longer than any other Private Sector outfit. Pinkerton's files are by no means limited to jockeys and touts, however. The private detective firm also claims files on 1.5 million "known criminals." And some of that information comes directly from police records.

The information pipeline between official law enforcement agencies and the Private Sector flows both ways. Private detective firms like Pinkerton's are often hired by large companies to run background checks on prospective employees, a job that includes finding out if the applicant was ever arrested. In most law enforcement agencies, arrest records are supposed to be confidential; an arrest is not a conviction, and disseminating the fact that an individual has been arrested can amount to reaccusing him of a charge on which he was found innocent. However, most large Private Sector firms have contacts in police departments ready to furnish arrest records or any other information regarding the applicant they may have on file. Sometimes such cooperation is done as a professional courtesy to a police alumnus working in the Private Sector; in other cases the information is simply sold by enterprising police officers as a means of supplementing their salaries.

In 1971, a New York City detective was convicted of selling police records to banks, airlines, private detective agencies, and other companies. The officer reportedly earned more than $10,000 per year selling such confidential files. Several of his customers were convicted of "giving unlawful gratuities" and "rewarding official misconduct." Among them were Pinkerton's, the Wackenhut Corporation, the William J. Burns International Detective Agency, and the Retail Credit Company.

The last member of this foursome is not, strictly speaking, a private detective agency as are the other three (although it holds private detective agency licenses in some states). Retail Credit is the leading consumer investigation service in the country and probably the most voracious data-grabber in the Private Sector. The company maintains files on 47 million Americans. If you've ever applied for life, medical, or auto insurance, filed a claim against an insurance company, taken out a mortgage, or financed a new car, Retail Credit probably has a file on you. And there is a real chance the information in that file is false or defamatory, or both.

A Caro, Michigan, woman discovered her insurance had been cancelled because a Retail Credit report falsely described her as an excessive drinker. She sued and was awarded $321,750.

A Martin, South Dakota, woman inherited some money and used it to purchase a new Chevrolet. She was rejected for automobile insurance by three companies which had received a Retail Credit report implying the money for the car had been earned through prostitution. The woman sued; Retail Credit settled out of court and cleaned up the record.

A member of the faculty of Princeton University was refused auto insurance by State Farm Mutual Insurance Co. when Retail Credit reported, accurately but irrelevantly, that she was living with a man out of wedlock.

A Retail Credit investigator checking out a California insurance broker talked to one of the man's competitors and got an earful of completely false allegations regarding his subject's honesty. The investigator included the calumny in his report and the broker sued for libel. The jury awarded him $250,000.

It goes on and on, and, even allowing for the huge volume of snooping done by Retail Credit, there are enough similar horror stories in the record to suggest that there may be something basically wrong with the way Retail Credit goes about its investigations. The major problem seems to be that the company tries to use the techniques of the assembly line to assess the character and worth of human beings.

Detectives and other professional investigators know that the job of digging out and verifying reliable information about anyone is a time-consuming and expensive process. If you were to hire a reputable private investigator to check into the background of some John Doe, you wouldn't expect to hear anything from him for at least a couple of days; when you did you'd probably also get a bill for several hundred dollars. But Retail Credit will tell you all about John Doe's solvency and morals at the bargain-basement price of five dollars.

How does the company work this inflation-fighting miracle? Mass production is the answer. When the Retail Credit gumshoe starts out on his daily rounds, he goes armed with a list of persons to be investigated. The list is constructed so that all the subjects live in the same neighborhood, or at least along some geographically coherent route that permits the gumshoe to minimize his travel time. Before our man calls it a day and heads for the barn, he is expected to have investigated and reported on every person on the list. Retail Credit officials admit that the list averages sixteen or seventeen names (former Retail Credit employees put the number as high as forty).

According to company officials, the legman investigates the seventeen people by talking to approximately forty neighbors, landlords, local merchants, or others who profess to know them. The average interview, they say, lasts about ten minutes. In other words, the man from Retail Credit "investigates" you by talking, on the average, to 2.3 people for a total of 23½ minutes.

Retail Credit was the target of a recent probe by the CBS news program "Sixty Minutes." The television reporters interviewed former Retail Credit investigators, and even arranged for a journalism student to work undercover and take a job with the company. "Sixty Minutes" reported that the people Retail Credit investigators list in their reports as sources of information in an investigation often have never even been contacted by Retail Credit.

Given such brief and sometimes imaginary interviewing, it might well be wondered how the Retail Credit investigators can report anything of substance about the people on their lists. Nevertheless they manage to, and four former field men testified to a Senate investigating committee that they were given quotas requiring them to turn up derogatory information on from 6 to 10 percent of all insurance applicants. Obviously the harried gossip brokers of Retail Credit are under considerable pressure to come up with some dirt; when none can be found, there must be a strong temptation to invent it.

As a result of the many lawsuits filed against it by its victims, as well as a major action by the Federal Trade Commission, Retail Credit Co. has received a great amount of unfavorable publicity. In order to escape its unsavory reputation, the company has resorted to the same ploy used by many individuals who find themselves afoul of the law; it changed its name. Retail Credit now goes under the name Equifax, Inc. Unfortunately, everything else seems to have stayed the same.

Considering the questionable reliability of the information contained in many credit files, it's surprising that government or police investigators would have any interest in seeing the inside of dossiers complied by Retail Credit/Equifax or similar consumer investigation services. However, *Where's What* says such files can be a useful source of leads—the names of neighbors and others allegedly willing to gossip about a person—and specific information such as date of birth or former addresses, items probably supplied by the subject himself. A former Retail Credit investigator told me that the company routinely made its files available to the FBI and other government investigators. This practice has presumably changed since May 1971, when the federal Fair Credit Reporting Act restricted the information that may be given to government agencies without court order to names, addresses, and places of employment. The federal law pertains only to "consumer reporting agencies,'' however, and in no way limits other Private Sector information sources.

Insurance companies comprise the largest group of Retail Credit/Equifax's customers. The Prudential Insurance Company of America, for example, does $5 million per year with the company. But the big insurers aren't satisfied with what your next-door neighbor or the neighborhood gossip might have to say about you; they also want to know what your doctor knows about you. And for this they are likely to turn to outfits like the Chicago-based Factual Service Bureau, Inc.

Suppose you were injured in an automobile accident and filed a claim against the other driver's insurance company. The insurance company wants to know from the outset how much they are likely to have to pay you. But that's impossible to say without a look at your medical records, information that is supposedly protected by the confidentiality of the sacred doctor–patient relationship. And that's where Factual Service Bureau comes in; according to its own sales pitch, it specializes in "securing medical records and information without patient authorization." In plainer language, it steals private medical records.

FSB agents pose as doctors, nurses, welfare workers, and sometimes even clergymen in order to work their scam. The fellow decked out in white coat and stethoscope who saunters into a hospital's records office may be a staff doctor on a legitimate errand. On the other hand, he may be a clever FSB agent about to brazenly con a clerk into turning over your folder to him. An NBC News investigative team got hold of a little handbook FSB furnishes its agents, giving them tips on impersonating doctors.

"In introducing yourself, say as little as necessary," quotes NBC from the handbook. "Write down the name of the doctor you are using, to avoid forgetting it," the manual adds.

When not playing doctor, some FSB agents pose as cops, the NBC investigation disclosed. The ingenious gumshoes actually figured three separate ways to inveigle their way into the National Crime Information Center, the coast-to-coast computer network operated by the FBI, providing state and local law enforcement agencies with access to hundreds of thousands of arrest records and similar data. Not all police forces are equipped with the computer terminal equipment needed to gain direct entry into the NCIC system; those without such gear rely on neighboring departments to relay their inquiries to the system by telephone. According to NBC, the Denver Police Department and at least four other police forces in Colorado were conned by FSB agents posing as local officers into handling NCIC requests over the phone.

Alternatively, the FSB agents would call a police department, identify themselves as New York City police officers, place their request for information, and leave a call-back number—a telephone in FSB's offices in lower Manhattan. When the police department called back with the information, the FSB agent manning the telephone would announce, "One hundred and first precinct," as he answered.

If all else failed, FSB turned to a private investigator in Columbus, Nebraska, who had access to the NCIC system through a friend in the local police department. FSB would make a flat payment to the man for the information.

FSB's activities in the Denver, Colorado, area attracted the attention of the local authorities, and eventually brought it under the scrutiny of the FBI and the IRS. The limelight put a definite crimp in the detective agency's activities, but did little to thwart the theft and sale of confidential medical information by similar outfits. According to Dr. Alfred M. Freedman, president of the National Commission on Confidentiality of Health Records, the Denver affair is "only the tip of a nationwide iceberg."

Ever been called to jury duty? If so, there's a good chance someone built up a dossier on you containing such information as your tax returns, the state of your marriage, your bill-paying methods, your personal habits, plus neighborhood gossip about you. In most large cities specialized investigative firms dig up such information on prospective jurors and sell it to the lawyers representing the plaintiff or the defendant. After pouring over your personal life, the lawyers will decide whether you're likely to be disposed toward their clients. If they think not, they'll work to keep you off the jury hearing the case.

In addition to those who traffic in confidential data about your bank balance, your bedroom, and your body, there is yet another category of Private Sector snoop; his files are chock full of information regarding your ideological purity. If you have ever written a letter to the editor, attended a protest rally, or subscribed to a radical newspaper, he may have started a dossier on you. The keeping of dossiers on suspected subversives, wrong-thinkers, and other troublemakers by private and self-appointed guardians of national security is a practice dating back at least to the 1930s, but it reached its peak during the McCarthyite panic of the 1950s. It was during the latter period that one of the largest and most powerful Private Sector "red squads" was formed—the American Security Council.

The Council started out in 1955 as the Mid-American Research Library, a dossier service to a group of member firms that provided its financial support; the Library advised them on employees and prospective employees who might not share their free enterprise philosophy. In 1956, ex-FBI agent John M. Fisher left his position in the security department of Sears, Roebuck and Co., one of the charter member firms, and became president and executive director of the Library, which soon changed its name to the American Security Council. The ASC augmented its own snooping with the purchase of a one-million-name file from the estate of Harry A. Jung, the late publisher of *American Vigilante* and a notorious anti-Semite. The ASC staff continued to update the dossier collection with reports from the security departments of member corporations and other right-wing groups, plus names gleaned from the hearings of congressional committees investigating "internal security." By the early 1970s, the files had blossomed into a gargantuan data collection requiring an index of six million cards.

More then 3000 dues-paying member firms have full access to the ASC's hoard of information on suspected enemies of the free enterprise system. Among the subscribers are Sears, Roebuck and Co., Lockheed, Motorola, Allstate Insurance, Honeywell, U.S. Steel, and General Dynamics, companies whose security staffs were well represented in the FBI's Old Boy Network, the Society of Former Special Agents of the FBI. Some of ASC's most generous support has come from the Schick Safety Razor Company, owned by right-wing millionaire Patrick J. Frawley. Besides helping member companies weed out lefties and other infidels who might apply for work, the ASC carries on a very active lobbying and public relations operation in behalf of such Pentagon pet projects as the anti-ballistic missile and the B–1 bomber.

The American Security Council has no monopoly on political dossier keeping within the Private Sector. The Western Research Foundation, for example, was founded nearly ten years before ASC by a group of ex-FBI agents. Western Research was formed to provide the same political dossier service to a clientele of West Coast–based companies, including the Southern Pacific Railroad, Pacific Gas and Electric, Standard Oil of California, and the Hearst newspapers. Some of the names in Western Research's files came from mailing lists and other files snatched by Jerome Ducote, ex-cop and freelance political burglar, during seventeen break-ins he carried out against leftist political and labor groups in California between 1966 and 1968. (Ducote also shared the fruits of his "after-hours research" with the American Security Council.) Since 1969, the Foundation's files have been taken over by Research West, Inc. The firm is licensed to operate as a private detective agency, but seems to be carrying on the same kind of work as the Foundation. Research West has been named in a multimillion-dollar libel suit filed by Synanon, Inc., the drug rehabilitation agency.

The supply of such subversive tracking outfits seems to exceed the demand, and some of the smaller ones just fade away. A Dayton, Ohio, firm, Agitator Detection, Inc., boasted only a few short years ago "complete computerized files on every known American dissident," as well as "all 160 million of their friends, relatives, and fellow travelers." Now the company is gone from the local telephone directory. In Southern California, the Fire and Police Research Association recently folded. "Fi-Po," as it was called, was headed by a former Los Angeles Police Department police officer and was staffed by Los Angeles Police and Fire Department volunteers. It provided the usual political dossier service, at a charge of $10 per name check, to such clients as the John Birch Society, as well as a host of corporate subscribers. Fi-Po's files were inherited by the United Community Churches of America of Glendale, California, yet another Private Sector clearinghouse for dossiers of the supposedly subversive.

The oldest established private political dossier service in the United States is probably the Church League of America, which was founded in 1937 by a group of Chicago right-wingers and Christian fundamentalists to combat the "Communist influence" they perceived among the American clergy. Since the 1950s, the Church League has been headed by former Air Force intelligence officer and ordained Baptist minister Edgar G. Bundy. Although the Church League's *bête noire* has always been the liberal National Council of Churches, it reserves an ample supply of vitriol for attacks on people it considers Communists, "fellow travelers," or "Communist dupes." The Church League boasts that its Research Library contains "the largest and most comprehensive files on subversive activity, with the single exception of the FBI." The zeal of the League's researchers is described in the organization's brochure:

The uniqueness of the Church League files is that every name of every person, organization, movement, publication, or subject of significance has been put on a reference card with one incident per card, each referring back to the original document in the files. Full-page ads in newspapers, such as the *New York Times,* calling for the abolition of Congressional investigating committees, or attacking our security laws, have sometimes carried names running into the thousands. Each one of these names has been carded and indexed with the reason for its appearing in the ad put on the card. Likewise, if an individual made a speech or wrote an article or book attacking and ridiculing a major doctrine of the Christian Faith or the American way of life, that individual's name and the article were each carded.

The League is much more than a clipping and indexing service, however. According to its brochure some of the information in its files was acquired by its "undercover operatives" sitting in on leftist meetings with miniature tape recorders and photographing the participants with tiny cameras. "Copies of file materials were also acquired by Church League agents," the brochure says, "who ingratiated themselves with leftists that accepted their volunteer help to work in various headquarters." Among the services the League offers to its supporters are background checks of suspected leftists and even attempted infiltration of left-wing organizations. For a "contribution" of $50, the League will give you a full political run-down on up to three of your neighbors.

Lest such offers be taken for the puerile Walter Mitty antics of a bunch of grown men playing counterspy, it should be noted that the League is taken very seriously by some segments of corporate America; the organization has received financial support from such large companies as Abbott Laboratories, Armour and Company, the Greyhound Corporation, Monsanto Chemical, Borg-Warner, and the Celanese Foundation. In January 1977, an official of the Wackenhut Corporation admitted under questioning by the Privacy Protection Study Commission—a panel appointed by the government under the 1974 Privacy Act—that the detective agency sometimes used the Church League's files while conducting background investigations for its corporate clients. Relations between the League and the right-wing rent-a-cop outfit seem, in fact, to be very cordial; Wackenhut recently made a present to the Church League of approximately 700,000 of its political dossiers.

The Church League puts out several publications, including the monthly *News & Views,* and the bi-weekly *National Layman's Digest.* The latter publication is described by the League as "dealing with individuals, organizations, publications, and subjects in religion, education, entertainment, political life, and youth groups." In 1969 and 1970 the *Digest* was edited by John Rees, a mysterious figure of the right-wing underground.

According to a report issued by the New York State Assembly's Office of Legislative Oversight and Analysis, Rees was born in Great Britain in 1926, came to the United States in 1963, and is still a resident alien. The report states that he was "an orderly in a Massachusetts nursing home before becoming a beneficiary of the will of Grace Metalious, author of *Peyton Place.*"

In 1968, Rees formed National Goals, Inc., which, according to its incorporation papers, was supposed to "provide an investigative service for various branches of government, State, Federal, and local, and to prepare memoranda, reports, books, pamphlets, and bulletins with respect thereto." Under the National Goals aegis, Rees began publishing a periodical called *Information Digest,* which was distributed by the Church League for a brief period around 1970. The *Digest* was a newsletter concerning the activities of the New Left, labor, civil rights, and other movements causing alarm on the Right.

Some of the information in *Information Digest* seems to have come from informers and undercover investigators within these organizations. In 1971, in a move apparently designed to protect such sources, the newsletter ceased general distribution through the Church League and was sent to a limited mailing list of some forty police red squads and other interested agencies around the country, including the New York State Police, the National Security Agency, and the CIA. The November 19, 1971, issue of *Information Digest* contained the following warning:

"It will be apparent to the 40 people now receiving the *Information Digest* that much of the information is obtained by sources active in radical, so-called revolutionary groups. Uncontrolled dissemination of this information can have the most serious consequences. . . . It is requested that you keep *Information Digest* for use within your own organization and do not share it with others. . . . If, in your judgement, material should be disseminated, please do not use it in I.D. format; scramble and rewrite!"

William F. Haddad of the New York State Assembly's Office of Legislative Oversight conducted an official investigation of the Reeses and *Information Digest,* and reported the following: Rees and his wife, Sheila Louise, may themselves have been two of the undercover sources for *Information Digest*. Under the pseudonyms of John Seeley and Sheila O'Connor, they opened a leftist bookstore called "The Red House" in Washington, D.C., in 1971. They also founded an organization called the Coordinating Center for Education in Repression and the Law, which was supposed to combat police repression and work to promote prisoner rights and abolish capital punishment. Sheila Rees also obtained a part-time job with the National Lawyers Guild, a civil-rights organization. All the while, the couple was turning out *Information Digest* and sending it to the restricted red squad mailing list.

It's not clear whether any police departments or other law enforcement agencies were actively involved with the Reeses in the *Information Digest* project, but the Baltimore post office box used by the newsletter was opened by the Maryland State Police. Rees reportedly has worked with several police departments across the country, as well as with the Wackenhut Corporation. Sheila Louise Rees is employed in the office of the ultra-right Georgia congressman Lawrence P. McDonald, a member of the John Birch Society's National Council. McDonald's accusations against prominent people regularly appear in the *Congres-*

sional Record, where the congressman has immunity from libel suits. *Information Digest* is then free to repeat the charges without risk of litigation. The newsletter's targets have included such figures from the entertainment world as Eddie Albert, Candice Bergen, Leonard Bernstein, Dick Cavett, Dustin Hoffman, Shirley MacLaine, Carl Reiner, and Richard Widmark. Rev. Ralph David Abernathy, Ramsey Clark, John Lindsay, and Leonard Woodcock have also been smeared by *Information Digest.*

It is not known whether the Reeses and *Information Digest* have retained any formal ties to the Church League of America, but it seems reasonable to assume that dossiers are freely swapped among the League, the *Digest,* the American Security Council, and all other similar "subversive"-watchers. These groups are not, in essence, competitive with one another; they share a common objective: to denounce as subversive those people of whose philosophy they disapprove.

In his handbook *Where's What,* investigator Murphy makes no reference to these groups; in a preface he states that he has deliberately omitted all reference to investigating subversive activities because "the inclusion of sources of information on subversive activities would have necessitated a higher security classification and the book would not receive the distribution the author hopes it deserves." (The handbook was classified "Confidential," the lowest security classification in general use in the government.) But we know that there is considerable contact between the political dossier services and federal, state, and local law enforcement and intelligence agencies.

The Church League's brochure includes "government security personnel" among the kinds of people who regularly visit its Research Library. The American Security Council and Western Research were founded by ex-FBI agents who are disposed to cooperate with their old alma mater. And *Information Digest* seems to exist primarily to disseminate dossier data to official police agencies. It seems a very safe bet that all the Private Sector political dossier services are willing sources of information for any official investigator.

Even the author of *Where's What* probably has not fully charted the labyrinth of the American dossier establishment. Are there hidden passageways linking the credit bureaus, the corporate security departments, the private detective agencies, and the political dossier services with government intelligence agencies, police red squads, and organizations like the Law Enforcement Intelligence Unit? Undoubtedly the answer is yes, but who, even among the "authorized persons" of the file exchanges, can say he knows every such interface?

The Private Sector's dossier establishment has taken on a life and momentum of its own. With the single exception of credit bureaus, the private file builders are completely unregulated. Privacy and freedom of information laws give the citizen the right to examine whatever files the government keeps on him, and to have erroneous information corrected. The laws strictly limit the circumstances in which such information can be released or even exchanged among government agencies. But the Private Sector filekeepers are free to collect every sort of gossip, misinformation, or outright lie about you and to traffic in the most intimate details of your private life, and there is virtually no legal rein on their actions. You have no legal right to demand to see the files they're keeping on you, or to insist that they correct the falsehoods contained therein.

The Federal Privacy Act of 1974 set up the Privacy Protection Study Commission to investigate the problem of Private Sector filekeeping. In July 1977, the Commission issued a 650-page final report, containing 162 recommendations to correct Private Sector misuse of personal information. The Commission's recommendations will probably produce some new laws restraining some of the more outrageous abuses of the dossier establishment. But no one expects legislation to correct all the problems; much of the activity of the file fanciers is, after all, protected by the right of free speech and other constitutional guarantees. The power of the Private Sector's gossip mongers will only be broken when they are recognized for what they are and society refuses to buy their trash.

9

The Hardware Merchants

In Washington, D.C., at any given moment of the business day, the same scene is repeated thousands of times, from one end of the federal bureaucracy to the other; a salesman—in government jargon, a "vendor"—pays a visit to a middle-level official and exhibits his wares. The hopeful merchant may be selling anything from rubber stamps to raincoats—somewhere Uncle Sam has a need for almost everything. But to most people who later learned about it, the merchandise offered to the Drug Enforcement Agency that day in May 1974 was something the United States government should very definitely not be in the market for. The man from B. R. Fox, a tiny electronics firm in suburban Virginia, was selling sudden death in several flavors.

The senior DEA official who was the prospective customer took more than a passing interest in the items; there must have been many times in his career when they would have proved extremely useful. Col. Lucien Conein is a veteran of the French Foreign Legion, the OSS, and the CIA. He fought alongside the Corsican Mafia in France in World War II and describes himself as a member of that underworld brotherhood. In 1963 he was the CIA's liaison man with the South Vietnamese army officers who planned and executed the assassination of President Ngo Dinh Diem. These days Conein is head of DEA's "special operations" group. It's not surprising then that he found the Fox merchandise, as he put it, "fascinating."

The lethal goodies included a booby-trapped M–16 rifle designed to kill its user, plus an exploding flashlight that did the same thing. There was also a cigarette package guaranteed to be hazardous to your health; it was packed with explosives and contained a tiny electronic trigger to set off the charge when the pack was moved. A photosensitive bomb could be planted in the dark, set to go off at sunrise or when someone turned on the light, whichever came first. But the *pièce de résistance* was called a "telephone handset insert." The device is planted in your telephone receiver and triggered when you pick up the phone. A short-duration timer gives you a couple of seconds to place the receiver next to your ear. Then, bang, you're dead.

Col. Conein says he had no intention of buying any of the deadly gadgets; apparently he was just window shopping. But had he placed an order, the B. R. Fox Company was prepared to deliver the goods on two weeks' notice.

The purveyor of this widow-making equipment was a company formed by the late Bernard Spindel, a leading Private Sector wiretapper. As the B. R. Fox Company, Spindel built and sold bugging gear in a small brick building behind his Alexandria, Virginia, home. After his death in 1971, the company was run by Spindel's young assistant and Mitchell Wer Bell III, a Georgia arms dealer who specializes in such items as machine gun silencers, cigars that shoot bullets, and a swagger stick that can launch a rocket. Wer Bell, an old OSS buddy of Conein, appears to have dreamed up the assassination gear.

The B. R. Fox Company, now defunct, was a small, if dangerous, fish in the large pond that is the security equipment market. Fortunately, most makers of police and security gear don't manufacture anything nearly as treacherous as Fox's booby-traps; the largest segment of the market is comprised of industrial security items, things like safes, vaults, security lighting systems, closed-circuit television, and burglar alarms. A study conducted several years ago by the Rand Corporation projected annual sales of such items to reach over $1.2 billion by 1978. A smaller, yet rapidly growing segment of the market is made up of police equipment, including everything from complex communication systems to fingerprint powder.

The boom in the security equipment industry is the result of several factors. First, of course, there is the well-known increase in the rate of all kinds of crime, especially crime against American business. Understandably, businessmen are willing to spend a great deal of money on locks, fences, and burglar alarms if the alternative is to lose all their profits to pilferage and hijacking.

Another stimulus to the industry's growth was the Vietnam War. The war, totally different from previous American experience in the kind of fighting involved, created a market for special counterinsurgency weapons and other gear. After the war, the aerospace and electronics industries that developed this special equipment convinced domestic law enforcement agencies they needed such things as helicopters, short take-off and landing aircraft, night vision instruments, and other such big-ticket items heretofore sold only to the Pentagon. Persuading the cops was easy, because much of the gadgetry was supplied free of charge, compliments of the federal Law Enforcement Assistance Administration. The LEAA itself is the third, and perhaps largest, factor behind the recent boom in the police hardware industry.

The LEAA was created by the Johnson administration in 1968 as a means of providing federal money to fight crime and upgrade the criminal justice systems in the cities and states. The agency started out with a $63 million budget for fiscal year 1969. By 1975 it was spending $880 million per year, and as of 1977 the total cost of the agency over its nine-year history was more than $5.5 billion. Some of the projects funded by this federal largesse were, to put it mildly, a bit dubious.

Loyola University was given $293,700 to determine whether a loose-leaf encyclopedia on law enforcement was needed. Forty-eight thousand four hundred sixty-five dollars were allocated to a former Washington, D.C., police chief to write his memoirs. A $541,623 grant was allocated to promote physical fitness among police officers; $200,000 of the money was earmarked for the development of a wristwatch-like device that would show the police officer his blood pressure, pulse rate, and temperature. Three and a half million dollars went to Florida law enforcement agencies to help them keep the peace during the 1972 Republican convention; $24,786 of it was used to replenish tear-gas stocks. Two and a half million dollars was given to police departments to buy electronic surveillance gear; $1.3 million of that was spent by the police in states where such bugging is illegal. And more than half a million dollars was given to the San Clemente, California, Police Department to help protect Richard M. Nixon.

It is, of course, unfair simply to cite such apparent extravagances out of context; some of them might really seem quite sound, were all the facts known. Others, however, must be judged prima facie examples of fourteen-karat boondoggles, such as the $27,000 study conducted by North Carolina with LEAA funds to determine why prison inmates want to escape (the study found that escapers tended to be prisoners turned down or otherwise ineligible for parole).

Even some worthwhile LEAA projects became the victims of bureaucratic mania. In the interest of developing a light-weight bulletproof vest for police officers, the agency decided to explore the use of Kevlar, a bulletproof plastic used in automobile tires. The Army Land Warfare Laboratory was commissioned to test the material, using goats dressed in Kevlar jackets as test subjects. After 100 of the animals had been dispatched by army marksmen, the experimenters concluded that, while Kevlar stopped bullets, it didn't save lives. The armor, under the impact of a bullet, was possibly more dangerous than the slug itself, and, if one were to be shot, the chance of survival was better *without* the Kevlar vest. This discovery, although negative, was valuable in establishing that the material should not be used as body armor. Had matters ended there, the LEAA could have claimed the project as a limited success. However, someone in the agency, exercising the bureaucratic logic of *Catch 22,* then distributed 3000 Kevlar vests to rural police officers for field testing.

Many of the LEAA-funded fiascoes that make the news should not be blamed on the agency, however, because it has little or no responsibility for them. Most of the LEAA money given to law enforcement is dispersed through a system of block grants to states. Every state has a planning agency which is supposed to come up with a plan for using federal funds to upgrade its criminal justice system. Although LEAA has a role in approving the plan, the state is given an outright grant, usually in the millions or tens of millions of dollars, which it is pretty well free to spend any way it wants. Often this gives the cops a kind of purse string power they've never known before. In 1975, when the LEAA along with most other federal agencies underwent a budget cut, a police magazine cheerily urged its readers, "Don't start counting pennies yet—there's still $800 million in the [LEAA] kitty."

LEAA money is supposed to help improve the criminal justice system. To the President's Commission on Law Enforcement and the Administration of Justice that originally recommended the establishment of the agency back in the 1960s, such improvement included things like better trained police forces, speedier and fairer trials, and better correctional institutions and programs. But to many of the local cops and LEAA bureaucrats, improving the criminal justice system means just one thing: snazzier hardware.*

The hardware merchants know where the money is, of course, and lose no opportunity to make their pitch to the cops. Their full-page ads can be found in such police magazines as *Police Chief, Law and Order, Law Enforcement Communications,* and *Industrial Security.*

"Bring crime to light. . . . With JAVELIN's full range of night viewing devices," exhorts one West Coast electronics manufacturer. Bell and Howell extols its "Roving Robber Stopper," an electronic robbery alarm system, with the claim, "It's like having 20 stakeout teams on duty around the clock." Burlington Industries offers a variety of bulletproof garments, including a groin protector, proof against .45 Caliber, .357 Magnum, and 12 guage 00 Buckshot assaults; "Keeping you alive is our business," says the ad. And Nikon offers the police its cameras, reminding them of the value of photographs, "when you can't take a jury to the crime scene."

Most of such gear does have some degree of genuine usefulness in law enforcement, and if the question of how best to spend federal funds

---

* The LEAA may have gone too far when it earmarked $2.5 million for a brochure telling local police departments how to apply for LEAA funds. Attorney-General Griffin B. Bell heard about the project shortly after taking office in January 1977, and decided reform of the agency was to be given top priority. He fired LEAA administrator Richard W. Velde and two of his deputies, and appointed a seven-member panel to study the agency and recommend what should be done with it. Reportedly, at least one member of the panel suggested that the LEAA should be junked and its funds directed to other projects, a sentiment some say is shared by the attorney-general. However, the many beneficiaries of LEAA largesse comprise a powerful lobby that will probably keep the agency in business. The best that the many critics of the LEAA now can hope for is some degree of reform.

to improve criminal justice is temporarily suspended, some of the new police gadgetry seems truly impressive. The program to develop bullet-proof clothing, for example, produced Kervan, a miracle fabric now used by more than twenty clothing manufacturers producing "fashionable armor." The material was used to protect President Ford after two assassination attempts in 1975. A Kervan vest can be had for about $50, a sport coat made from the material sells for about $150, and a custom-tailored bulletproof suit will cost several hundred dollars.

Matching latent prints found at a crime scene against a large fingerprint file used to be a time-consuming task that could take weeks to complete. By then the identified individual might be long gone. The New York City police, however, working with a $300,000 LEAA grant, developed a computerized system which can make the match in a few seconds. The system employs such up-to-the-minute features as laser photography, microfilm, and optical scanning.

A West Coast company with its eye on the police market has been breeding marine bacteria. The bacteria are bioluminescent, i.e., they emit light like fireflies, and they have been bred to respond to the presence of certain vapors in the air by varying their light output. Among the 500 different vapors to which the bacteria respond are explosives and heroin. When placed in a portable photoelectric detector, the bacteria can be used to sense the presence of bombs or drugs.

Among the most impressive of the new police gadgetry are the "night viewing devices," which were developed by the military for use in the nighttime jungles of Southeast Asia. The devices differ from the earlier "sniper-scopes," which have been around since World War II, in that they don't employ infrared or ultraviolet spotlights in order to work. The new devices are termed "passive," meaning they use moonlight, starlight, or whatever other faint illumination happens to be available. The heart of the night viewing devices is an electronic component called an "image-intensifier tube." The tube amplifies available light by a factor of 60,000 or more, turning a virtually pitch-black scene into noontime brilliance in the eyepiece of the device.

The devices are lightweight, compact, and portable, and can be carried by a foot patrolman or in a squad car, or attached to a closed-circuit television camera. Since much crime, ranging from drug dealing to break-ins, is carried out under cover of darkness, the police have had no trouble finding applications for the instruments. Most law enforcement agencies using night viewing devices are very close-mouthed about the kind and extent of their use, suggesting the equipment is widely used for covert surveillance. A Canadian police officer using one of the devices in a helicopter at night while looking for a lost child remarked that from an altitude of several hundred feet he could "almost see the spikes in the railroad track" below. Since there are no laws restricting their use, some of the night viewing devices have gotten into the hands of private detectives for unofficial snooping jobs.

Some of the most controversial items on the cops' shopping list are the so-called "nonlethal" weapons. One manufacturer's ad in a police magazine shows a police officer decked out in riot gear and confronting a mob. "Less lethal response . . . you could do worse," says the ambiguous tag line. "Write today for our complete catalog of Less-Lethal Weaponry. It's the better way."

The most common nonlethal weapons are incapacitating chemicals, such as tear gas, dispersed from a variety of cannisters, sprays, and other projectors. There are two kinds of tear gas, CN and CS. CN, which has an aroma faintly reminiscent of apple blossoms, causes tears to form, forcing the eyelids to close. It also irritates or burns the neck, armpits, and genitals. But CN is considered mild compared to the newer CS, an odorless gas that produces all of the same effects as CN plus coughing, respiratory distress, and general irritation of the sinuses. While tear gas is considered nonlethal, it does not always live up to that description; in New York City in 1975, for example, there were three instances in which the gas killed by causing a condition called "chemical pneumonia" in its victims.

In violent confrontations with demonstrators, police sometimes use a mixture of CS and DM. The latter is an orange-colored gas that smells like cheap licorice and causes severe sore throat, chest pains resembling a massive coronary, and uncontrolled vomiting and defecation. A police manual advises, "The use of DM should be a last resort proposition."

The gasses are disseminated through grenades, blowers, and spray devices. CN and CS can be burned, releasing the chemicals in very small particles carried by the hot air; CN is sometimes dissolved in a liquid to form a solution that can be propelled at a target in a water-pistol-like stream. The solution is known commercially as Chemical MACE and is widely used by police forces. MACE comes in spray cans, fountain pen projectors, and special police nightsticks that spray the chemical. The effect of MACE on its victim is the same as a very heavy dose of tear gas—quite unpleasant and guaranteed to put him out of commission for at least twenty minutes.

For several years MACE sprays were a popular item with people who felt the need for a self-defense weapon, but were unwilling or unable to carry firearms. Then, in 1975, the Federal Bureau of Alcohol, Tobacco, and Firearms reclassified tear gas sprays as firearms, thus effectively eliminating the private consumer market for such devices. At the same time a new nonlethal weapon appeared on the market and, for a time, filled the vacuum left by the outlawed MACE. The new weapon was called the TASER.

The TASER is made of molded plastic, weighs a little over a pound, and looks like a type of flashlight, which it is. The device is also a kind of dart gun which fires two small, barbed darts. The darts remain connected to the device by fifteen-foot wires which transmit an electrical charge of 50,000 volts from the TASER's batteries into the victim. The charge causes uncontrollable muscle spasms, which completely immobilize the victim in three seconds. A Florida service station attendant who was robbed by a TASER-wielding assailant reportedly said, "It was like sticking your finger in a wall socket. I fell to the floor and couldn't move."

The weapon was originally called a TSER, which stood for Tom Swift's Electric Rifle, the original inspiration of the TASER's inventor, Jack Cover, a California aerospace engineer and businessman. Cover remembered the Tom Swift story while trying to come up with some kind of anti-hijacker weapon that could be used without the danger of firing a gun in an airliner in flight. When the TASER was finally ready for production, domestic hijacking in the United States had been drastically reduced by screening passengers prior to boarding, so Cover offered the weapon to the private citizen self-defense market, instead. It was an instant hit. Five thousand of the weapons were sold at a price of about $200 each before state and federal authorities decided the TASER is a firearm, subject to all the licensing controls of a handgun.

Tear gas and electric shock are two of the more prosaic entries in the nonlethal weaponry field. In 1967, the Institute for Defense Analysis, a Pentagon think-tank, surveyed the techniques then in use or being tested as nonlethal weapons. The survey report is still considered one of the standard works on the subject. Many of the ideas described range from the mildly sadistic to the downright psychopathic.

"Pain has potentialities as a nonlethal weapon," the report reads, introducing an account of some experiments:

Intradermal injection of solution of inorganic or organic acids are very painful. Organic acids such as formic, acetic, and lactic produced great pain on injection, which was followed by analgesia for 6 to 22 min, depending on the nature of the acid.

One manufacturer is exploring this approach to chemical weapons development. A small, self-injecting syringe with ½ to 1 ml of acetic acid would be injected under the skin. He claims this causes rapid, intense, and immobilizing muscle pain.

The IDA researchers concluded, "This pain agent might be quite attractive for incorporation into dart guns for use by the individual policeman," but warns, "The use of pain weapons will certainly arouse indignation in some quarters." One should hope so.

It should be noted that the IDA study was not conducted for the Pentagon or as a means of devising new weapons of war. It was done for the President's Commission on Law Enforcement and Administration of Justice, the panel that conceived and recommended the establishment of the LEAA. The IDA report is entitled "Nonlethal Weapons for Use by U.S. Law Enforcement Officers." Let's take a look at some of the other gadgets under consideration for use by the cop on the beat.

"One investigator is exploring an approach to tranquilization through a combination injection of scopolamine and apomorphine," the IDA researchers report. "The latter induces severe vomiting in about 1 to 2 min. The subsequent effect is one of mild sedation when the retching has stopped. This is a possible method for dealing with the fleeing criminal and is a relatively new approach to the concept of weaponry in which immobilization depends on vomiting rather than some other more life-threatening response. . . . Indirect incapacitation may be achieved by improved vomit agents, the use of sneezing powders, or other rapidly acting materials whose physiological effects cannot be ignored.''

Much of the weaponry considered by the IDA study is designed for use against rioters or crowds of protesters, a major source of law enforcement concern during the late 1960s and early 1970s. The study notes, for example, that itching powder might be used to clear an area of sit-ins, and recommends that "research be supported on the application of itch-inducing agents to crowd and mob control and sit-ins.''

Another anti-crowd weapon considered by the study is the Cold Brine Projector. The device delivers a stream of cold brine which soaks its victims to the skin. "The objective of the device is to discharge a slug of liquid sufficiently below body temperature and in sufficiently large quantities to cause an incapacitating shock. . . . The sudden immersion in cold water results in topical and deep pain from massive vascular spasms. This effect occurs at immersions below approximately 50°F. One of the initial effects of such immersion is the reflex arrest of breathing lasting about 1 min. While not in itself dangerous, it is most distressing.''

Plastic confetti is still another anti-crowd weapon. It consists of tiny flakes of Teflon, which, when spread in large quantities on the ground, cause people to fall down. The study tells us that "slippery liquid and semi-liquid polymers" can be used the same way, as can fire extinguisher foam. The IDA researchers suggest that such material could be spread by projectors mounted on cars or trucks, or even from a helicopter overhead.

Not all of these brainstorms successfully completed the journey from laboratory to police arsenal, but at least one of the more exotic varieties of nonlethal weapon seems to have gone into production, judging from a brochure offered by a British company. The London-based firm Allen International produces military and police equipment, and their brochure offered something called "The Photic Driver—A non-violent weapon." The weapon is described as "intended to interfere with the natural rates of the alpha and beta rhythms of human brains and to cause temporary malfunctioning but does not, generally, have side effects nor can it do damage except to persons subject to epilepsy.''

The Photic Driver is a powerful light projector that can be made to flicker at rates of from three to twenty-five times per second. For many persons, exposure to flickering light—especially red light—at these frequencies produces a ''flicker fit,'' an epileptic-like seizure; for others, the attack is less intense. The Allen International brochure noted, ''Red light at a suitable flashing rate incapacitates 6% to 15% of persons exposed. Incapacity varies in degree from a feeling of slight or considerable uneasiness, gastrointestinal symptoms, nausea, fainting, and in cases of exposure to epileptics, the device can induce an attack.'' The brochure quotes experimental results showing that up to 28% of a crowd exposed to the Photic Driver would be immediately incapacitated, and adds, ''When used as a crowd dispersing device, it is considered that a degree of panic would be induced by a relatively small percentage of persons being visibly affected by the flickering light. This is a cumulative effect because those not immediately and directly affected would develop a condition of anxiety and would become easily and rapidly affected.'' In other words, the Photic Driver could start a human stampede.

It can be argued that, no matter how brutal and sadistic any specific nonlethal weapon happens to be, it is much less likely to cause death or permanent bodily harm than a lead slug from a police special. From that viewpoint it seems desirable that the police have the option of a nonlethal response in law enforcement situations. It may be just such a line of reasoning that prompted Senator Edward Kennedy of Massachusetts, a liberal, to pressure the National Science Foundation to sponsor research and development of new nonlethal weaponry in 1971.

The other side of the issue is the great potential for abuse of nonlethal weapons. There is relatively little police abuse of firearms in the United States, if only because of the administrative burden involved in explaining the presence of dead bodies. But someone can be given an entirely gratuitous dose of tear gas by the police, suffer considerably from it, and yet will probably be none the worse for wear the next day. In fact, MACEing a prisoner locked in a cell has replaced the rubber hose treatment in some jurisdictions. In Northern Ireland, the British army has tortured political prisoners with light and sound inside its concentration camps, then used rubber bullets to put down the street demonstrations inspired by such outrages. Had the British not devised a way to crush dissent without shedding much blood, even the most ardent American anglophile might now recognize the resemblance between Her Majesty's goons and their spiritual cousins in the Soviet KGB, the Chilean DINA, and the Iranian SAVAK. What the nonlethal weapon lacks in firepower, it more than makes up in political power.

Nonlethal weapons and other police equipment made in the U.S.A. have found their way into the hands of some of the most repressive regimes in the world. Military weapons of mass destruction require an export license, and the Departments of State and Defense are empowered to veto the deal if the customer country's foreign policy suggests the arms might be used for aggression. But until very recently, police equipment, i.e., weapons designed for use by the state against the individual, were routinely shipped overseas without regard for the condition of human rights within the borders of the purchasing nation. The record of many other Western democratic nations is no better.

In 1974, sixty-six police technology dealers from eleven countries, including the United States, exhibited their wares in Moscow at Krimtekhnika–74, a Soviet-sponsored exhibition of police gear. Admission to the Stadium of the Young Pioneers was by invitation only; the only Soviet citizens permitted to tour the exhibits were government officials, police officers, and KGB agents. Among the items displayed were teargas guns, handcuffs, black leather gloves with weighted knuckles, a TASER-like club that delivered an electric shock, and a variety of electronic surveillance gear. There was, in fact, just about everything a secret policeman might desire for dealing with Russians who didn't fully appreciate the Paradise of the Proletariat.

When plans for American participation in the exhibition were made public a month earlier, the project was attacked by Congressman Charles A. Vanek of Ohio from the floor of the House of Representatives. "This is a most shocking, unconscionable action in which American businesses are deeply involved," said Vanek. "For the sake of sales and profits, a group of American businessmen will be placing their wares on sale in Moscow for examination by the KGB." Senator Henry Jackson of Washington termed the affair "an outrage," and publicized it during a national television interview.

Spurred by congressional and public pressure, the Department of Commerce announced it was extending existing rules to require export licenses for the sale to the Soviet Union and other Communist countries of "any instruments and equipment particularly useful in crime control and detection." Also in response to the adverse publicity, most of the estimated thirty American companies planning to exhibit in Moscow withdrew from the show. Only two American firms participated: Infinetics, Inc., the maker of magnetic airport screening devices, and Search Products, Inc., which sold a mobile crime laboratory to the Soviet Ministry of Internal Affairs at a price of $28,000. However, other American-made police equipment was brought to the Moscow exhibit by Western European dealers.

Congressional sensitivity to the sale of American police gear to the KGB has not always been matched by concern over the massive exporting of the same kind of equipment to the oppressive governments of "friendly" countries. In fact, the State Department's Agency for International Development, through its Office of Public Safety, *gave away* hundreds of millions of dollars of police equipment to such regimes between 1961 and 1975. By making presents to the local police of tear gas, pistols, shotguns, gas masks, walkie-talkies, patrol cars, computers, and other hardware, AID hoped to counter Communist insurgency in countries like South Korea, Brazil, Uruguay, and Chile. For the most part, however, the American largesse was used instead to facilitate the murder, torture, rape, and enslavement of the local citizenry. After some especially unsavory examples of these results became public in 1974, Senator James Abourezk of South Dakota succeeded in writing into law a prohibition against "the use of foreign assistance funds to provide training, advice, or financial support for police, prison, or other law enforcement forces of a foreign country."*

The hardware merchants have not abandoned the foreign police market, however. For example, Rockwell International recently tried to fill an order from the military junta currently in control of Chile for a $5-

---

* The legislation resulted in closing down AID's Office of Public Safety, which no longer had a function. Lauren Goin, the director of the Office, made a quick transition to the Private Sector and formed Public Safety Services, Inc., a consulting firm which provides police expertise to foreign governments.

million fingerprint identification system. According to Rockwell officials, the Chilean Ministry of Defense intended to use the system for "crime detection," failing to add that the list of acts currently considered crimes by the generals who recently overthrew the legally elected government includes speaking against the military regime, or even possessing banned books. Chilean citizens are now routinely fingerprinted for the identification cards they are required to carry, and the Rockwell system would provide the junta with a powerful electronic tool for keeping track of potential dissidents who had not yet been thrown into the prisons and torture chambers. Fortunately, the State Department denied Rockwell an export license for the fingerprint system.

One of the most powerful police weapons manages to evade export controls by going abroad in disguise. Computers ostensibly ordered for innocuous administrative or commercial tasks are actually employed in police intelligence systems. For example, American-built computers are used to form a police intelligence network in Latin America for the exchange of political dossiers among the dictatorships of Chile, Argentina, Brazil, and Uruguay. South Africa's apartheid government uses American computers to keep track of dissident blacks. For the American companies that peddle these electronic shackles to the dictators, it's a matter of "see no evil."

IBM is a major offender. When interviewed on the subject by a computer industry journal, a company spokesman offered this bit of sophistry: "We are in a position similar to a car manufacturer. If General Motors sells you a car, and you use it to kill someone, that doesn't make General Motors responsible. Once the manufacturer sells the automobile, there's no guarantee it won't be used to commit a crime."

To anyone with a background in computer technology, this alibi is transparent nonsense. The simple fact is that, in order to make any computer installation work at all, the purchaser or renter of the equipment requires the service of a team of technicians, systems engineers, and programmers. Even in the United States it is almost a universal practice of IBM customers to obtain these so-called "customer engineering" services from IBM. In countries such as Chile, Brazil, or Argentina, IBM personnel are almost continually on hand to service the company's computers. It would be impossible for the IBM customer engineers to be ignorant of any major task to which the computer was being put. And, of course, were IBM to withdraw its people from the computer installation, the operation would soon grind to a complete halt.

Unfortunately, IBM is not the only American computer manufacturer guilty of turning a blind eye to the acts of foreign governments that use its equipment to abuse human rights. In fact, only one computer maker, the Control Data Corporation, has a corporate policy of refusing to provide computers to be used for such purposes. In Congress, Senator Edward Kennedy of Massachusetts has raised the question of tighter controls on the export of computers, but there is little prospect of legislation in the near future.

There are few controls on any part of the police and security equipment industry, partly because the whole subject seems as remote from our everyday lives as nonlethal weapons in Belfast or police computers in Buenos Aires. But in fact security gear abounds almost everywhere we look; we don't see it because it arrived so inconspicuously over the last two decades that it's virtually invisible. Nonetheless, security and police gear touches and influences our lives daily. Consider a typical day in the life of a hypothetical businessman.

As he leaves for the office in the morning, his wife closes the front door behind him, turning the dead bolt and fastening the chain; both pieces of hardware were recently installed following reports of prowlers in the neighborhood. Recalling this, plus the fact that he is going on an overnight business trip this evening, he makes a mental note to investigate the residential burglar alarm he saw advertised on television the night before.

On the way to the office, he stops at the local bank to buy some traveler's checks. Total time in line and at the teller's window is twelve minutes; his picture is taken twenty-four times by each of the two time-lapse surveillance cameras mounted high on the wall behind the tellers.

Putting his car in the company parking lot, he approaches the rear entrance to the office building where he works. There is no guard or receptionist on duty, so he gains admittance by inserting a magnetically coded identification card in a slot and pressing several numbered buttons in a coded sequence. As he opens the door, the security guard in the front lobby sees him on a closed-circuit television monitor and recognizes him as a company employee.

At lunchtime he drives to a local shopping center and enters a tobacco shop. A one-way turnstile immediately inside the door insures that he will have to leave by a different door, one near the check-out counter where the cashier can watch for customers leaving with merchandise. Beyond the turnstile, he steps on an annunciator mat, causing a chime to ring softly in the front of the store. As he walks among the aisles, he is temporarily hidden from direct view of the cashier by stacks of cartons, but a system of convex detection mirrors gives a clerk a "fisheye" view of him.

Next to the tobacconist is a department store, which he enters in order to buy some extra shirts for his trip. He walks through the store and a security guard in the basement watches impassively as he appears on a succession of closed-circuit television monitors. He pays for his purchase by check, identifying himself with a driver's license bearing his photograph and thumbprint. Nonetheless, the cashier takes a picture of him and his check with a special camera standing on the counter.

Later that day he's tied up in a meeting well past the time he should leave to catch his flight. On the way to the airport, he knows he was speeding when the policeman parked beside the highway flags him down, but he wonders how the officer could tell; he didn't see a second car with the telltale radar dish. The policeman shows him the new gadget that caught him—a hand-held radar gun with a digital readout.

He produces his driver's license and auto registration, and the trooper takes the documents back to his car and calls in to his dispatcher. The information is entered into a terminal of the computerized National Crime Information Center. His name is checked against the wanted persons file to see if there is an outstanding arrest warrant for him, and his registration is checked against the license plate and vehicle files to make sure it isn't stolen. A computer 200 miles away in the state capital gives him a clean bill of health, the trooper gives him a warning and returns his documents, and he is again on his way to the airport.

He just barely makes his flight, first passing through the metal detector and handing in his suitcase to be x-rayed. On the flight, the restroom seems to be occupied every time he tries to enter it, so on arriving at his destination he goes directly to the restroom in the airport. Fortunately he has a dime to get into the stall; the airport management found that coin locks reduce vandalism and help defray the maintenance costs.

He checks into a motel and, after dinner, settles down for an evening of watching television on the color set in the room. After the late news he can't find the right button to push on the unfamiliar set to turn it off. Finally, in desperation, he pulls the plug from the wall socket, turns off the light, and goes to bed. A few minutes later there is a knock on the door. The TVs must not be unplugged by the guests, the security guard tells him. The motel had a lot of expensive sets ripped off, so it installed this alarm system that sounds a buzzer at the front desk if the set is unplugged. The guard replugs the set and shows him how to turn it on and off. After he returns to bed, he is a long time getting to sleep; high-intensity lighting turns the parking lot outside into high noon, and enough of the light seeps past the window drapes to keep him awake well into the early morning hours of tomorrow.

As he drifts into slumberland, our businessman might well reflect on the events of the day. He was photographed by his bank, televised by his employer, spied on by the local merchants, radared and computered by the cops, scanned and x-rayed by the FAA, and tattled on by a television set. He was photographed more times in a single day than his grandfather was in a lifetime, and he has appeared on television screens more often than the average talk show guest in a year.

He isn't likely to think twice about any of this, however, because none of it is particularly remarkable. The police and security gear he keeps running up against during his daily routine has come upon the scene so gradually that he may be only dimly aware that almost none of it was around twenty years ago. If these gadgets infringe on his privacy and freedom, perhaps he has no objection. After all, even he is a customer for locks and burglar alarms, so he might understand the imperatives of a society under siege. No one can say for sure, however; when the shopkeepers bought their hidden cameras, when the police procured their radar and night viewing devices, when the airlines installed their x-ray machines, he was not consulted.

Someday in the future it all may become too confining for him. Maybe some new gadget he finds poking into his privacy will be the last straw. Or perhaps it will be something small, like that turnstile in the tobacco store that dictates which door he may use. But whatever it is that finally gets to him, if he goes a little crazy and starts smashing things, there'll be a full record of the incident on videotape for use by the court. And if instead he joins with others to picket the shopkeepers or demonstrate against the police, he may find out all about the Cold Brine Projectors, the Plastic Confetti, and the Photic Driver.

10

Breaking and Entering

The Watergate burglaries have been driving the police crazy. No, not the 1972 break-ins at the Democratic National Headquarters; the police walked in on the second of those and caught the five CIA-trained burglars in the act. What's confounding the cops is the string of unsolved burglaries in the plush Watergate condominium complex right next door to the scene of the historic caper. The first apartment was hit in May 1974. During the following twenty-six months, thirty-nine more were entered, and some $200,000 in jewelry, silverware, cash, and other valuables was taken.

The historic Watergate break-in was led by James McCord, a former senior official and technical expert in the CIA's Office of Security. The four Cubans he led had also carried out covert missions for the CIA, and one was a professional locksmith. Yet despite all their expertise, they were easily detected by an alert security guard and caught by the metropolitan Washington, D.C., police. By contrast, the apartment burglar seems like the Invisible Man. In fact, the cops have nicknamed him (or her) "The Watergate Phantom."

A visit to the Watergate apartment buildings makes it easy to see how the burglar earned his title; the complex is one of the most security-conscious in the District of Columbia. All visitors must come to the front entrance where they are met by a desk clerk, who calls the tenant and announces them by name. All other entrances to the building are kept locked—tenants have keys—and are under twenty-four-hour surveillance with closed-circuit television cameras.

The apartment doors are secured with deadbolt locks. An FBI expert called in to examine the locks on the burgled apartments discovered something that made matters even more interesting: the locks had not been picked. The police theorized the Phantom has a master key that will open any of the Watergate doors. The apartment management says that can't be. True, they say, the locks were initially set for a master key system when the building was first built, but all master keys were later destroyed, and most of the locks have since been changed. If that's so, then the cops really have a mystery on their hands: it seems they're looking for someone who can crawl through a keyhole or slip himself under a door.

Locks, safes, vaults, and burglar alarms are among the most traditional paraphernalia of the Private Sector. Locks date back to ancient Greece. They were throughly commonplace in the mid-nineteenth century when American locksmith Alfred Hobbs challenged his English colleagues with the boast that he could pick the best of their products, but no English locksmith could defeat a Hobbs-built lock. He made good on both claims. Such contests of ingenuity advanced the art of locksmithing, even as competition between electronic eavesdroppers and countermeasures technicians elaborated audio surveillance techniques a hundred years later. Edwin Holmes, who invented the first electric burglar alarm in 1853, put it this way: "The whole history of bank burglary and vault building is competitive; and in the same manner that a new system is devised to protect armor plate, so the burglar finds or devises a new method of attack."

Defeating locks and burglar alarms has since developed into a highly specialized craft practiced by a small, elite group of specialists. When done for profit by an individual entrepreneur like the Watergate Phantom, it's called burglary; when practiced by government employees, it is referred to, in the wonderful euphemistic language of bureaucracy, as "surreptitious entry." Government picklocks and cracksmen learn their craft in federally operated burglary schools. Some who migrate to the

Private Sector on retirement apply their knowledge to designing defensive measures for their clients. A few have been known to use their skills for the occasional illegal entry into a business office or a political campaign headquarters. Those who turn to illegal bugging often employ burglary techniques to conceal hidden microtransmitters in their victim's premises. However, most simply retire their burglary tools and eschew doors to which they hold no keys.

Colonel James Valentine (USAF, Retired)* is a former surreptitious entry expert. I asked for his professional guess about the Watergate Phantom's *modus operandi*.

"If there really is no master key in existence," Colonel Valentine said, "then my guess is your Phantom has impressioned his own set of keys."

"Impressioning" is the technique of making a duplicate key, generally from a wax or clay impression of the original. In the case of the Phantom, I couldn't see how he could get access to all those original keys. I said as much to Colonel Valentine.

"You don't need the original key to make the impression," he replied. We were sitting in his office at the private security firm where he works. He selected a blank key from a supply hanging on hooks on the wall behind his desk.

"Observe," said Valentine. "This blank is made to fit the kind of lock I have on my office door."

He took a pair of pliers from a black leather case and grasped the blank with them. Then he flicked a large Zippo lighter to life and held the key blank over its billowing yellow flame. After a few seconds the key was covered by a thin layer of black soot. Still holding the blank with the pliers, he went over to his office door, opened it, and inserted the blank into the lock. He twisted it back and forth several times, but it didn't turn. Withdrawing it, he held it up for me to see.

"See those bright spots?" he asked.

Bright brass showed through the carbon at several points along the

---

* "Colonel James Valentine" is a pseudonym for a man who has served as an entry expert for both civilian and military investigative agencies. I have no knowledge that "Colonel Valentine" has ever carried out any break-ins within the United States of America or any of its territories or possessions.

edge of the blank. ''That's where the tumblers rubbed off the soot.'' He took a small rat-tail file from his case and proceeded to rub it against the blank at each of the bright spots. Next, he blackened the key blank with his lighter again, then reinserted it in the lock. When he withdrew it, the brass spots had reappeared. He filed them again.

Colonel Valentine repeated this process about a dozen times, whistling silently to himself, as he worked. I had just about lost patience with the demonstration when he gave a grunt of satisfaction and turned toward me with raised eyebrows. He was turning the key back and forth in the lock. The deadbolt was sliding in and out of the door.

''Voila,'' said Valentine, ''the Phantom strikes again.''

''Impressive,'' I remarked, ''but wouldn't the Phantom make himself conspicuous by spending so much time lurking in apartment doorways with his file and cigarette lighter?''

''That's not how it's done,'' Valentine replied. ''Our man fits the blank to the lock as he happens past the door; the carbonizing and filing take place offstage. It may take ten or fifteen trips spread out over two or three weeks, but from what you tell me of the loot that's missing, it's worth the trouble. The Phantom may be a Watergate tenant himself; with what he's collecting tax-free, he could certainly afford it. And that would make it much easier for him to be often seen in the hallways without arousing suspicion.

''Also, if the Phantom really knows his locks, he may be able to impression a master key that will open any of the apartments that are still on the original master system. But he'd have to be pretty good to do that—as good as me.''

Few picklocks are as good as Jimmy Valentine. His deft fingers and powers of concentration could be the envy of a concert violinist, and, like a musical virtuoso, he nurtures his skill through daily practice. His training ground is a table-top array of locks, each mounted in a miniature door, hinged to swing closed in a scaled-down doorjamb. The collection spans the full range of pick resistance, from the simple to the nearly impossible.

The easiest lock to open is the spring-latch variety, Valentine explains. It often takes the form of a key-in-the-doorknob arrangement. A tapered, spring-loaded latch slides into the lock as the door is closing then snaps back into the recess—it's called a "mortise"—in the door-jamb when the door is fully shut. The lock is popular with users because it saves them the trouble of using a key when they leave their house or apartment; it's popular with apartment house owners because it's cheap; and it's popular with burglars because it requires almost no skill to open. The spring latch yields to a simple tool called a "loid" (probably after celluloid, the material out of which it is commonly made). The loid is simply a strip of plastic or celluloid that can be inserted between the door and the doorjamb and used to slide the spring latch back into the lock, thus opening the door. Plastic credit cards are popular among burglars for use as loids. Colonel Valentine disdained to demonstrate such an elementary technique as loiding a spring latch, and declared that, when encountering such a lock, he preferred to pick it and so spare his credit cards as well as his self-respect.

Having raised the subject of lockpicking, which, of course, is his favorite, Colonel Valentine directed our attention to a wall poster showing a cutaway view of a standard pin-tumbler cylinder lock. The same drawing is contained in most encyclopedias, and I have often enjoyed contemplating the ingenuity of Linus Yale, Jr., the obscure portrait painter who invented this type of lock in the 1860s. Nonetheless, I listened carefully to Colonel Valentine's disquisition on the functioning of the cylinder lock, for I knew it was a preamble to his explanation of how it can be made to misfunction.

The heart of the lock, Colonel Valentine explained, is the cylinder, which, when turned, moves the deadbolt to lock or unlock the door. The cylinder is normally kept from turning by a series (usually five) of metal pins of differing lengths which protrude from the body of the lock into the cylinder. Each pin is actually two separate pins end to end; the two are pressed together and held in the cylinder by a spring. Inserting the proper key into the cylinder forces each pin pair upwards to the point where the lower pin is entirely within the cylinder, and the upper pin is entirely within the lock body. The cylinder is then free to turn and move the bolt. Lockpicking, Valentine explained, consists simply of accomplishing the same result without a key.

You may have read of fictional picklocks who use such homely artifacts as a straightened hairpin or a paperclip. It is possible to open a lock with such gear, Valentine allows, but he advises anyone inclined to try it to bring along a box lunch, because it will take all day (or night). He withdrew a zippered leather wallet about the size of an eyeglass case from his jacket pocket, and opened it. The wallet was crowded with instruments vaguely reminiscent of what one sees on the circular shelf next to a dentist's chair. This, said Valentine, was professional lock-picking equipment.

A few dozen of the tools were variations on a single basic theme: a flat metal strip of the general shape and dimensions of a small nail file, with a narrow, tapering tail about two inches long. Each tail had a differently shaped tip; some terminated in a slight curve, others in a zigzag or "S" curve, and others in one or more tiny knobs. These, Valentine explained, were picks, and they were made to be inserted into a keyhole—the technical term is "keyway"—and used to push up each of the pin tumblers to the point where the cylinder is free to turn. Each was designed for a particular situation, and a master picklock selects a pick as thoughtfully as a champion golfer calls for an iron.

The other instruments in Valentine's leather case were tension wrenches—small metal rods, each bent at one end into an "L" shape. Selecting a pick and a wrench, Valentine demonstrated the fine art of lockpicking.

He first inserted the short end of the tension wrench into the keyway of one of his practice locks and pressed a finger against the tip of the long end; this had the effect, he explained, of exerting about the same degree of twisting pressure on the lock's cylinder as the turning of a key. With his other hand he inserted the pick in the keyway, above the tension wrench. (Despite what we see on television, lock picking is a two-handed job.) The hand holding the pick moved almost imperceptibly. After no more than thirty seconds he moved the tension wrench through a full circle, turning the cylinder and opening the lock. The lock was a high-quality, deadbolt device, probably superior to what can be found on the average front door. Valentine had picked it in less time than it usually takes me to find my key.

Valentine then proceeded to demonstrate an even faster way of opening the lock, using a technique known as "raking." Again he inserted the pick and the tension wrench in the keyway, but this time he quickly withdrew the pick, repeating the action several times, and making a faint scraping sound as the instrument encountered the pins. After raking the keyway five or six times in about as many seconds, Valentine again turned the tension wrench and opened the lock. Raking, he explained, is faster and easier than picking, and a preferable technique when a little noise can be tolerated.

Colonel Valentine made the whole business look easy, but when I tried my hand at the pick and tension wrench, the lock stubbornly refused to yield; it seems it takes a lot of practice to develop the right touch. I was a little more successful with the automatic pick, a gun-like device with a thin, straight pick attached. One simply inserts it into the lock and pulls the trigger. It took me several tries, but I succeeded in opening the lock. The big drawback of the automatic pick is that it's really noisy. And Valentine assures me that there are some difficult locks which can only be defeated through the old-fashioned pick and tension wrench technique.

"Is there a lock that can't be picked at all," I asked.

"Show-offs like me are fond of saying there's no such thing as a pick-proof lock," Valentine replied. "In theory, that's probably true. But whenever I hear someone say it, I ask if they're prepared to bet money I can't show them a lock they can't pick. I've never gotten any takers."

"If you did, what lock would you show them?"

"Oh, there are several that I'd hate to run into in a true surreptitious entry. There's one called the Illinois Duo that has three sets of pins, instead of only one. There's no way to rake the thing, so you have to pick fourteen separate pins. Five are in the top of the keyway, five in the bottom, and four in the side. You have to be a contortionist to move the pick around the tension wrench. If you can pick it at all, it'll take you all night.

"Then there's the Miracle Magnetic. The pins aren't moved by the mechanical action of the key; they're magnetized and set to respond to a special magnetic coding in the key. It may be possible to defeat it, but not with the good old pick and tension wrench.

"And the Medico lock is guaranteed to drive you nuts. It's another one you're not going to open with a pick and wrench. And there are a few others that will also give you real trouble. They may not, strictly speaking, be 'pick-proof,' but if you have one of those locks on your front door, and you come home to find someone has picked it . . . well, at least you have the distinction of having been robbed by an aristocrat among burglars.''

A dubious consolation, but one that few professional writers such as myself are likely to need. The aristocracy of burglars won't waste their talents on the modest digs of a freelance scribbler; the elite among picklocks visit only the homes of the wealthy. In fact, the curious thing about such high-class thievery is that both victim and criminal are likely to belong to the same economic level.

Such top-notch burglars rarely get caught. Lock-picking is only part of the complex of skills they bring to their work; careful planning is essential to keeping out of trouble. For example, the professional will employ a number of tricks to insure the premises he's going to enter are unoccupied and likely to remain so while he carries out his task. After opening the lock, he will insert a small obstacle, such as a pin, in the keyway, so that a key cannot be inserted, then lock the door from the inside. If the tenant returns unexpectedly, he won't be able to walk in on the burglar, and his fumbling with the key will alert the intruder to the unforeseen development. When the tenant finally goes off in search of a maintenance man to open the door, the burglar will make good his getaway. Aristocratic thieves almost never resort to violence.

High-class ''burglars'' limit their take to small, very valuable items, disdaining such things as color television sets or stereos. In their search for jewelry, cash, and negotiable stock certificates, they try to avoid leaving any indication that they have been on the premises. Some go as far as to photograph areas of a home with a polaroid camera before searching, so they can put things back in place exactly as they found them. Such precautions can pay important dividends; the thief may be sipping vintage wines and sunning himself on the Riviera for several days before his victim is even aware he's been robbed.

Two such jewel thieves were caught recently, but only through the exceptional efforts of a Florida police detective. Sgt. Thomas Blake of the Dade County police had developed a mild obsession with a pair of burglars who specialized in luxury high-rise apartments in Florida and elsewhere on the East Coast. Often posing as prospective tenants, they would visit an apartment house to case it and inquire about the security arrangements. Later they would return to burgle the buildings. Sgt. Blake used his vacations and days off to drive as far north as Washington, D.C., and interview apartment managers and rental agents who might have come in contact with the duo. Also at his own expense, he distributed wanted flyers instructing those who thought they saw the pair to contact him. After a year his efforts paid off.

Sgt. Blake received a report that two men fitting the thieves' descriptions had checked into a motel in Fairfax County, Virginia, a Washington, D.C., suburb. Blake alerted the Fairfax police, who rented the room next door to the pair and set up an observation post. The next day they trailed them to a luxury high-rise building in the Maryland suburbs and watched in amazement as the two, dressed in tennis whites, sauntered past security guards and entered apartments with such speed and ease that the casual onlooker would never doubt they were using keys.

The next day the police followed the two as they paid a similar visit to another plush apartment house in northern Virginia. As the pair left the building, this time dressed in expensive business suits, the cops moved in and arrested them. The police searched the suspects and found them to be carrying $2500 worth of stolen jewelry and an assortment of picks, wrenches, and other burglary paraphernalia. In their car, the officers discovered the take from the previous day's break-ins in Maryland: $17,890 in hot jewelry. Down in Dade County, Florida, Sgt. Blake alternated between elation and dismay. His year-long hunt had come to an end, but he wasn't there to take part. Blake had seriously considered flying up to Washington at his own expense, but abandoned the idea when his wife pointed out what it would do to the family budget. Unlike the pair of *bon vivants* he helped catch, Blake has to live on the salary of a police sergeant.

Apart from relentless, hard-working cops like Sgt. Blake, the elite burglar's major nemesis is the intrusion alarm system. While most jewel thieves who confine themselves to private homes aren't likely to get caught this way, the burglar who specializes in bank vaults, strongrooms, and other commercial establishments where millions in cash and merchandise are held, must take special pains to avoid tripping a silent alarm system that will summon the police. But the potential payoff from such burglaries is so great that a new kind of criminal specialty has developed: the electronic burglar.

The burglar who specializes in defeating intrusion alarm systems plays for much higher stakes than the picklock who restricts himself to premises not guarded by burglar alarms. A picklock who fails in his task simply doesn't get inside, but the electronic burglar outsmarted by an ingenious alarm system stands a good chance of getting caught in the act. And there are a wide variety of traps set to catch a second-story man who gets careless.

The simplest and cheapest intrusion detection system consists of magnetic switches that register when a door or window is opened, or when someone steps on a specially constructed floor mat. Metal foil attached to the inside of the glass will signal if a window is broken. These systems are most often used in private residences and are not really intended as protection against the elite burglar.

Banks and strongrooms may employ similar devices to register whenever the vault is opened, but generally more sophisticated detectors are used. Since opening or cutting into a vault usually involves some noise and vibration, contact microphones are commonly installed inside. Vibration or pressure sensors can also be installed in the floor and set to go off if someone walks across it. Two electrical engineers recently patented a device for use with such an alarm system; it can discriminate between human footsteps and other vibrations, thus reducing the chance of false alarms.

Movie burglars are often shown frustrating footstep sensors by lowering themselves within reach of the loot on a rope suspended from the ceiling. In real life, however, such acrobatics would likely attract an audience of police officers, if the premises were also protected by any of several motion detection devices that are gaining increasing popularity in burglar alarm systems. Ultrasonic waves or microwaves are projected from a transmitter in the wall or ceiling and completely fill the room. Any motion produces frequency changes that trigger the alarm.

Moviegoers and television viewers are also familiar with photoelectric beam systems, set to go off if the intruder breaks a beam of visible or infrared light. The sensitivity and effectiveness of these systems has been increased through the use of lasers. A new motion-sensitive device attaches to a chain-link fence and will trigger an alarm if someone begins to climb it anywhere along its length. And a robot-like instrument, which is wired into a closed-circuit television system, frees the security guard from the need to sit glued to the monitor screen; if anything moves within the camera's view, the device sounds the alarm.

In the face of such technological obstacles, the electronic burglar's job may seem impossible. But the recent record of break-ins at premises guarded by sophisticated burglar alarm systems reveals that they are far from infallible.

The Henry Kay Jewelers on Michigan Avenue in Chicago was protected by what police called "a sophisticated alarm system." But burglars used electronic means to neutralize the alarm in January 1977, and made off with three suitcases of quality watches, diamond rings, gold bracelets, necklaces, pendants, and lighters. Value of the loot: $500,000.

The offices of the SRS Jewelry Casting Corporation in mid-Manhattan was considered physically impregnable. Additionally, the SRS vault had a special intrusion detection system: an electric blower continuously pumped air into the vault, keeping the pressure inside slightly higher than the surrounding office space. If the vault was opened or penetrated in any abnormal way, the slight drop in pressure would trigger the burglar alarm. Yet in July 1974 burglars defeated the alarm system and made off with $600,000 in gold. Three days earlier the same electronic burglary team bypassed the alarm system of the L and S Plate and Wire Corporation in Queens, New York, and took $508,000 in gold from the vault.

In 1968, a team of sophisticated burglars neutralized the burglar alarm in the Forest Hills, New York, branch of the Manufacturer's Hanover Trust one weekend in March. Proceeds from the two-day job: an estimated $4.5 million, including the contents of hundreds of safe deposit boxes. In October 1974, electronic burglars bypassed the alarm on the vault of the Purolator Security Inc.'s vault in Chicago and got away with $4.3 million. And the all-time record haul was made in July 1976 in Nice, France, by a gang of burglars who tunneled into a bank from a nearby sewer, defeated the alarm system, and made off with an estimated $8 to $10 million from 300 safe deposit boxes. In view of the ease with which the electronic burglars pulled off these capers, it's not surprising that a San Francisco jeweler now uses a tarantula to guard his display cases, or that a gold coin collection on display at a New York jewelry trade show in 1976 was submerged on the bottom of a fish tank containing a school of flesh-eating piranhas.

The electronic burglars who racked up this list of successful jobs did not resort to magic to overcome the sophisticated alarm systems. They all approached the problem of getting inside undetected in basically the same way: they attacked the alarm system at its most vulnerable point. The motion detectors, the sound detectors, the footstep detectors, and the other sensing devices are virtually invulnerable; a burglar who tried to sneak inside and disable them would be detected before he could get near them. The sensing devices are linked to a control box, also generally inside the protected area and safe from attack. But beyond the control box the system is exposed, and it is there that the electronic burglar goes to work.

Alarm systems are either local or remote. A local system simply sets off a loud bell or siren when it's tripped, supposedly to attract the attention of neighbors or passersby. But in a time when it's possible to be mugged or murdered in broad daylight on a public street while passersby discreetly avert their eyes, the businessman or banker holding a fortune in his vault cannot rely on the willingness of someone to ''get involved'' and telephone the police. Therefore, he opts for a remote system, which silently summons the police or private guards from a central station some distance away.

The remote burglar alarm system was invented by Edwin Holmes, who used a telegraph-like arrangement to connect banks, jewelry stores, and the home of an occasional millionaire to central guard stations in Boston and New York City in 1858. The Holmes Electric Protection Company (which is still doing business 119 years later) erected its own poles, over which it strung insulated wire of its own manufacture. When the first commercial telephone exchange was installed in New York City in 1877, Holmes switched to this new medium to link his clients with his central stations. Telephone lines are still used for this purpose, and they comprise the weakest link in the remote alarm system. They are the prime target for the electronic burglar. The Forest Hills bank job is a good illustration of how it's done.

Although the burglary of the Manufacturer's Hanover Trust branch in Forest Hills took place on a quiet Sunday morning in March 1968, planning for the job began over two years earlier. The superintendent of an apartment house a few blocks from the bank received a telephone inquiry regarding a certain apartment on the second floor of his building. The flat would be ideal for his mother, the caller said. The superintendent told him the apartment was occupied, with no immediate prospect of being vacated, but suggested the caller leave a number where he could be contacted if things changed. The caller replied that he was usually out of town on business, and promised to call the superintendent regularly to check on the apartment's availability. True to his word, the man called every month for more than two years. In January 1968, the apartment was finally vacated; the man signed the lease and moved in. The new tenant's furnishings included what the FBI was later to call "a portable electronics laboratory."

The attraction of the second-floor apartment had nothing to do with the preferences of the renter's mother; it consisted of a telephone cable that ran beneath the kitchen window. The new tenant and a few of his friends had determined that the Manufacturer's Hanover alarm system was linked to its central station by way of this cable. Exactly how they learned this is unknown, but investigators familiar with the *modus operandi* of the electronics burglar can make some pretty reasonable guesses.

The gang may have paid a nocturnal visit to the bank building when they first cased the job two years earlier. By picking a lock or impressioning a key, they could have gained entry to the bank building (while most banks install intrusion detection sensors within their vaults, few blanket the entire building with such instruments). Once inside, they would have been free to search for the telephone terminal box, where the control unit of the vault alarm system was linked to the telephone lines. Alternatively, one of the gang may have posed as a telephone repairman, and climbed a pole to a junction box where he located the cable and pair for the alarm system. In either case, the job may have been unwittingly simplified by the telephone company, which routinely flags the alarm lines with red insulating sleeves to guard against the possibility of a repairman's triggering a false alarm by accidentally breaking or shorting them.

Many residential burglar alarm systems use automatic dialing devices to call the police or alarm service with a recorded message when the system is triggered. These can be circumvented through the simple expedient of cutting the telephone line before breaking in. Commercial alarm systems are in continuous, around-the-clock connection with the central station over telephone circuits that are dedicated to the task. Breaking or tampering with the line will, in itself, cause an alarm to sound in the central station.

One of the burglars may have triggered the alarm when he carefully selected the pair of wires among the hundreds twisted within the cable beneath the window and gingerly patched them to the electronic rig he had assembled in his kitchen. If so, it probably aroused little suspicion, since false alarms are commonplace events. It is an elementary principle of the design of burglar alarm systems that anything done to make them more sensitive to the presence of an intruder also tends to make them more prone to accidental triggering.

Air-conditioning units, ringing telephones, and other noises have been known to trigger ultrasonic motion detectors. Crowds of people walking in the street outside can set off microwave sensors. And fog, seeping into a building through an open window, can obscure the light beam in a photoelectric system exactly as would the shadow of an intruder. A severe thunderstorm passing over a city can set off burglar alarms all over town. In Beverly Hills, California, where the remote alarms are signaled to the police rather than to a private alarm service, an average of seven to ten alarms is received every day, and 98 percent of them prove to be false. Police departments in other parts of the country report similar statistics. Given these circumstances, our electronic burglar can afford to trigger a few "false alarms" on purpose in order to study the system and observe how long it takes the police or private guards to respond, without risk of arousing suspicion.

Once our burglar has successfully tapped into the alarm line, he can observe at his leisure voltage variations and other kinds of electrical activity taking place over a twenty-four-hour period. The central station will periodically check the line by sending a signal over it; equipment in the bank's alarm system must respond with a characteristic reply. Our electronic burglar observes all this on his meters and scopes.

For the Forest Hills Gang, D-Day was 2:00 A.M. Sunday morning. In the kitchen of the second-floor apartment, the alarm specialist connected a specially built "black box" to the telephone line; the device was designed to imitate the electrical characteristics of the alarm system control unit in the bank. Next, he severed the line, disconnecting the bank's alarm system from the central station. Miles away, in the central station, there was no indication that anything unusual had happened. The burglars were now free to enter the bank and open the vault with impunity.

The alarm man stayed in the apartment while the rest of the gang entered the bank. The technician monitored his black box and prepared to simulate a response to any test signals sent from the central station. He also tuned a special radio receiver to the local police channel; if somehow his accomplices were discovered, he'd hear the police dispatcher order a squad car to the bank to investigate reports of "a burglary in progress." A pair of walkie-talkies kept him in contact with the team in the bank in case that happened.

Inside the bank, the gang set to work getting inside the vault. The day of the cracksman with sandpapered fingertips and stethoscope who opens combination locks through sheer finesse is, alas, gone. Some older vaults are still susceptible to this approach, but those installed since 1965 respond only to brute force delivered in massive amounts. Today's bank burglar simply brings along whatever equipment is necessary to cut a hole in the wall of the vault. This may include drills, chisels, sledge hammers, hydraulic jacks, tanks of compressed oxygen and acetylene gas, and perhaps a supply of burning bars.

The burning bar, or as it is called in Europe where it originated, the thermic lance, is a long steel tube containing a dozen or so ferrous alloy rods. Pure oxygen is pumped into one end of the tube, and the other end is ignited with an acetylene torch. The burning alloys produce little smoke, but temperatures as high as 10,000°F. can be achieved. The burning bar can boil away the steel wall of a safe, or melt the reinforced concrete of a bank vault. Whatever the Forest Hills burglars used to cut the three-foot hole in the side of the vault, they came prepared. They left behind a small vial of nitroglycerine, presumably to be used on the vault if all else failed. Fortunately that last resort was unnecessary; police estimate the quantity of nitro found in the bank could have demolished the entire block.

As the burglars worked, it began to rain. The tape on the opening they made in the telephone cable beneath their kitchen window started to leak. It gradually soaked through and shorted out some telephone wires. After the telephone company received several complaints, a pair of servicemen were sent to investigate. They quickly discovered the unauthorized patch and the wire running into the second-floor window. As they prepared to climb a ladder to the window, the lookout inside radioed to his accomplices, who were almost finished emptying the vault and its safety deposit boxes. The team left hurriedly, and about the same time the telephone men cut the patch wire from the apartment. Of course, in the central station, the bank alarm went off. But the thieves were gone by the time the police arrived, and the officers, failing to notice the hole in the vault wall, reported the incident as a false alarm. When the burglary was finally discovered on Monday morning, the break-in team, together with $4.5 million, were long gone.

Does the sophisticated burglar alarm, then, serve any purpose besides transforming clever thieves into millionaires? At least, as Colonel Valentine might observe, it keeps out the riff-raff. Most burglars are far less skillful than the Forest Hills Gang, and are closer to the Seat Pleasant, Maryland, man, who, in September 1976, was arrested while pushing a 200-pound safe along the sidewalk in front of his home (the safe had been removed from the rental office of a nearby apartment house with something less than the finesse used by a first-class bank burglar). Central station burglar alarm service is estimated to be a $200-million-per-year industry in the United States, and it may be assumed that the thrifty merchants and bankers who pay most of this tab believe they are getting something worthwhile for their money.

Generally, they get the kind of security they pay for. Underwriters' Laboratories, the nonprofit testing service that has been evaluating everything from toasters to building materials since 1894, has a Burglary

Protection and Signaling Department which tests and certifies alarm systems. Alarm and vault specialists from the UL Burglary Department even conduct no-notice ''break-ins'' at some of the protected premises they've certified, to make sure everything is working as it's supposed to. But meeting UL's tough certification standards is expensive; of the estimated one million alarm systems in the United States, only 75,000 are UL-certified.

Virtual impregnability is there for anyone prepared to pay the price. Two hundred thousand dollars was the bottom line for one of the tightest security systems in the world, recently installed in a new office building in East Hanover, New Jersey. Not a secret installation of the Pentagon, the CIA, or the National Security Agency, the curious X-shaped building is the corporate headquarters of Nabisco, and the bakery company's management went to some extraordinary lengths to keep strange hands out of the corporate cookie jar.

The hub of the Nabisco system is a huge semicircular console within the building, from which a lone Pinkerton's guard orchestrates security as an old-time movie organist might match music to mood on his giant keyboard. Thirteen television monitor screens show critical zones in the building and the surrounding 121-acre tract. Every fifteen seconds the scenes shift, as a different set of cameras is switched into the console. Eleven television cameras in the building scan the four entrances, the computer, payroll, and vault areas, and the service elevators. Four cameras, equipped with night viewing devices, are mounted on the roof, where they can watch the surrounding landscape, even in near-total darkness. Fourteen other cameras, some with low-light-level capability, watch other areas beyond the walls of the office building. Seven of them can be made to pan and zoom by the guard at the central console.

A security status board at the console is shaped in the overall floor plan of the building. Seventy-five light-emitting diodes flash on and off as doors within the building are opened or closed. Unauthorized entries cause an audible signal to alert the guard. A two-way audio system enables the guard to converse with people at various locations both inside and outside. A sensitive audio alarm system listens for the slightest sound in the company's vaults.

Two other Pinkerton's guards patrol the grounds in a jeep. Walkie-talkies keep them in touch with the guard at the console, whom they relieve in a system of one-hour watches.

The 950 white-collar employees who work in the building carry special identification cards. The card carries a full-color photograph of the employee, his signature, and other printed information. It also bears the magnetically encoded dimensions of his right hand, which comprise a unique pattern. To gain entry to the building, the employee inserts his card into the slot of a reader device, which relays the hand dimensions to a central computer. At the same time he places his hand on the surface of the reader device, which automatically measures and compares it to the information on the card. If it matches, the door is automatically unlocked.

Burglarproof, or merely burglar-resistant? Old hands in the business have learned never to say never. Right now some underworld genius may be busy in his workshop trying to crack the magnetic code on one of those ID cards, picked from a passing wallet. A larcenous electronics whiz may be dreaming up ways to fool the television cameras. And a master crime planner may have concluded that the only way to be invisible to those electronic eyes is to look like you belong; a trusted seamstress may already be studying a picture of a Pinkerton's uniform. In the long run, it reduces to a question of what's inside and how badly someone outside wants it.

Love laughs at locksmiths, the poet said.

Especially love of country, Colonel Valentine adds.

But most often love of fine things, the good life, and the joy of beating the system, say the long-gone members of the Forest Hills Gang.

11

Private Eyes and Politicians

On an August night in 1970, three men dressed as telephone company repairmen entered an office building in downtown Indianapolis and rode the elevator to the eighth-floor suite of U.S. Senator Vance Hartke. One of the three, a former air force intelligence agent, picked the lock on the office door and the trio entered. While one man rifled the files in search of lists of campaign contributors, another hunted for Hartke's personal income tax returns, and the third attached a tiny microphone and FM transmitter to the underside of a desk used by one of Hartke's aides.

The break-in at Senator Hartke's offices marked the beginning of a secret five-year campaign of burglary, bugging, wiretapping, and political dirty tricks in the Midwest only recently uncovered by a grand jury probe in Indianapolis. But the operation was not a purely regional affair; before they completed their work, the grand jurors heard sworn testimony linking the spy program to the highest levels of the FBI, the Justice Department, and the Veterans Administration in both the Nixon and Ford administrations. According to indictments handed down in the case, the dirty work was done by a small private detective firm called International Investigators, Inc.

International Investigators was formed in the early 1960s by two former FBI agents, George W. Ryan and George Miller. Ryan and

Miller hired a staff of former agents from the Office of Special Investigations, the air force's counterintelligence department. The company is reported to have carried out some very sensitive work for the Kennedy administration, including the surveillance of Otto Otepka, a State Department security chief who was fired for leaking information to a congressional committee, and the wiretapping of Jimmy Hoffa on orders from Attorney-General Robert Kennedy.

After a few years Ryan and Miller sold the company (Ryan became security manager for Aramco, a consortium of American oil companies in the Middle East), and it subsequently changed hands several times. By 1970, it was nearly defunct and owned by a former air force OSI man who sold it to C. Timothy Wilcox. Wilcox is a pleasant, clean-cut, and articulate young man who once worked as a buyer for an Indianapolis department store. His only experience with security work was a long stint as a burglar alarm salesman. But he was also a Republican precinct committeeman who viewed politics as the key to success, especially in the private detective business.

From the first, Wilcox courted the cops. He realized that it is almost impossible to do effective private investigative work without the cooperation of the local police, and that it is frequently useful if they can be relied upon to look the other way. Wilcox didn't waste his time ingratiating himself with the cop on the beat; he went straight to the top, which, at the time, was a police chief who answered to the distinguished moniker of Winston Churchill.

Churchill was police chief in the administration of Indianapolis mayor Richard Lugar, whom President Nixon once described as his "favorite mayor." Wilcox may have approached Churchill through a local Republican party contact, such as GOP National Committeeman L. Keith Bulen, whom Wilcox listed as a character reference in his application for a private detective agency license. However he made the contact, Wilcox chose an opportune moment to knock on Churchill's door.

Chief Churchill suspected one of his police lieutenants of taking bribes from a local madam and dealing in drugs. He had assigned two of his officers to watch the suspect. For three months the detectives had videotaped the cop and the madam through a telephoto lens, but they failed to obtain evidence to prove the chief's suspicions. Churchill decided he would get better results if he used an investigator who did not work for the police department, so he chose Wilcox for the job.

A short time after Churchill assigned International Investigators to the case, a neighbor who lived in the same apartment house as the suspect policeman noticed a man dressed as a phone company repairman working on a telephone terminal box in the building. The neighbor, who happened to be an employee of Indiana Bell, noticed a few things about the "repairman" that didn't seem genuine, so he asked to see some identification. When the man couldn't produce any phone company credentials, the neighbor called the police.

A state trooper arrived and questioned the "repairman," who identified himself to the officer as C. Timothy Wilcox. He flashed his private detective's license and told the trooper he was working for the Indianapolis police chief. The trooper confirmed this with a telephone call to Chief Churchill and turned Wilcox loose.

The next step in the surveillance consisted of breaking into the police lieutenant's apartment, searching it, and planting a concealed bug. According to several former employees of International Investigators, Wilcox headed the three-man entry team, which included a former air force lock-picking specialist who had taught courses in surreptitious entry to students from the FBI, the CIA, and Army Intelligence.

The surveillance of the suspected cop by International Investigators continued for three months, but apparently the results were not sufficient to prove Chief Churchill's suspicions, for no action was taken against the officer at that time. International was paid $450 for the job, which may seem an extravagant fee to charge for coming up with nothing, but was actually a bargain-basement price for the risks Wilcox and his people took. The break-in, bugging, and wiretapping were done without warrants (in fact, Indiana law prohibits anyone but a federal agent from conducting electronic surveillance under any circumstances), and left the International team open to prosecution on several federal and state charges. To Wilcox, the value of good relations with the Indianapolis police outweighed any prospect of financial reward for the job.

Wilcox continued to cultivate senior police officials whenever he could. He checked their offices and telephones for bugs and wiretaps. When International's offices were located near a pawnshop run by a suspected fence, the firm's staff recorded the numbers of all police cars visiting the shop, and Wilcox turned them over to a senior police officer. Wilcox even took out a private detective's license for a police captain so that the man could moonlight for International. Free of charge, Wilcox helped Chief Churchill prepare an application for a federal grant to set up a criminal intelligence unit; the plan involved hiring former Secret Service agent Kenneth Hale as a consultant. Hale, a friend of Wilcox, eventually succeeded Churchill as chief of police. One measure of Wilcox's success in wooing the cops can be seen in the private detective's license applications of employees later hired by the firm; whenever such an application was filed, one or more senior Indiana police officials would be listed as references to vouch for the applicant.

With the cops in his corner, Wilcox set out in pursuit of the thing he saw as the key to success: political influence. The first opportunity that presented itself was the Indiana senatorial election of 1970. Richard Roudebush, a Republican congressman who served on the House Un-American Activities Committee, was challenging the Democratic incumbent, Senator Vance Hartke. Roudebush's campaign coordinator was Edgar L. (Nick) Longworth, a local party worker and an old friend of C. Timothy Wilcox.

Longworth retained Wilcox to serve as security officer for the Roudebush campaign. Wilcox checked the campaign headquarters for bugs and wiretaps, but former employees of International Investigators claim the sleuthing services he provided went well beyond such defensive measures. They charge him with masterminding a dirty tricks operation that almost succeeded in capturing Hartke's Senate seat for Richard Roudebush.

Two former agents of International Investigators have admitted taking part in the August 1970 Hartke break-in, as well as a second entry into the senator's offices a month later to replace the fading batteries in the bug they installed during their first visit. They say the third member of the team was Wilcox, and that he planned and directed the operation. They revealed that the Hartke break-ins were only part of a series of burglaries they carried out with Wilcox during the 1970 campaign.

Edward D. Lewis, an Indianapolis attorney and a close friend of Hartke, was the target of another of the political break-ins. Lewis's offices were entered and his files searched. Cancelled checks covering a three-year period were taken, and a microphone–transmitter was concealed under Lewis's office chair. The intruders parked a car in a nearby street and concealed in its trunk a special FM receiver coupled to a voice-activated tape recorder. Every conversation held in Lewis's office was recorded by the hidden device. An International agent periodically removed the tapes and replaced them with fresh reels.

In yet another break-in, the former International detectives say they and Wilcox entered a building near Hartke's offices and broke into a room used for meetings by his campaign workers. They concealed another bug in a potted plant and positioned it to pick up conversations anywhere in the conference room. In this case, the receiver and recorder were installed in the nearby Republican State Headquarters, inside the office of a senior Roudebush campaign official.

Not all the dirty tricks involved illegal entry. In one case several mailbags awaiting pick-up in the lobby of Democratic Headquarters were stolen. The bags contained a mass mailing of invitations to a $100-a-plate Democratic fundraising dinner. According to a former International detective, the invitations were delivered to Roudebush campaign workers who later remailed them shortly before the dinner, to insure a poor turn-out.

Nineteen seventy was the year of the Kent State Massacre and the two-month invasion of Cambodia. The November elections were viewed by the Nixon administration as an opportunity for an endorsement of its policies, a kind of ideological referendum. Nixon personally campaigned for Republican candidates in twenty-one states in a bid to increase his support in the Democratically controlled Congress.

In Indiana, the state's normal roughhouse politics escalated into a bitter name-calling match in the Senate race. Roudebush's supporters accused Hartke of being "a supporter of the Vietcong" because of the senator's opposition to the war, while the Hartke campaign focused on Roudebush's ties to organizations affiliated with the John Birch Society. The race for Hartke's Senate seat was close, finally settled by a recount which gave Hartke a thin lead of 4500 votes.

Informed of the recent disclosures of the 1970 break-ins and buggings, Hartke recalled that he suspected leaks in his campaign organization. The Roudebush people seemed to have advance notice of every
campaign maneuver he made. Hartke now believes the dirty tricks
operation nearly cost him the election.

According to several former International employees who took part in
the operation, the break-ins and buggings were intended to cost Hartke a
great deal more than his Senate seat. One of the objectives of the operation was to obtain evidence proving that Hartke had been involved in a
number of illegal deals. A Roudebush campaign worker recalled Wilcox's boasting on Election Night 1970, ''I have enough to put Hartke in
jail for the rest of his life.''

The efforts of International Investigators, Inc., to obtain evidence of
criminal wrongdoing by Senator Hartke actually antedate Wilcox's
1970 purchase of the firm. When Wilcox acquired the company, he
found among the detective agency's many dossiers a thick file on Hartke
compiled during the 1960s. The client who had paid for the investigation was a major Midwestern utility company that suspected Hartke of
selling political favors to some of its competitors.

The theory the company sought to prove was that Hartke had received
payments from Hoosier Energy, Inc., an Indiana electric utility, in
exchange for using his influence in Congress to advance the business interests of the company. The payments were supposed to have been
channeled through UNITO, Inc., a public relations firm with close ties
to Ed Lewis, a friend of Hartke and a target of one of the 1970 break-
ins.

The grand jury probing dirty tricks in the Hartke–Roudebush contest
apparently heard testimony that Indiana utility interests had played a
role in the 1970 anti-Hartke operation. It subpoenaed the top officials of
Public Service Indiana—Indiana's largest electric utility—and demanded records of payments by the company to the lockman who had
taken part in the break-ins. The grand jury also subpoenaed Gerald R.
Redding, the senior partner of the law firm that represented Public Service Indiana, and later indicted him for conspiracy in the break-ins.

Did the repeated efforts of International Investigators and its
clients—carried out for almost a decade—ever manage to prove the
theory that Hartke was involved in wrongdoing? Apparently not. One

veteran of the 1970 operation recalls, "We weren't able to make a good enough case, so we let it drop." In fact, there is nothing to indicate they were able to make any case at all.

The Hartke operation was only the first of a long series of political dirty-tricks campaigns conducted by International Investigators. A former Republican campaign worker recalls Wilcox's boasting to her that he had broken into more than 100 offices in Indianapolis. A detective who worked for the firm for five years described his participation in more than a dozen "political investigations." Often, he said, such investigations were aimed at compiling derogatory information to be used for political blackmail.

"You wouldn't believe how political philosophies change," he said, "when you show someone a photograph of himself in bed with the wrong person."

And what if he couldn't get such a photo?

"Indianapolis is a small town," he replied. "You'd be surprised what a little innuendo can do."

Several months after the loss to Hartke, Nick Longworth, the Roudebush campaign official who had recruited Wilcox, resigned his local government job and declared his intention "to devote full time to Republican politics." It's not clear what kind of political work he had in mind, but three weeks before his resignation he applied for a private detective's license in order to work with International Investigators.

The next important political contest in Indianapolis was scheduled the following November, when John Neff, a local attorney and former Democratic state legislator, would challenge incumbent mayor Richard Lugar. Lugar appointed as his campaign manager L. Keith Bulen, then county GOP chairman. Bulen's aide was Nick Longworth.

Meanwhile, International Investigators had acquired a new client—the Marion County License Branch. The Indiana License Branch System is a private corporation that handles the administration of motor vehicle and driver's licenses under contract to the state. Each branch is controlled by the county chairman of the political party in power. The Marion County Branch was controlled by L. Keith Bulen, Longworth's boss in the Lugar campaign organization. International was put on a monthly retainer of $500 by the branch for "security work."

Whether or not International Investigators ever did any security work for the branch is unclear, but about this time the firm began to work on behalf of Mayor Lugar's reelection campaign. Once again Nick Longworth brought in his friend Wilcox to check the mayor's office and campaign headquarters for bugs and wiretaps, and once again the detective agency's services went beyond defensive measures.

An International detective was assigned to infiltrate the Neff campaign. In the guise of a volunteer worker, he went to Neff headquarters, expropriated copies of the candidate's speeches and speaking schedules, photographed the real campaign workers, and scouted the locations of the telephone lines. Two other men climbed to the roof of Neff headquarters to see if taps could be placed on the campaign telephone lines where they emerged from the building. Whether they succeeded in tapping the lines is not known, but a tap was discovered on Neff's home telephone, and his campaign workers believed their own telephone conversations were being overheard. Mayor Lugar was reelected in a landslide victory.*

Nineteen seventy-two—the year of the Watergate break-in and the presidential election—was a busy time for International Investigators. Longworth and Wilcox took a trip to San Diego and brought along an electronic eavesdropping specialist—a former TV repairman who custom-built the bugs and taps used by International. The purpose of the trip was to reconnoiter what was then the proposed site for the Republican National Convention. Later Longworth served as Mayor Lugar's advance man at Miami Beach, the actual site of the convention.

On the Indiana scene, former governor Matthew E. Welsh was running for his old office against Republican Otis R. Bowen. An International agent was sent to infiltrate the Welsh campaign. The anti-Welsh

* Apparently Lugar was himself the victim of an elaborate and vicious dirty-tricks operation in 1976 when he ran for Senator Hartke's Senate seat. During the campaign, Hartke repeatedly charged Lugar had a secret Swiss bank account. Some months after the election, in which Lugar defeated Hartke, documents surfaced indicating that Lugar had opened an account with the Union Bank of Switzerland and deposited $1.35 million on April 10, 1972, three days after a federal campaign law went into effect requiring disclosure of campaign contributions. The documents seemed to imply that Lugar may have laundered money for Richard Nixon, and also linked the Swiss account to a prominent Nazi war criminal living in Spain. However, handwriting analysis indicated that Lugar's signatures on the documents had been traced, and internal inconsistencies in the information they contained proved that the papers were fraudulent.

operation seems to have been comparatively tame, involving only the use of a concealed recorder to tape some of the Welsh campaign meetings.

At the same time, Indiana Congressman Andrew Jacobs, Jr., was challenged by Republican William H. Hudnut. An elaborate anti-Jacobs operation was considered, including a plan to send a female campaign worker to Washington to seduce Jacobs in a hotel room before hidden cameras. However, the plan was abandoned when it became apparent that Jacobs was going to lose to Hudnut without any encouragement. (Jacobs regained his seat in 1974; Hudnut is now mayor of Indianapolis. Informed of the recent disclosure of the planned seduction, Jacobs remarked whimsically that it seemed preferable to being bugged.)

Nineteen seventy-three was an off year and a doldrums for political dirty tricking in Indiana. The one high point during the year was the break-in at Democratic State Headquarters in August. Unlike the Hartke operation, which employed the expert services of a military-trained lockman, the Democratic headquarters break-in was accomplished through the crude measure of jimmying a door. A bug was planted, then retrieved two days later. The objective of the operation may have been to observe some intramural shafting going on within the Democratic party at the time.

It would be unfair to conclude that only Republicans indulged in the Midwestern political hijinx. International Investigators worked for the Democrats in Indiana, although in every known instance the target of the operation was another Democrat. In neighboring Ohio, however, International was briefly employed by the Democrats to work against the Republicans. The operation came to an abrupt end when Wilcox drove to Ohio to visit one of his Democratic clients. The client recognized a special coding on Wilcox's Indiana license plate number which indicated that the detective had political connections in the Republican-controlled state.

Political investigations represented only a part of International Investigators' business, and, in terms of the company's income, it was a small part. Conventional private sleuthing paid better, especially when the firm used the same "direct approach" it employed in political matters. In 1972, for example, International was hired by the chancellor of Indiana Northern University, which was then under investigation by the Indiana Private School Accrediting Commission on suspicion of being a diploma mill. A former International detective says he and another employee of the firm, without their clients approval or knowledge, broke into the Commission's offices in the Indiana State House and removed, copied, and returned the Commission's files on Indiana Northern. The university paid several thousand dollars to International to conduct the investigation.

In addition to its sleuthing services, International Investigators also offered its clients a complete line of electronic surveillance equipment for do-it-yourself investigative work. The bugs and other devices were constructed by Melvin Freeman, a former television repairman who has been described as an "electronic genius." Freeman, a close friend of both Wilcox and Nick Longworth, is at least a very talented tinkerer who can whip up a listening device in a matter of hours from readily available electronic components. Why Wilcox chose these homemade bugs over the more professional products of Bell and Howell, Audio Intelligence Devices, or Martin Kaiser, Inc., seems obvious. The 1968 Omnibus Crime Control and Safe Streets Act outlaws even the possession of such equipment by anyone except official agencies permitted to eavesdrop by court order. In Indiana, where even the police are forbidden to bug and wiretap under any circumstances, it would be impossible for Wilcox to order the equipment from established suppliers.

Freeman's tinkering ran him afoul of the law on several occasions. In 1972, he was convicted of conspiracy to steal equipment from the telephone company to build "blue boxes," those contraband devices that are used to cheat the phone company on long-distance calls. Two years later he was convicted of using a "blue box" and received a three-year sentence. Freeman, whose bugs were planted in the offices of Senator Hartke and his aides during the 1970 campaign, invoked the Fifth Amendment when called before the grand jury investigating International's dirty tricks operations.

The downfall of C. Timothy Wilcox, like that of Richard Nixon, was caused by some embarrassing tapes. In 1975, investigators discovered a collection of reels locked in a storage room in Indianapolis Police

Headquarters. On listening to the tapes, the investigators discovered that they were the product of the illegal wiretapping and bugging of the police lieutenant carried out by Wilcox on behalf of Chief Winston Churchill in 1971. Some of the reels bore labels indicating they were the property of International Investigators, Inc.

The matter was turned over to a strike force from the Marion County, Indiana, prosecutor's office, which began questioning some former employees of International. At the same time, the Pulitzer Prize–winning investigative team from the *Indianapolis Star* got wind of the probe and began digging in parallel with the strike force. At first the reporters and investigators focused on the affair of the cop and the madam, but as the former detectives began to talk freely in exchange for immunity from prosecution, the story of International's dirty tricks program began to unfold.

As the investigation progressed, Wilcox launched a counterattack. While interviewing a former International employee at his apartment, two strike force investigators discovered a tape recorder concealed in a wastebasket. Outside the house they found Wilcox slouched down behind the wheel of a parked automobile, carrying a pair of high-powered binoculars and a variety of bugging equipment. The strike force also discovered that Wilcox had begun to compile dossiers on several of its members as well as a reporter from the *Indianapolis Star*'s investigative unit. Wilcox may have found some comfort in going through the motions of turning the tables on the investigators, but he was just whistling in the dark. The grand jury indicted him on several counts of burglary, conspiracy, and illegal eavesdropping.

Also indicted was Wilcox's friend and political crony, Nick Longworth. Longworth had been long gone from Indianapolis and had been working in Washington, D.C. In 1973, his service to the campaign of Indiana governor Otis R. Bowen was rewarded when the governor appointed Longworth co-director of the state's Washington, D.C., liaison office. Later, when President Nixon appointed former Congressman Richard Roudebush as director of the Veterans Administration, Roudebush hired his former campaign coordinator to serve as his administrative assistant. Informed by the *Indianapolis Star* that Longworth had been indicted for taking part in the break-ins and dirty tricks carried out during his 1970 campaign against Senator Hartke, Roudebush said, "It is appalling to me to hear these things, because I don't really believe they are true. I think the whole thing is somebody's imagination. It sounds like Watergate to me."

Before long it began to sound very much like Watergate. The strike force investigators discovered that the fruits of the anti-Hartke operation—checkbooks and memoranda stolen during the break-ins and tape recordings of the bugged conversations—had been turned over to senior officials of the Department of Justice immediately after the burglaries. There were strong indications that the Justice Department had covered up the affair.

In October 1970, two International agents went to Washington and personally delivered the anti-Hartke materials to Gary Baise, a senior administrative official in the Department of Justice. Baise now recalls that the materials "appeared to be part of a political vendetta," and decided not to act on them. Apparently he did not feel the materials were clear evidence that Hartke had been party to a felony, otherwise he would have had no choice but to turn them over to others in the Justice Department for prosecution.

However, it seems obvious that the stolen documents and bugged conversations were clear evidence that the International detectives who obtained them had committed a string of felonies, including breaking the federal laws against electronic eavesdropping. Baise says he didn't examine the materials closely enough at the time to realize how they had been obtained, and he claims he doesn't even remember who gave them to him. When Baise consulted his appointment calendar for 1970, he says he discovered a mysterious gap, a missing page covering the two-week period during which the International agents visited him in Washington. However, the strike force has been able to establish that Wilcox and another detective flew to Washington on the day Baise received the materials. In any event, Baise does recall discussing the anti-Hartke materials with his boss in the Justice Department, William D. Ruckelshaus.

Ruckelshaus, a former Indianapolis attorney, was deputy attorney-general in charge of the Justice Department's Civil Division at the time. He held a string of jobs in the Nixon administration, including director of the Environmental Protection Agency, acting director of the FBI, and special assistant to Attorney-General Elliot Richardson. He resigned during the "Saturday Night Massacre"of October 1973, when Nixon fired Richardson and Special Prosecutor Archibald Cox. Ruckelshaus and Baise are partners in a Washington law firm today, and the former EPA director defends the paper, plastics, and metals industries in pollution lawsuits.

Ruckelshaus says he doesn't recall Baise's telling him about the anti-Hartke materials. He told an Indianapolis press conference, "It is possible that Mr. Baise had mentioned it to me, but I will say that if I was told this information was illegally obtained or damaging to Hartke, I would have remembered that. I cannot rule out the possibility that Mr. Baise had mentioned some information to me, but I don't think that he would have even mentioned Senator Hartke because he knew how I would feel about using the Justice Department to get involved in a political campaign."

Ruckelshaus, a Republican, had considered running for Hartke's Senate seat in 1970, but deferred to Roudebush several months before the bugging incidents.

Both Baise and Ruckelshaus were called to testify before the grand jury investigating International's political dirty tricks programs. In a report it released after hearing all witnesses to the Hartke affair, the grand jury expressed considerable reservation regarding the account presented by the two former Justice Department officials:

. . . we are convinced that when the documents which had been stolen out of Edward Lewis's office with the tape recording of the electronic eavesdropping device placed in Mr. Lewis's office were delivered to Gary Baise in Washington, that he was told said documents and tape recording were illegally obtained.

We further believe that, as a member of the United States' Department of Justice, he then had an obligation to take some action to determine what illegal acts had been committed and who was involved.

It is unclear if this material was brought to the attention of Mr. William Ruckelshaus; but it is clear that Gary Baise kept the materials and did nothing to determine if any laws had been broken or crimes committed.

If persons occupying high positions in our system of justice in our country have such a casual disregard for the law, how then are our children to learn proper respect for the law, and how is our society to maintain order?

The grand jury noted that it had no jurisdiction in the matter of Baise and Ruckelshaus, but urged the Justice Department to make "a complete and thorough investigation for any possible crimes including, but not limited to, obstruction of justice and receiving stolen goods."

The grand jury may have really believed that the Justice Department was going to explore possible wrongdoing by a former deputy attorney-general and his aide, but its faith was not warranted by past performance in the case; the Department pulled off a stunt at a critical point in the strike force's investigation which almost kept Ruckelshaus and Baise out of the matter entirely.

The Indianapolis strike force had been cooperating with the FBI in the case because the bugging and wiretapping carried out against Hartke was a violation of federal law. In fact, the Indianapolis investigators learned that the Bureau had known about International's involvement in the Hartke break-ins for over a year, but inexplicably had failed to prosecute the case. In any event, the Bureau was aware of Gary Baise's involvement in the case, and knew that subpoenas had been issued for him and the tapes and materials turned over to him by International Investigators in 1970. Shortly before Baise was due to appear before the grand jury, agents from the FBI visited him and, on orders from the Justice Department, seized the tapes and materials.

The maneuver had the effect of a delaying tactic, since there was little point in taking Baise's testimony if the materials were not available to be entered as evidence before the grand jury. But a delay at this point would be fatal, because the five-year statute of limitations on the 1970 campaign offenses was within days of running out. Confiscating the tapes and stolen documents served not only to keep Ruckelshaus and Baise out of the case, but to deny the strike force essential evidence that any crime had been committed at all. Without the materials, there was a good possibility that no indictments whatsoever would be handed down in the 1970 anti-Hartke break-ins.

The *Indianapolis Star*'s investigative reporters learned of the development and published the story of the Justice Department's delaying maneuver. The affair was beginning to take on the odor of a Washington cover-up, and the national press was showing signs of interest in the case. Apparently someone in Washington used his better judgement, for

the day after the story appeared in the *Star,* the Justice Department released the materials and had them flown to Indianapolis. They arrived in
the prosecutor's office only minutes before Gary Baise walked into the
grand jury room.

Although they believed any possible wrongdoing by Ruckelshaus and
Baise was beyond its jurisdiction, the grand jury handed down indictments in the Hartke affair against Roudebush campaign coordinator
Nick Longworth; Gerald Redding, the attorney for Public Service Indiana; Buena Chaney, a former GOP state chairman; Eston Perry, a
former aide to Chaney; and C. Timothy Wilcox. Named as unindicted
co-conspirators were the former air force lockman and the International
detective who had admitted their parts in the break-ins.

The statute of limitations question was raised again when the five defendants moved for dismissal of the charges on grounds that more than
five years had elapsed since the break-ins. The burglaries had, in fact,
occurred between August and October 1970, and the indictments were
handed down November 1, 1975, just barely beyond the five-year limit.
The defendants also charged that the Indianapolis prosecutor had no jurisdiction to prosecute the bugging and wiretap charges, since electronic
surveillance is prohibited by federal law and isn't covered by any Indiana statute.

The prosecutor maintained that the break-ins and eavesdropping had
been part of a criminal conspiracy that lasted at least until the evening of
November 3—Election Day—when Wilcox is reported to have visited
Roudebush headquarters and flashed copies of Senator Hartke's per-
sonal income tax returns to the workers there. The state also argued that
Indiana law permits prosecution of violations of federal law.

In the end the judge found that the statute of limitations had expired
and decided that the local prosecutor had no jurisdiction over the federal
wiretap charges. The indictments against the five defendants were dismissed, ending any chance that some of the more interesting questions
in the case will ever be answered.

If Richard Roudebush's campaign coordinator, Nick Longworth,
helped plan the Hartke break-ins as the prosecution charged, what did
his boss know about it, and when did he know it? Why did the FBI,
which learned from several sources about the International Inves-

tigators' role in the Hartke break-ins more than a year before the investigation by the Indianapolis strike force, fail to follow up on the matter at the time? Was the Justice Department's confiscation of the fruits of the Hartke break-ins and buggings a deliberate attempt to protect former deputy attorney-general Ruckelshaus from having to answer some embarrassing questions before the grand jury?

And the most perplexing question may be this: Were the striking parallels between Watergate and the five-year program of dirty tricks in Indiana mere coincidence? Was there any real connection between the White House Plumbers and their Indianapolis counterparts? Senator Hartke seems to suspect there was. Commenting on the 1970 break-ins he observed, "In one sense, my campaign was a training ground for the masterminds of the Watergate burglaries, buggings, and dirty tricks. There was a conscious effort on the part of the Nixon-dominated Republican National Committee to sabotage the re-election of myself and a number of other senators who opposed the Nixon administration."

But while there are striking similarities between Watergate and the Indianapolis affair, they very probably are the product of coincidence. If the break-ins, the buggings, the attempted blackmailings, and the other dirty tricks are linked at all, it is in the same way that two or more cases of smallpox are related: the conditions are right, so the disease spreads.

Like C. Timothy Wilcox, most of the International detectives who took part in the Indianapolis operations are in their mid-thirties—bright young men, articulate and well-tailored. They are of the same generation and were shaped by the same social mold as the young men of Watergate. They could be the fraternity brothers of John Dean, Jeb Magruder, Donald Segretti, or Gordon Strachan. They believe in law and order, but they define those concepts in the same terms used by G. Gordon Liddy or E. Howard Hunt. They are furtive, yet proud, for while they must practice their trade in the political back alleys of America, they are unswerving in their belief that God is on their side.

Radical right-wing ideology was also the motivation of Jerome Ducote, a California political detective with a somewhat different background from the International detectives. Ducote was a police officer with the Santa Clara County Sheriff's Department until 1964, when he left in a dispute over his activities in the John Birch Society. He had been an investigator with the Burglary Squad, and he made considerable use of his knowledge of breaking and entering after leaving the Sheriff's Department; between 1966 and 1968, Ducote and two associates carried out seventeen political break-ins.

The ex-cop was hired by the Santa Clara County Farm Bureau, a growers' group opposed to the efforts of Cesar Chavez and the United Farm Workers to organize the migrant farm workers in California. Ducote was paid $800 per month to compile information on political radicals supporting the UFW. His reports labeling the Farm Bureau's targets as Communists were handed over to the late James B. Utt, an ultraconservative congressman from Orange County, who read them into the *Congressional Record,* thereby permitting them to be published elsewhere with immunity from libel.

Ducote's work came to the attention of the Western Research Foundation, a nonprofit organization formed by ex-FBI agents and right-wingers during the early years of the Cold War. The Foundation operated a private intelligence network, collecting information on left-wing radicals and dissenters and supplying these data to California corporations and government agencies. Western Research was reputed to have close ties with the FBI, and officials of the Foundation told Ducote that the Bureau would be grateful to him for his help. Shortly thereafter, Ducote was approached by a man he believes was an FBI agent and asked to burglarize the San Jose Peace Center, an anti-Vietnam War organization.

Ducote and his accomplices carried out the break-in, the first of the series of seventeen they would commit during the next year and a half. In each case the ex-cop would be approached by a stranger—an FBI agent, according to Ducote—who supplied money and plans for the break-in. The assigned targets included the United Farm Workers, *Ramparts* magazine, the home and office of the late radical labor organizer Saul Alinsky, and the Student Non-Violent Coordinating Committee. Ducote says his Bureau contacts instructed him to turn over the fruits of the burglaries to an official of the Santa Clara Farm Bureau, although the official now denies he played any role in the affair. Whatever Ducote did with the materials he took during the break-ins, copies of some of the items turned up in the hands of the federal government: somehow the FBI got hold of a mailing list Ducote took from the San Jose Peace Center, and the State Department, while refusing visas to two Soviet officials, produced some letters the ex-cop had stolen from the American-Russian Institute in San Francisco. Of course, this falls short of proving Ducote's charge that the FBI sponsored his escapades, since copies of these materials could have reached the Bureau through one of its many other sources.

Not all of Ducote's missions involved breaking and entering; in 1968 he trailed Saul Alinsky to Washington, D.C., where, dressed as a priest, Ducote listened to the labor organizer address the National Liturgical Conference. Even the ex-cop's nocturnal forays were sometimes more hilarious than sinister, such as the time he was tipped that the subscription list of a left-wing San Francisco newspaper was due to be dumped in the trash. Ducote staked out the dumpster for three nights running before he saw the list discarded. As he approached the bin, three other figures also emerged from the shadows. An FBI agent, an Army Intelligence officer, and a San Francisco policeman had all received the same tip and came to claim the subscription list for their respective agencies. The cop settled the dispute by grabbing the list from the trash and threatening to arrest his competitors if they didn't bug off.

Word of Ducote's exploits eventually got around, and in 1975 an investigator from the California attorney-general's office asked to talk to him. Secure in the knowledge that the statute of limitations on the burglaries had long since run out, Ducote gave the investigator a long and detailed account of his crimes. The FBI has denied any part in the affair, and in fairness to the Bureau it should be noted that no real evidence has been offered supporting Ducote's belief that the mysterious strangers who ordered the break-ins were, in fact, FBI agents. But if Ducote can be believed at all, someone exploited the ex-cop's right-wing politics and professional knowledge of the art of breaking and entering in order to conduct an extensive political spy operation.

Sometimes it's almost impossible to tell the difference between private political snooping and official spying. In June 1968, a Palo Alto, California, banker arrived at his office one day to find he had an unexpected visitor. The man identified himself as Franklin R. Geraty, an investigator for a New York City private detective firm called Fidelity

Reporting Service. Geraty told the banker that Fidelity had been hired by "the Republicans" to conduct routine background investigations of some aides to Richard Nixon, then a leading contender for the Republican presidential nomination.

Geraty asked the banker for any personal information he might have concerning Richard V. Allen, a local resident. Allen was a senior staff member of the Hoover Institution on War, Revolution, and Peace, a conservative research center of Stanford University. Two weeks prior to Geraty's visit, Allen had left the Hoover Institution to become national security advisor to candidate Nixon. Geraty said he was checking Allen out on behalf of the Nixon campaign.

The banker's suspicions were aroused. He told the private detective it would take some time to find out if he had any information about Allen, and he asked Geraty to call back later. The banker happened to be well connected in Republican circles, so after Geraty left he called Nixon's office and spoke to his secretary, Rose Mary Woods. Miss Woods checked and told the banker neither Geraty nor Fidelity Reporting were working for Nixon.

Nixon's staff wondered what was going on, so they called in John Caulfield, the former New York City policeman who later earned national notoriety during the Senate Watergate hearings. Caulfield made some inquiries in New York and turned up some fascinating information about Fidelity Reporting Service.

Fidelity was owned and operated by Albert Palocsik, a long-time New York private eye whose clients were often listed in the Social Register. Palocsik also served as bodyguard and escort for celebrities such as Judy Garland and the Beatles. Other clients of Palocsik's protective services included Svetlana Stalin and certain U.N. officials, and the assortment of visas in the detective's well-thumbed passport suggested he was no stranger to international intrigue. Palocsik was, in fact, a contract employee of the Central Intelligence Agency, and Fidelity Reporting Service provided cover for some of the Agency's New York–based operations. Franklin R. Geraty may have been a private detective, but he was also a CIA agent.

Nixon's people reached the very understandable conclusion that President Johnson was using the CIA to spy on the Nixon campaign. They decided not to make the matter a public issue for fear that an attack on

Johnson might spur him on to more enthusiastic support for Hubert Humphrey's presidential bid. They chose to ignore the matter, instead, and it stayed buried until after President Nixon's resignation, when it was surfaced by former Nixon speechwriter William Safire.

Called upon by the press to explain the incident, the CIA denied that the motive for investigating Richard Allen was to spy on the Nixon campaign. Six months before the incident, a CIA spokesman said, Allen, in his capacity as a Hoover Institution researcher, approached the Agency to request certain unclassified information. The CIA gave him the data he requested and, several months later, decided to furnish him with additional, classified information. First, however, it was necessary to get him a security clearance. That, said the CIA, was the reason for Geraty's investigation.

However, Richard Allen disputes some details of the Agency's explanation. It's true, he says, that early in 1968 he contacted the CIA and asked Director Richard Helms to have his staff review a forthcoming Hoover Institution publication in the interests of accuracy; but, says Allen, he never requested any information from the CIA, classified or unclassified.

Was the CIA merely conducting a security check of Richard Allen, or was it fishing for political blackmail material to give to the Democrats? Or could there have been some other reason for the probe? Allen, after all, was due to step into the position of national security advisor to Richard Nixon, a job actually filled by Henry Kissinger after Nixon was elected. The CIA must have realized that if Nixon succeeded in reaching the White House, his national security advisor would be the presidential aide responsible for, among other things, the CIA. The officials in Langley would certainly want to find out everything they could about this man who might one day be their most important channel to the president. The motive for the Agency's spying on Richard Allen may have been bureaucratic, rather than precautionary or political. But if that is the real reason for the incident, it raises another intriguing question: did the CIA also compile a personal dossier on Henry Kissinger?

Perhaps the most intriguing aspect of the Allen affair was the revelation that the CIA uses private detective agencies, a fact barely hinted at in the past. In 1963, Hollywood private eye Fred Otash compiled and published an international directory of private detective firms. Curiously, one customer that bought several copies of the book was the CIA. Of course, it's not really remarkable that the Agency would be interested in a comprehensive compilation of overseas private eyes listed by country, since such people can be enormously valuable in foreign intelligence operations. But Otash may not have realized his CIA readers were equally interested in the state-by-state listing of domestic private detective agencies operating within the United States.

When the CIA first considered the very sensitive question of operating within the United States, someone must have pointed out that firms like Fidelity Reporting Service could offer ideal cover. Private detective agencies are licensed to snoop, and they provide a confidential service, routinely refusing to disclose their clients' identities. They could provide perfect camouflage for the CIA's domestic intelligence activities.

Anderson Security Consultants, Inc., is a small company in northern Virginia that advises its clients—government agencies and private businesses—on such workaday matters as the safe disposal of office trash that might contain confidential information, or how to make sure no one plants a bug in the walls of that new office building while it's under construction. It was just the latter service that Anderson Security provided to the Central Intelligence Agency when the CIA's new headquarters building was going up in Langley, Virginia, in the early 1960s. The CIA officials must have had every confidence in Anderson Security; after all, they had created and staffed the company themselves. The private security firm was a CIA proprietary.

Anderson Security did an assortment of detective jobs for the CIA, including watching Agency and Pentagon employees whose loyalty came into question, and recruiting undercover agents for the Bureau of Narcotics and Dangerous Drugs. It also took on standard private eye assignments for nongovernment clients.

In 1967, the CIA decided to use Anderson Security for Project MERRIMAC, an operation aimed at infiltrating anti–Vietnam War groups in the Washington, D.C., area. Detectives from the private security firm joined the Women's Strike for Peace, the Washington Peace Center, the Congress on Racial Equality, and the Student Non-Violent Coordinating Committee. By 1968, the list of target organizations had been expanded and Anderson Security agents were sent to New York, Philadelphia, and Baltimore to spy on the peace movement for the CIA.

The official reason for Project MERRIMAC was to obtain advance warning of political demonstrations in the Washington, D.C., area that might pose a physical threat to CIA buildings. However, the expanded spy program included such things as getting lists of contributors to peace organizations, information that had little bearing on supposed threats to CIA installations. Anderson Security was assigned to spy on political dissidents who disagreed with the war policy of the Johnson administration, and that is but one small tactical step away from outright dirty tricking in a partisan political campaign.

The CIA may never have used its own private detective agencies for political campaign work within the U.S., but the Agency certainly took a great interest in one private eye who played a mysterious and little-known role in the Watergate affair. In January 1975, Senator Howard Baker of Tennessee revealed he had learned that the CIA had compiled a dossier on Arthur James Woolston-Smith, a New Zealand national employed by the New York private investigative firm of Science Security Associates. The reason for the CIA's interest in Woolston-Smith was not disclosed, but it may have been because the private detective learned of the Nixon campaign's plans to bug the Democrats several months before the Watergate break-in.

Woolston-Smith, who specializes in anti-bugging techniques, somehow learned of the CREEP (Committee to Reelect the President) plans in December 1971 or January 1972. He passed the word about the planned bugging operation to a former client, William Haddad. Haddad, then the publisher of a small New York weekly, had been an associate director of the Peace Corps in the Kennedy administration and was on close terms with many Democratic Party officials, including party chairman Lawrence O'Brien.

Haddad wrote to O'Brien and repeated Woolston-Smith's warning. The Democratic chairman assigned party communications director John Stewart to follow up on the matter, and on April 26, 1972, Stewart met with Haddad and Woolston-Smith in Haddad's New York office. The two men told Stewart that the Republicans planned to bug the offices of the Democratic National Committee in the Watergate, and that they were going to use Cuban emigrés to carry out the operation. They suggested ways in which the funding of the operation might be used to trace the operation back to the Republicans and prove they were behind it. The names James McCord and G. Gordon Liddy were mentioned during the meeting.

It seems incredible, but nearly two months before the arrest of McCord and the four Cubans inside the Watergate offices of the DNC, the Democrats had been fully briefed on the CREEP operational plans to bug them.

The Democrats say they took no action in response to Woolston-Smith's warning because there were no secrets worth stealing in party headquarters. They also point out that electronic eavesdropping countermeasures can be expensive. Whatever their reasons, the Democrats' inaction turned out to be the best political tactic. Nixon would have won reelection without the Watergate bugging; with it, he lost the presidency and brought disaster to the Republican party.

A tantalizing question remains: How did Woolston-Smith learn of CREEP's plans? The detective says he heard through the wiretapping fraternity that James McCord had purchased some bugging equipment. This is entirely plausible, but it fails to explain the detailed knowledge of the planned bugging exhibited by Woolston-Smith and Haddad in their meeting with Stewart. Fred Thompson, minority counsel for the Senate Watergate Committee, suspected that the detective, who had past connections with both British and U.S. intelligence, may have received a leak from the CIA, a theory that presupposes a degree of CIA knowledge of the planned operation that the Agency has repeatedly denied. Other scenarios have columnist Jack Anderson learning of the operation from his friend, Watergate burglar Frank Sturgis, and passing the story along to Haddad, or a Democratic "double agent" within CREEP blowing the whistle on the operation. But the most interesting theory is that the Democrats learned of the planned Watergate operation through some wiretapping and bugging of their own, a possibility that could have strongly bolstered the Republicans' Watergate defense, "They all do it."

The curious lack of curiosity about the affair on the part of the press and the Democratic majority on the Senate Watergate Committee led to cries of outrage from such conservative quarters as Accuracy in Media, Inc., a press watchdog group that has worked hard to get the story out. But the national news media have remained indifferent to the mystery and it seems destined to remain one of the unanswered questions of Watergate.

Whatever lessons have been drawn from such incidents as the Watergate affair and the anti-Hartke campaign, they don't seem to include the idea that political crime doesn't pay. As the 1976 presidential campaign got into gear, there were abundant indications the political private eyes were up to their dirty old tricks. George Wallace's Georgia campaign coordinator discovered two bugs hidden in his Atlanta office and accused the Carter campaign of having put them there. Jimmy Carter's New York campaign headquarters was broken into and copies of Carter's political master plan were stolen. A senior aide to Congressman Dawson Mathis of Georgia admitted planting a bug in the congressman's Albany office to spy on a fellow staffer. A Connecticut Democratic official posed as a newspaper reporter to interview Republican Senator Lowell Weicker.

It doesn't seem to matter that most bugs and wiretaps collect nothing more than hours of boring chit-chat, that break-ins almost never yield anything worth the risk of a sojourn in the slammer, and that dirty tricks have a way of backfiring. Spying seems to have become as much a part of American political campaigns as straw hats, bumper stickers, and lapel buttons.

And 1984 is going to be an election year.

12

The Police–Industrial Complex

A few days before the inauguration of his successor in January 1961, President Eisenhower delivered his farewell address to the American people over national television. The major theme of the president's speech was the continuing dangers of the Cold War, but many listeners were startled to hear this added warning from the nation's foremost old soldier:

. . . We have been compelled to create a permanent armaments industry of vast proportions. Added to this, three and a half million men and women are directly engaged in the defense establishment. . . .

Now this conjunction of an immense military establishment and a large arms industry is new in the American experience. The total influence—economic, political, even spiritual—is felt in every city, every state house, every office of the Federal Government. We recognize the imperative need for this development. Yet we must not fail to comprehend its grave implications. . . .

In the councils of Government, we must guard against the acquisition of unwarranted influence, whether sought or unsought, by the military–industrial complex. The potential for the disastrous rise of misplaced power exists and will persist.

We must never let the weight of this combination endanger our liberties or democratic processes. . . .

The military–industrial complex. It was a new term and a new idea. A moderate Republican president had perceived the invisible and unofficial links between the military establishment and the private sector. He saw a new center of power forming in a society responding to the threat of foreign aggression. It was a necessary danger, the president said, but a danger nonetheless. Build a strong fortress, but be careful it doesn't become a prison.

Is there a useful parallel between the military–industrial complex President Eisenhower warned us of in 1961, and the ties we have seen linking the public law enforcement establishment to the Private Sector today? Is there a police–industrial complex? I believe the answer to both questions is yes.

The $5-billion-per-year private police industry is tiny when compared to the defense–aerospace industry. But it is growing at a steady 10 to 15 percent per year. And the estimated one million public and private police are due to double during the next decade. President Eisenhower saw the military–industrial complex as only a potential threat to freedom, but, as I have tried to show in these pages, the police–industrial complex already encroaches on our liberties in small ways. If freedom is already forced to retreat, what do the remaining decades of this century have in store for us?

There are some legislative remedies to the Private Sector abuses I have described. A stringent model licensing law for private guards and rent-a-cops can be formulated by the federal government and adopted by the states. The privacy laws can be strengthened to control the hired snoops and gossip merchants. The loopholes in the wiretapping laws can be plugged (and the existing laws enforced). All these steps can and should be taken, but none deals with the root of the problem. The police–industrial complex poses a threat to individual liberties, not because we haven't enough laws, but because we have too little regard for The Law.

Our criminal justice system has ceased to work. Of course this means that the most dangerous kinds of street criminals—muggers, armed robbers, rapists, even murderers—are receiving light sentences or probation, and are being returned to society. But it also means that white-collar criminals are getting even more lenient treatment. Perjury, illegal campaign contributions, income tax evasion, bribery, and other favorite crimes of the powerful rarely seem to be punished by any prison time at all. Big companies violate anti-trust and anti-pollution laws, then evade prosecution through their highly paid legal departments.

For the rest of us, the widespread lawlessness at the top and bottom of the socioeconomic heap seems to have sparked a resolve not to be alone in respecting the law. A decade ago, one rarely saw "No Smoking" signs disregarded in buses, trains, and other public places; now it's a common sight. Today, most people driving on the public highways deliberately flaunt their disdain for the speed laws. And affluent, well-educated people shoplift, walk out of restaurants without paying, crawl under turnstiles, and steal from their employers. Later they boast to friends of things which a generation ago would have been profoundly shameful. The rip-off has become chic.

For the average person frightened by the direction things are taking, the only recourse is to put more locks on the door and petition for more public police. But public police forces are competing with other government services for the tax dollar, and some cities with the highest crime rates in the nation have been forced to lay off police officers.

For business and other private economic interests, the solution is easier. They spend part of what they have in order to protect the rest. In a way, we have come full circle. The Private Sector was born in the nineteenth century amid rampant lawlessness that threatened the railroads and other private interests. Public law enforcement was inadequate to the task of protecting private assets, so private security evolved into a kind of national police force. Now, as we enter the last quarter of the twentieth century, we are moving back toward those bad old days.

The vigilantes have returned, ten thousand strong. They are joined by the private eye, the rent-a-cop, and the company police. More and more of our names find their way into privately compiled dossiers. Public law enforcement may take a back seat, but it stays in touch with the private police through secret societies and Old Boy Networks.

Before we move into the next century, the police–industrial complex may reteach us all an important, but bitter lesson: when the criminal justice system stops working, the Private Sector moves in to fill the vacuum.

Bibliography

BOOKS

Barlay, Stephen. *The Secrets Business.* New York: Crowell, 1973.
Brown, Robert M. *The Electronic Invasion.* Rochelle Park, N.J.: Hayden, 1967.
Caesar, Gene. *Incredible Detective: The Biography of William J. Burns.* Englewood Cliffs, N.J.: Prentice-Hall, 1968.
Coates, Joseph F. *Nonlethal Weapons for Use by U.S. Law Enforcement Officers.* Arlington, Va.: Institute for Defense Analysis, 1967.
Carroll, John M. *Confidential Information Sources: Public and Private.* Los Angeles: Security World, 1975.
Cowan, Paul; Egleson, Nick; and Hentoff, Nat. *State Secrets: Police Surveillance in America.* New York: Holt, Rinehart and Winston, 1974.
Center for Research on Criminal Justice. *The Iron Fist and the Velvet Glove: An Analysis of the U.S. Police.* Berkeley, Calif.: 1975.
French, Scott R. *The Big Brother Game.* San Francisco: GNU, 1975.
Greene, Richard M., editor. *Business Intelligence and Espionage.* Homewood, Ill.: Dow Jones–Irwin, Inc., 1966.
Haddad, William F., and Burton, Thomas M. *Report to the Standing Committee on Governmental Operations, regarding "Information Digest."* New York: New York State Assembly, Office of Legislative Oversight, 1976.
Harris, Don R. *Basic Elements of Intelligence.* Washington, D.C.: U.S. Government Printing Office, 1976.
Horan, James D. *The Pinkertons: The Detective Dynasty that Made History.* New York: Crown, 1967.

Institute for Local Self Government. *Private Security and the Public Interest.* Berkeley, Calif.: 1974.

Jones, Raymond R. *Electronic Eavesdropping Techniques and Equipment.* Washington, D.C.: U.S. Government Printing Office, 1975.

Kakalik, James S., and Wildhorn, Sorel. *Private Police in the United States.* 5 vols. Santa Monica, Calif.: The Rand Corporation, 1972. (Available from the U.S. Government Printing Office, Washington, D.C.)

Lapidus, Edith J. *Eavesdropping on Trial.* Rochelle Park, N.J.: Hayden, 1974.

Le Mond, Alan, and Fry, Ron. *No Place to Hide.* New York: St. Martin's, 1975.

Lipman, Mark. *Stealing.* New York: Harper's Magazine Press, 1973.

Lipson, Milton. *On Guard: The Business of Private Security.* New York: Quadrangle, 1975.

Miller, Arthur. *The Assault on Privacy: Computers, Data Banks, and Dossiers.* Ann Arbor: University of Michigan Press, 1971.

Moolman, Val. *Practical Ways to Prevent Burglary and Illegal Entry.* New York: Cornerstone Library, 1970.

Murphy, Harry J. *Where's What: Sources of Information for Federal Investigators.* New York: Warner Books, 1976.

National Action Research on the Military-Industrial Complex (NARMIC). *Police on the Homefront.* Philadelphia: American Friends Service Committee, 1971.

Overstreet, Harry, and Overstreet, Bonaro. *The Strange Tactics of Extremism.* New York: Norton, 1964.

Pollack, D. A. *Methods of Electronic Audio Surveillance.* Springfield, Ill.: Charles C Thomas, 1973.

Report of the National Commission for the Review of Federal and State Laws Relating to Wiretapping and Electronic Surveillance. Washington, D.C.: U.S. Government Printing Office, 1976.

Robertson, Elizabeth, and Fechter, John V. *Directory of Security Consultants.* Washington, D.C.: U.S. Government Printing Office, 1975.

Texas State Senate Subcommittee on Consumer Affairs. *Final Report of the Senate Subcommittee on Consumer Affairs into the Activities of Southwestern Bell Telephone Company.* Austin, Texas: 1976.

Turner, William W. *Power on the Right.* Berkeley, Calif.: Ramparts Press, 1971.

Twentieth Century Fund Task Force on the Law Enforcement Assistance Administration. *Law Enforcement: The Federal Role.* New York: McGraw-Hill, 1976.

Weber, Thad L. *Alarm Systems and Theft Prevention.* Los Angeles: Security World, 1973.

PERIODICALS

Law Enforcement Communications. Six times per year; United Business Publications, New York, N.Y.

Police Chief. Monthly; International Association of Chiefs of Police, Gaithersburg, Maryland.

Security Management. Bimonthly; American Society for Industrial Security, Washington, D.C.

Security World. Monthly; Security World Publishing Co., Los Angeles, California.

Vigilante: The Magazine of Personal Security. Quarterly; Vanguard Associates, Phoenix, Arizona.

Index

233